TO MY FATHER-IN-LAW
AND GOOD FRIEND
LEWIS WETZEL PIERCE

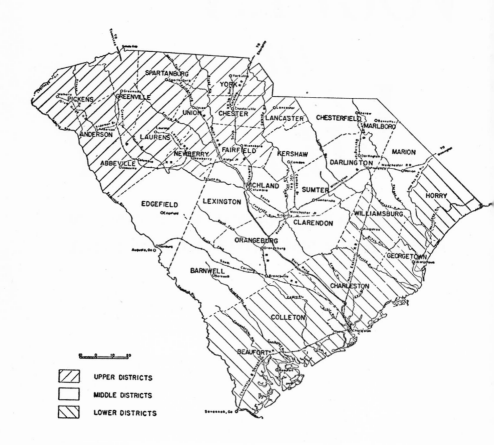

SOUTH CAROLINA, 1860

Vogues in Villainy

in

Villainy

CRIME AND RETRIBUTION IN ANTE-BELLUM SOUTH CAROLINA

by

JACK KENNY WILLIAMS

UNIVERSITY OF SOUTH CAROLINA PRESS
COLUMBIA
1959

THE AUTHOR

Jack Kenny Williams, author of *Vogues in Villainy: Crime and Retribution in Ante-Bellum South Carolina,* received his B.A. degree in 1940 at Emory & Henry College at Emory, Virginia and his M.A. and Ph.D. degrees at Emory University in Georgia. He has published numerous articles in historical magazines and has been president of the South Carolina Historical Association.

Williams was born in Galax, Virginia, in 1920. He taught public school in Virginia, 1940-42. In 1942-46 he was an officer in the United States Marine Corps, serving overseas with the fourth Marine Division. In September, 1947, he was appointed an instructor of history at Clemson College and in 1957 was made Dean of the Graduate School.

He is married to the former Margaret Pierce and they have two children, Katherine and Mary.

Copyright © 1959 by the University of South Carolina Press, Columbia.
Printed by the State Commercial Printing Company, Columbia, South Carolina.
Library of Congress Catalog Card Number: 59-8430

CONTENTS

ILLUSTRATIONS

Foreword

THE PURPOSE OF THIS BOOK IS TO TRACE THE PATTERNS OF LAW-lessness and the mechanics of law enforcement within South Carolina during the ante-bellum decades, 1790-1860. As such the book is an investigation of an isolated facet of the complex social and cultural history of the State. The author hopes that the study may suggest a fuller understanding of the South as a whole, and especially of the less favored white citizens.

South Carolina was selected for this presentation because in many respects the state was typical of the Old South. Certainly South Carolina was not characterized by exceptional lawlessness; nor could the State boast of any unique legal institutions.

For the most part the book is concerned only with white citizens. Slaves and free blacks were tried by special minor courts and were punished in accord with special codes of written and unwritten laws. The history of their criminal activity is therefore a distinct and separate study, one done skillfully in 1914 by the late Professor Howell Meadoes Henry. His *Police Control of the Slave in South Carolina* (Emory, Virginia: privately printed), is a pioneer work in the historiography of the American slave system. Admittedly the separation of Negro and white crime is at times difficult; and numerous instances in which whites and blacks were comingled in crime, as partners or as villain and victim, are of necessity given space.

This study was begun under the direction of Professors Bell Irwin Wiley and Walter Brownlow Posey of Emory University, and whatever merit it may have is attributable in large measure to their suggestions and criticism. This is not to imply, however, that they share responsibility for errors of fact or judgment.

Among those who assisted in the processes of research and to whom particular gratitude is due are Dr. J. Harold Easterby of the South Carolina Archives Department; the late Dr. Robert L. Meriwether of the South Caroliniana Library, University of South Carolina; Miss Marella Walker of the Emory University Library; and the research staffs of libraries at Clemson College, Duke University, the University of North Carolina, Vanderbilt University, the Alabama Historical Archives Commission, the South Carolina Historical Society, and the Charleston Library Society.

The author is obligated to the editors of the *South Carolina Historical Magazine,* the *Journal of Southern History,* and the *Journal of Criminal Law, Criminology, and Police Science* for permission to use material from his articles on criminals, printed in those publications. Special permission to use quotations has been granted by the following: Duke University Press for material from Lillian Kibler's *Benjamin F. Perry, South Carolina Unionist* (Durham, 1946); Vanderbilt University Press for material from Giles J. Patterson's *Journal of A Southern Student* (Nashville, 1944, edited by Richard C. Beatty); Hugh F. Henry for material from his father's *Police Control of the Slave in South Carolina* (Emory, Virginia, 1914); Mrs. R. F. Bradley for material from her mother's *Traditions and History of Anderson County* (Atlanta, 1928); Columbia University Press for material from Herbert Apetheker's *American Negro Slave Revolts* (New York, 1953); Rinehart and Company, Incorporated, for material from Thomas L. Stokes' *The Savannah* (New York, 1951); Bobbs-Merrill Company, Incorporated, for material from Charles M. Wiltse's *John C. Calhoun, Nationalist* (New York, c. 1944); The Johns Hopkins Press for material from Elizabeth Merritt's *James H. Hammond* (Baltimore, 1923); University of Oklahoma Press for material from Shields McIlwain's *The Southern Poor White* (Norman, 1939); Duell, Sloan and Pearce, Incorporated, for material from Beatrice St. Julien Ravenel's *Charleston Murders* (New York, 1947); University of North Carolina Press for material from Rosser H. Taylor's *Ante-Bellum South Carolina: A Social and Cultural History* (Chapel Hill, 1942); and University of South Carolina Press for material from Daniel W. Hollis' *South Carolina College* (Columbia, 1951). Permission to quote from articles in the *South Carolina Historical Magazine* was given by the editor, Mrs. Mary Prior.

The author owes special thanks to Mrs. Louise Jones DuBose, Director of the University of South Carolina Press, for editorial assistance: and to Hugh H. Macaulay, Daniel W. Hollis, Mae S. Ringold, and Margaret Pierce Williams for reading this work in printer's proof.

Publication of this book is made possible by a grant from the Claude W. Kress Research Fund, Clemson College.

November, 1958   J. K. W.

I. The Face of Crime

CRIME WAS FAR TOO PREVALENT IN SOUTH CAROLINA, DEPLORED the editor of the Laurensville *Herald* in June, 1850, and he was tired of writing about it. Believing that his readers were equally weary of the subject, he avowed his determination no longer "to sicken the heart of the too sensitive by dwelling on the dark deeds of the guilty."

Few citizens of pre-Civil War South Carolina agreed with this newspaperman's intention—if, for that matter, he agreed with it himself. Then as now, in South Carolina as elsewhere, crime and punishment were subjects of high interest. Then as now, the exploits of lawless men and the successes or failures of police officers made prime newspaper copy and first rate conversation pieces.

But the Laurensville writer was apparently quite correct when he said there was too much crime in his State. No completely accurate records of crimes were kept, but a sampling of criminal courts' journals indicates that during the forty years preceding the Laurensville editorial the average crime rate in South Carolina had nearly doubled. Sessions courts' indictments for 1850 were in a ratio of approximately 1 for every 350 citizens. In 1800 the ratio had been about 1 to 600.[1] Thus the pattern was clear and the *Herald* was not alone in taking note of it. Legislators, ministers, and lawyers joined with editors in a demand for action aimed at halting the spread of lawlessness. The Attorney General, late in the ante-bellum period, strengthened their mandate with his frank admission that the problem of steadily increasing crime was an "obvious and alarming" one.[2] Grand juries also expressed grave concern over the "growing criminal class" and the apparent inability of police to cope with its members. As early as 1812 a Chester District grand jury deplored what it termed a vast advance in the number of unpunished offenses against person and property; and from then until 1860 numerous juries made the subject of increasing crime a prominent feature of their semi-annual presentments.[3]

[1]

Grand juries were understandably protesting situations which existed within their own districts, and it is true that certain of the State's jurisdictional areas were more victimized by criminals than others. Charleston District, for example, which contained the State's chief seaport and boasted of eight times the population of any other district, had more than its share of assault and battery, murder, and larceny. Indeed, with an average indictment ratio of about 1 to 285, it was exceeded as a center of criminal activity only by Horry District, a Low Country area on the North Carolina border which, being off the main roads, did not attract the full attention of the critics. Horry's ratio of indictments was 1 to 238.

Most travelers to South Carolina visited Charleston, and many of them commented publicly on the widespread lawlessness of the urban area. As a result, the whole State suffered in reputation. Visitor William Faux, for instance, wrote that his few days in Charleston had convinced him that the city was being disgraced by bands of thieves and cutthroats. "In the street where I sleep," he declared, "for two nights successively, our slumbers have been disturbed by the cries of murder!"[4]

The irrepressible Anne N. Royall was more severe. "Charleston, S.C.," she wrote, "from being the garden spot of the United States, is now a receptacle for the refuse of all nations on earth; not only nations, but of jails, penitentiaries, pirate dens, &c." The inns and hotels, she said, served as headquarters for the criminal gangs which plagued the city, and existed "for the especial accommodation of ruffians, gamblers, pick-pockets, and swindlers—the landlord the greatest swindler of the whole."[5]

Such outbursts, while exaggerated, were doubtlessly believed by many readers outside the State; but the reputation of Charleston also suffered from the disparagement of some native South Carolinians. Up country Calvinists, in particular, looked on the port city as being akin to the Biblical Sodom and Gomorrah. The young John C. Calhoun was expressing the sentiments of a number of his neighbors when he wrote to his wife in the early 1800s that he believed Charleston to be "intemperate and debauched."[6] Similar attitudes were fostered in some cases by adverse reports from citizens of Charleston. One resident wrote: "Our city is infested by a gang of lawless and reckless vagabonds who prowl about, bent on mischief and destruction. . . . When a stop will be put to these evil doings we know not."[7]

Charleston had its infamous "French Alley" and its equally disreputable "Good-Bye Alley," both being hangouts for sailors; but the section of town which gave police officers most trouble was "The Neck," a long, narrow strip at the back of the city. After 1821 Charleston grand jurors complained bitterly of poor law enforcement in The Neck, and a jury in 1847 bluntly described the entire area as a vast "den of ill repute."[8] Such condemnations were supported by heated editorials in the city newspapers. By 1842 these attacks led to the enactment of special laws for the police of The Neck, but legislation failed generally to better circumstances and it remained the city's most lawless section.

Other than Charleston, the South Carolina district most frequently denounced as being overrun with criminals was Edgefield. Situated midway between the mountains and the seacoast, with its west line at the Savannah River, Edgefield was by comparison with its neighbors a populous district, and contained in addition to its "seat of justice" the bustling railroad town of Hamburg.

Sessions courts' records indicate that Edgefield's reputation for excessive crime was undeserved. With a 1 to 491 ratio of indicted lawbreakers to resident population, the district stood well above the State average; yet in contemporary opinion and current history it was and is roundly belabored as representative of the worst in lawlessness and moral temper.

One modern writer, for example, has concluded that Edgefield was a "profligate and undisciplined neighborhood" where a man might easily "find either a fight or a frolic." This writer emphasizes the fact that the district produced such typical hotheads as Preston S. Brooks, who caned Massachusetts Senator Charles Sumner in 1856, and "Pitchfork" Benjamin R. Tillman, the one-eyed radical agrarian of the late 1800s.[9]

Typical of the contemporary sources such writers have used in arriving at their conclusions is an 1850 committee report laid before the legislature. "A fact should be stated," the members were told, "which may be already known . . . [that Edgefield], for the last several years, has had to lament the perpetration of a vast number of crimes, and the number has become so great that the Grand Jury, at the last Term, actually reported that the Jail was too small for the number of inmates."[10]

No doubt such a report had been presented by the grand jury. About half the juries of the State were penning similar paragraphs.

Juries in Union District in 1806, Richland in 1825, Kershaw in 1829, Fairfield in 1835, Barnwell in 1844, and Abbeville in 1852 may be cited among those protesting the size of their jail buildings. Hence the critics who censured Edgefield on this basis were being unfair. For that matter, Edgefield District obtained a new jail in 1852, a brick structure with a capacity of "forty or fifty boarders," and a citizen of the district soon questioned the need for such a large establishment. "It stands this day entirely empty of prisoners!" he declared. "Taunt old Edgefield no more for her crimes!"[11]

But Edgefield did deserve an unsavory reputation in connection with homicide. About eight per cent of all the district's criminal indictments were for this major crime, whereas the figure for the State at large was nearer four per cent. The frequency of murder, owing to the spectacular nature of that offense, may have been responsible for Edgefield's badge of infamy. Some critics, at any rate, recognized murder as the district's special evil. Judge Thomas J. Mackey, to cite an example, is on record as having said on one occasion, "I am going to hold court in Edgefield, and I expect a somewhat exciting term, as the fall shooting is about to commence."[12]

Worse publicity than the judge's facetious remark was given by the incomparable Mason L. "Parson" Weems, who made Edgefield murders and murderers the theme for one of his popular small books. The following is taken from the Parson's introduction to *The Devil in Petticoats*:

> "Oh mercy!" cries the reader—"what! Old Edgefield again! Another murder in Edgefield! Why, 'twas but t'other day that you gave us a history sufficient to freeze the blood with horror— the story of a husband murdering his wife! And now you talk of a history ten times, if possible, more unnatural and horrible still— . . . . And all in Old Edgefield! *Well, the Lord have mercy upon Old Edgefield!* For sure it must be Pandemonium itself, a very district of Devils!"

That, certainly, was sufficient to condemn "Po' Old Edgefield" in the mind of Weems' eager readers.

Other towns and districts of South Carolina were at various times accused of considerable ill behavior but in general Charleston and Edgefield bore the brunt of such attacks. Columbia was now and then described as "a gathering place for fakirs, swindlers and idlers, etc.," and a resident who had moved there from Lexington reported shock at discovering the necessity for locking doors and windows.

Such a procedure, he declared, had not been his custom back in peaceful Lexington.[13]

Columbia was at times an attractive city for thieves and robbers. Travelers thronged Columbia, and crooks plied their trades among these visitors. One citizen wrote in 1855 that the criminals had even moved into the residential sections where they "entered and burglarized houses every night."

"What are our city authorities about?" he asked. "An extra patrol force ought to be put on duty at once."[14]

Three Up Country towns, Newberry, Greenville, and Chester, were also prominently mentioned as being rough in manner and on occasion seriously lacking in respect for law and order. Near Newberry was Mollohon's Tavern where "idle and vicious" persons congregated and plotted evil. Nearby, too, was John Kinard's whisky distillery, "a constant rendezvous for bacchanalian rowdyism." The problem of crime in the town and district was adequately delineated by the editor of the Newberry *Sentinel,* who in 1853 concluded an account of the fall court term with the following: "Some of the convicted were sent to jail, and others got off with a fine. We trust there is a time coming when peace shall reign in our border."[15]

Greenville and Chester were also remembered as gathering places for rioters and ruffians. Concerning Greenville, attorney Benjamin F. Perry recalled that his first visit to the mountain village provided him with the view of "two drunken blackguards throwing stones at each other, on the public square, cursing and abusing each other with gross epithets." And, "It was customary for the young men of the village and the old ones also to meet in the piazas [*sic*] of the stores, and sometimes on the sidewalks of the streets, and play cards all the morning or evening, drinking in the mean time toddy." Furthermore, "The people of the country [would] come into the village, hitch their horses to the fences, get drunk, strip in the streets and fight."[16]

The situation was but little better in Chester. According to a grand jury report in October, 1820, "vices . . . [in Chester] prevail to an extent not equalled in any other country on the globe to an extent which unless measures are adopted to prevent the increase of them threaten to subvert all law and order."

Such accounts were doubtlessly overstated, but the districts in which these towns were located did have comparatively poor criminal indictment ratios. This does not indicate that the Up Country was less law abiding than the Low Country. For though Greenville, Newberry, and Chester districts had heavy crime counts, neighboring Abbeville, Laurens, and York Districts had among the best records in the State. Indeed, Abbeville, with an indictment ratio of 1 to 1340, apparently set the pace for good behavior. In this connection, two Low Country districts with fine records were Williamsburg and Marion, having indictment ratios of 1 to 977 and 1 to 791, each well above average.

But if the over-all count was about the same for the geographical halves of the State, the two sections did report noteworthy differences in the types of their crimes. Thus, the English tourist, Adam Hodgson, was probably correct when he wrote in the early 1820s that the South Carolina citizens living above the Fall Line were "more rude and familiar, and their conversation more licentious and profane" than their flat land brothers.[17]

Low Country districts generally led in murder indictments and in all forms of larceny. The Up Country, on the other hand, had the bulk of assault and battery indictments and held the dubious honor of trying about sixty-five per cent of bastardy cases. In brief, an Up Country man was more apt to find himself involved in a fistfight or a morals issue; while a Low Country citizen was more likely to have his wallet stolen or to be shot in "sudden heat and passion." Each was quick to tell a stranger that the other was "worse off."

The ratio of criminal indictments to resident citizens in ante-bellum South Carolina is not of itself a fully accurate indicator of the face of crime within the State. Criminals were indicted for offenses both petty and serious; and it is a point in mitigation of South Carolina's record that of more than ten thousand indictments sampled, about sixty per cent were for the relatively minor offenses of assault, assault and battery, and similar breaches of the peace. It is true, of course, that a greater proportion of these petty criminals were apprehended by the law enforcement officials.

Contemporary Opinion on Causes of Crime

Ante-bellum South Carolinians who served as spokesmen in behalf of an orderly society offered a variety of reasons for the criminal activity within their State. Unaware of now popular psychological and sociological interpretations of such matters, they pinned to the problem of crime a number of loosely related, rather unimaginative, but perhaps accurate causes.

Most observers regarded whisky as the principal source of crime. "We are free in stating," wrote the Barnwell District grand jury in 1818, "that three-fourths of the indictments that fill the records of our Courts of Justice, have their origin at . . . Tippling shops." Jurors throughout the State expressed a general agreement. A Chester jury in 1827 declared whisky to be the root of every sort of evil from riot to murder; and a Greenville jury, as late as 1856, presented the "practice of drunkingness [sic] as the greatest nuisance that has fallen within their observations."[18]

These official fault-finding bodies were not alone in condemning strong drink as an instigator of crime. Lawyer Benjamin F. Perry believed in 1835 that "one half if not two thirds" of sessions courts' cases originated "in intemperance," and the editor of the Lancaster *Ledger* in 1853 wrote that four-fifths of all criminal indictments in his area were whisky-inspired.[19]

Most editors were resolute foes of drink. Such papers as the Lexington *Temperance Standard* and the Columbia *South Carolina Temperance Advocate* gave over the bulk of their print to tales of criminal excesses caused by drink, of poverty and ill health brought about by it, and of the need for strong laws concerning it. Other papers were similarly devoted to the theory that excessive drinking and excessive lawlessness were diabolical bedfellows. The Columbia *Southern Chronicle,* in January, 1842, concluded a murder account with the observation: "thus the accursed liquor suddenly sent another soul to the bar of eternal justice. How long shall this moral pestilence continue to desolate our land?" The Sumter *Banner* on October 18, 1848, invoked poetry to express its views:

> Ye sons of Cold-Water, your voices now raise,
> And speak of Cold-Water and sing to its praise;
> Its virtues are many, its vices but few,
> Its life-giving powers are offered to you.
> It will do you more good than Sherry or Port,
> And save you from quarrels, from fighting and court.

Editors and grand jurors were aided in their anti-drink crusade by the conversion to their program of several sessions courts' judges. John Belton O'Neall, an outstanding member of the State's antebellum bench, charged many of his juries with the information that the reign of "king spirits" was always followed by the reigns of "king larceny and king murder." As South Carolina's most ardent temperance leader, O'Neall organized numerous societies and was once elected president of the "Sons of Temperance."

The list of prominent jurists who publicly denounced the evils of liquor also included Joseph N. Whitner, Aedanus Burke, Thomas Lee, and Richard Gantt. Judge Burke, it was stated, tried to win drunks to sobriety by treating them kindly. On one occasion he freed a thief who claimed strong drink had driven him to crime, saying to the larcener, "When I was a boy, I sometimes drank whiskey, and if I happened to take a drop too much, I always felt a great inclination to steal."[20] Judge Gantt gained a measure of local fame for his grand jury charges against whisky. An instance was in Spartanburg in 1841. The drunkard, Gantt told the jurors, was in reality the most pathetic and hopeless of criminals for he could not, under any conditions, enter the gates of Heaven. "Imagine if you can," Gantt orated, "St. Paul *a straddle* of a whiskey cask measuring out half pints, & General Washington cavorting around . . . with his coat off wanting to fight like a bully at a petty muster ground."[21]

The clamor against whisky as a promoter of crime led on the one hand to a rash of temperance societies and on the other to a series of confused and sometimes contradictory laws. Of the two, the societies were perhaps the more effective. The temperance society movement was an early organization in South Carolina, but made little headway until 1830. Thereafter it spread with amazing rapidity. By 1860 few villages were without an active "Cold-Water Club." To cite examples, Laurens district listed twenty-two clubs in 1848; and the "wet" city of Charleston had at least three active societies during the late 1850s. In Charleston an ardent Cold-Water disciple could attend on Tuesday nights the "Marine Total Abstinence Society," on Thursday evenings the "Independent Order of Rechabites," and on Friday nights, "The Sons of Temperance." Singly and in unison these organizations worked with hot fervor. In addition to their regular meetings they distributed pledge cards, printed broadsides and pamphlets, and imported prominent speakers. They made temperance a popular subject and carried their messages even into the schools where adolescent orations against whisky and wine became literary society favorites.[22]

These groups consistently urged that existing laws regulating the sale and use of whisky be strengthened and others enacted. In this endeavor they had fair success. Such proposals as that of lawyer Albert Rhett, who would take all the property from a habitual drunk-

ard and give it to his next of kin, or that urged by the editor of the
Charleston *Observer,* who would hang any innkeeper caught selling
whisky to known alcoholics, did not become laws;[23] but during the
ante-bellum decades ten less drastic bills did successfully run the
legislative maze. For the most part these concerned the granting of
licenses to sell. Such licenses were granted by the courts until 1801
and thereafter by the "Commissioners of High Roads and Bridges"
or by town councils. The price of the license fluctuated from legislature to legislature but a figure set by the comprehensive whisky act
of 1835 represents an acceptable average. According to the provisions of this law all liquor dealers were to be bonded in the sum of
one thousand dollars and their permits were to be priced at fifty
dollars. These high figures were expected to cut down the number
of dealers but there is no evidence that such was the result.

In an effort to restrain drinking in barrooms and inns, the lawmakers in 1796 required a retailer of spirits to sell not less than three
gallons to each purchaser. This impractical law was restated in 1834
to read one pint per customer, and by 1849 the minimum was raised
to one quart. In no case was drinking allowed near the building
where the whisky was dispensed. In addition, some legislative effort
was suggested to halt the sale of liquor to soldiers and to "itinerant
traders," but such proposals failed to pass.[24]

In fine, whisky legislation, whether aimed at buyer or seller, had
little effect in South Carolina. Strong drink was far too popular with
most classes of people for law to halt its use. An early historian
summed up the matter with these words:

> Drunkenness may be called an endemic vice of Carolina. The
> climate disposes to it, and the combined influence of religion
> and education, too often fail to restrain it. . . . [Many citizens]
> drink water only when they can get nothing else. . . . The gen-
> eral position being once admitted that the addition of rum, gin,
> brandy, or whisky, is an improvement of water, it is no easy
> matter to stop at the precise point of temperance.[25]

One reason why drinking could serve as a catalyst for crime was
the practice, almost universal among South Carolina white men, of
carrying arms, for although some towns had local ordinances forbidding the promiscuous firing of guns, neither they nor the State
had any law against the carrying of weapons. Governor Pierce M.
Butler declared in 1838 that "only the unthinking part of the community" kept weapons on their persons,[26] but his statement, if meant

to be true, reduced the "thinkers" in pre-Civil War South Carolina to something of a minority. The sessions courts' records indicate that foreign travelers James Stirling and Carl D. Arfwedson were on this point better observers than the governor. Stirling wrote that the custom of carrying weapons was general throughout the State and was, to his mind, "proof of proneness to violence, and a provocative to it." Arfwedson declared that not only did most South Carolina males carry weapons, but in addition, "Any man is considered imprudent who does not."[27]

There were critics of this custom but their influence was small. A few church leaders, grand jurors, newspaper editors, and civic groups began attacks on "knife-and-gun-toting" in the late 1850s, but they met with little success before the end of the Civil War. A typical presentment of protest was offered by the Abbeville jurors in the fall of 1838. As these men viewed it, "The carrying of private arms such as the murderous Bowie knife Dirks Pistols Sword-canes &c" was a violation of the rules of civilization. An Edgefield jury wrote in October, 1845, that the custom of carrying weapons was directly responsible for "a majority of all the cases of bloody violence which have occurred in our District for many years."

Now and then independent citizen groups joined the jurors in protest. For instance, petitions from such groups were received by the State Senate in 1844.[28] Despite their heated verbal insistence, these documents were not acted upon and most males continued to consider a pistol or a knife as a necessary accessory to the daily costume. To at least one South Carolinian this appeared to be evidence of intellectual immaturity. "When will *the people* of South Carolina learn wisdom from experience?" he asked in a vitriolic letter to the Laurensville *Herald.*[29]

The writer of such a letter need not have singled out South Carolina for criticism. Sister states were similarly unenlightened. But the South Carolina censurer could cite an almost endless array of serious crimes occasioned by the odious practice of which he so bitterly complained. Newspapers chronicled them in issue after issue.

One case which vividly illustrates the fact that an armed citizen might become a menace to friend as well as foe concerned the tragic death in 1853 of a respected Columbia resident. According to the April 29 issue of the Columbia *Daily South Carolinian,* "As a Mr. Ridgeway was passing down the steps . . . of the M. E. Church, the right skirt of his coat, in the pocket of which was a loaded pistol, came in contact with the sidestone of the steps, causing the pistol to go off, the contents of which took effect on Mr. Summerfield Batts, who was standing a few paces in front."

The complaints against the carrying of arms became numerous enough by 1852 to warrant legislative action, and Senator Franklin J. Moses introduced a bill demanding severe punishment for those who for any reason made assaults with concealed weapons. Moses noted that while the federal Constitution granted citizens the right to bear arms, it did not give them the authority to hide their weapons. Hence he believed his proposal would rectify the evil situation of which the people complained, without depriving them of a "natural right."

The senate passed Moses' bill, but in the house of representatives it died silently in committee. A similar bill introduced in 1856 was tabled. Finally in 1858 a statute was placed on the books stating that one who attacked another with a concealed weapon of any sort would, upon conviction, suffer a six month jail term and a fine which might be as high as two thousand dollars. Such a law was not what the angry critics had in mind but it was sufficient, apparently, to halt their protests. And, while the act did not forbid the actual carrying of weapons, it did discourage the practice. That was fair progress.[30]

Ante-bellum citizens interested in criminology were quick to point out that the larceny, homicide, and assault and battery rates increased materially during public festivals. This was not a surprise. South Carolinians were a rural people and "public days" were events of great moment in their lives. The contagious exuberance of the crowd, the heady excitement of a change from the humdrum of everyday life, the inclination of the bully to become quarrelsome, all combined to insure that impolite and perhaps disastrous affrays would mar the celebrations. In addition, the pickpockets, "blacklegs and sharpers," gathered where the people gathered; and their presence was not conducive to order.

Muster day and race week were two events "especially calculated as times for trouble." One lawyer remembered the races in Columbia as being hangouts for the "cut throats from every port." They were assembled, he said, "to demoralize and pirate on the young and unwary."[31] An English tourist, Basil Hall, wrote from Charleston in the 1820s that the racing season there was filled with so much fighting that the track officials hired officers who, armed with long whips, lashed the fighters in an effort to quell their activity.[32]

Hall, an officer of the English Navy, would have been even more impressed with the pugilistic nature of South Carolinians had he remained in the State long enough to view a militia gathering. It was a commonplace throughout the South that little peace and quiet could be expected on these muster dates. Ostensibly for the patriotic purpose of military instruction and drill, the meetings too often turned into general drunken brawls.

Every South Carolina militia unit had its bully, and such men made fighting almost an order of the day. Indeed, one who reads contemporary accounts of these seriocomic affairs gains the impression that they were called essentially to furnish the troops with a rather rugged and unplanned form of combat training. Fair examples of the unsavory and violent aspect of muster day proceedings are such events as the riot staged by a Lancaster unit, which began as a personal struggle between Archibald Flemming and Jackson Gregory and ended as a club-swinging, rock-throwing, knife-slashing mass melée; and the murder of Henry Stone by Mabury Mitchell at a Spartanburg encampment. Mitchell's weapons were his bare fists, and he shouted as he mauled his victim, "This is the way to fight."[33]

The Fourth of July and the Christmas holidays were also apt to be rowdy occasions in South Carolina. The patriotic July date was described by one contemporary as a time set aside for eating bad food, listening to long speeches, and dodging wild bullets. In his opinion, he advised his brother, it would be "the safest as well as the most pleasant to stay at home and sit in the shade."[34]

Apparently it was also safer to stay at home during the Christmas season. It, too, might be a time for dodging bullets and bullies. The Charleston *Courier* regularly chronicled the holiday wave of stabbings, shootings, and acts of Hallowe'en-like rowdyism.[35] In the Up Country, too, the season was riotous and one newspaper editor lamented, "Our streets, during the . . . holidays have been full of mad-cap roystorers shooting off guns and so forth. Some of our wild boys have been guilty, too, of sundry peccadillos . . . such as stretching grape-vines across the road just high enough to decapitate some luckless night rider." Such conduct, the editor concluded, "deserves the severe animadversion of the law."[36]

Probably the public event which was accompanied by most assault and battery, larceny, swindling, and petty crimes of all types, was court week or court time. The "Courts of General Sessions of the Peace, Oyer and Terminer, Assize and General Gaol Delivery" were held at the "Seats of justice" in each district of the State for a period of four to ten days every spring and fall. For many people these biannual sessions were the high points of the entire year. The country folk—a "rude, unpolished race" they were called by some—came to town to sell the fruits of their labors, buy supplies for the half-year, meet old friends, gossip, and, in the words of a New England observer, spend the bulk of their free time "standing about in public places all day, gaping and staring at every body and every thing that was in any degree new."[37]

But the country people were not alone. The beggar came too, as did the patent medicine salesman, the Yankee peddler, the "faro-dealer," the traveling dentist, the professor who gave Shakespearean readings at the drop of a coin, and "Signor Spinetto" with his "exhibition of the one-hundred learned canary birds."

In fine, as described by one contemporary editor:

> The session of Court in our country villages creates as much sensation among the people as the rural fairs in England. . . . Almost every family in the village are expecting some of their kindred or friends—hotel keepers stow away an ample supply of provisions—store keepers "stir their stumps" to have goods up by Court—every body expects to be busy, every one thinks he will be the richer before its close. . . . Our streets are then busy; you wonder where so many people came from. Old wagons and carts, used up horses and other refuse articles are exposed for sale. . . . Here, there, and every where you hear the auctioneer's cry, "going, going, very cheap, gone"; then an inharmonious discord of most wretched music, ground out of a cracked organ, or may be a shrill voice accompanying a banjo sung by a woman a shade worse looking than her song is harsh; then above all, the constable's voice calling some tardy witness—this is Court time, this glorious epoch which occurs but once in six months.[38]

Lawlessness always increased in direct proportion to the size of the crowd. Brawls and riots were therefore expected during court time and extra constables were usually hired. They more than earned their pay.[39]

Indeed, it happened now and then that the special police were wholly unable to cope with the situation. The editor of the Yorkville *Citizen* as late as 1856 reported that the streets of his village during court time were "in a perfect riot by drunken sandhillers without any effort to quell."[40] And Judge Charles J. Colcock remembered the occasion in Spartanburg at which a large, uncontrolled fracas broke out, lasting well into the night. "Hundreds were . . . fighting by light-wood fires," he wrote. A young lawyer, riding his first circuit, wit-nessed this affair from a hotel window and was so unnerved by it that he hastened out of town the following morning, leaving his cases for others to handle.[41]

An indication of the violence attending court time may be readily obtained by consulting the sessions courts' journals. These point out that a regular part of criminal court business was the indicting, ar-resting, trying and sentencing of brawlers and petty thieves who disturbed the area with their nefarious activities. Rarely do the records fail to include such statements as "John McDaniell and Jacob Snipes having committed an Assault & Battery in the Court Yard were fined one hundred dollars each"; or, "A Great Riot having taken place last night in this village & the Court Being Informed that one Mitchell McMurphey a Mr. Boyd & Mr. Wallace were concerned in it, it is ordered that they be bound over for the next term."[42]

So it was that to a recognizable extent court week and public holi-days inspired the animal nature inherent in man. This lamentable at-tribute of the people was likewise noted during times of political activity. Political campaigns and election days were blood-boiling intervals during the ante-bellum decades. The terse statement of a Charleston grand jury in April, 1824, that twelve of the current in-dictments under consideration had originated during the spring elec-tions was not unusual. Throughout the State, by letter, petition, and oration, people complained of the same evil. An election was de-scribed by one newspaper editor as a "scene of revelling, and immor-ality," and a "debasing struggle of bribery, corruption, and intrigue." Another critic penned these acid lines:

> View the Election Levee—the door of every tavern spread wide . . . [and the voter being led] like a felon, to the ballot-box in a state of duplicity with less fortitude than Balaam's ass, Esau-like, to close the sale of his birth right! Nor does the scene close here. The evening farce ensues—the nooks and corners of every street, are lined with drunken men's bodies, covered with blood and filth. . . . Each tavern is now a modern Bedlam! —coats, hats, and shirts are scattered to the four winds; combat-ants arrayed for bloody fight, neighbor against neighbor, friend against friend, and not infrequently, brother against brother! The battle rages,—the air is rent with angry curses, and wolfish screams—oaths of defamation sound thro' the streets, like mar-

tial music, and the scene closes with broken heads, bloody noses and scratched faces.[43]

Numerous instances of the lawlessness attending elections might be cited. The murder of John Ashe, a Charleston ward-heeler who was said to control at least fifty votes, is a case in point; but the victim was not widely mourned. The struggle between Joseph Williams, Charles Farrelly, T. K. Darcey, and John McKenna is another. In the midst of a political argument at a tavern, Williams was threatened. He pulled a pistol from his pocket and, pointing it at the others, began backing toward the street. At the door he stumbled and fell. His opponents rushed toward him at once. He fired at McKenna, but missed. Farrelly fired at him with the same result. Then Darcey began to pummel him with a *"loaded* or *leaded* stick." The others joined in and beat and kicked him without mercy. Williams lived, but he refused to prosecute his attackers.[44]

A less serious disturbance was reported by George Brasington in 1816. Offering a ten dollar reward for the capture of his assailant, he wrote:

> On the night after the boxes was opened at our last election for Kershaw District, I peaceably walking the street—a villain overtook me at the corner of Col. Nixon's house and said *you God dambd Brasington,* and at the same time gave me a blow with his right hand on my left cheek, and he left a mark with blood—I ran after him and left a mark with a muddy shoe on his breeches behind.[45]

The South Carolina political campaign which engendered the most violence was the nullification contest of the early 1830s. This period of stress and strain was remembered by some South Carolinians as a time when many feared civil war within the State. The heated controversy left in its wake broken bones and broken friendships. It occasioned duels and less formal affrays and brought forth such belligerent group statements as the following from an Up Country "Union Society": "In defense of the Federal Union, we have drawn our swords and flung away the scabbards. . . . We have but two words by way of reply to the nullifers, which are these: 'Come on!' "[46]

Election disturbances and similar breaches of the peace were described by many Carolinians as being only the evidence of what they admiringly termed "hot blood." A quick temper, these home-schooled psychologists pointed out, was natural with their people, was a part and parcel of their virile manhood, and hence was not to be deplored. It cut vile slander to a minimum, they said, and put a high order of civility into all social intercourse. For that matter, it was not unusual for obituaries and biographies to note "hot blood" as a memorable attribute of the subject's personality. The Charleston *Courier,* in a eulogy concerning Colonel Joseph P. Dickinson, concluded a paragraph of praise with the note, "his temper was warm and irascible."[47] An early biographer of Judge David J. McCord observed, in similar manner, that the Judge was "a hot-tempered man" who "never hesitated to use a cane or his fist."[48]

Whatever the merits of this interesting theory, short tempers did their share toward filling sessions courts' dockets. The Lancaster citizen who was shot because he refused a free drink; or William Bailey, who was killed because he had inadvertently pulled a button from Thomas Prince's coat; or James Walsh, who was murdered in cold blood for walking across the corner of James Oliver's lot: these are gentlemen who ran afoul of that dangerous characteristic which some South Carolina contemporaries described as "the manly spirit of our citizens."[49]

At least two foreign observers of the South Carolinian's ready temper believed that weather was the cause of it. "Swashbuckling is a natural accompaniment to the effervescence of heads in a hot climate," remarked a French tourist. "The frequent occurrence of crime," declared traveler Louis F. Tasistro, "is probably the result of climate operating upon the brain, which, by rendering men restless and impatient under the sense of injury, causes them to adopt the theory of Bowie-knives and pistols as the readiest mode of redress."[50]

South Carolina citizens seeking further cause of excessive crime were prone to declare that unrestricted immigration of outlaws and malcontents from elsewhere was the major evil to be remedied. This argument was especially widespread during the late decades of the ante-bellum period. Not more than three per cent of South Carolinians in 1850 had been born outside the United States, but these few were regarded with deep suspicion. Added to the foreign born were those people who crossed the border from other states and were not a part of the census count. Many of these interstate travelers were openly accused of various crimes, and the apprehension in Edgefield District of Jack Morris, a New York citizen, plying his trade as a thief, or the capture and escape of three Virginians who had beaten an aged gentleman near Lancaster, were occurrences giving strength to such accusations.[51]

Charleston especially was considered by many to have an excess of "surplus population" whose "innovations upon private rights" were public scandals. Being a port city, Charleston was thought to collect a "flotsam and jetsam of rascals" not only from other areas of the nation but also from overseas. Up Country newspapers, for instance, expressed a groundless suspicion that "hordes" of immigrants "well trained in crime" were continuously arriving at Charleston from England, and they demanded some legislative action to put a stop to it.[52] Complaints notwithstanding, no legal moves were made by the State to control immigration. Any such attempt would have been in serious conflict with federal law. That may or may not have influenced the States' Rights minded legislators.

Concerning immigrants or visitors from elsewhere who were caught in crime or suspected of crime, South Carolina adopted an attitude of "pass them along." Juries and vigilance committees alike were insistent that such criminals or unpopular persons be "sent packing," and punishments were usually followed with an order, official or otherwise, to vacate the State immediately.

The listing of presumed causes of crime was a favorite literary pastime for many South Carolinians and for most visiting tourists. A majority agreed that drunkenness, exaggerated tempers, the habit of carrying weapons, the excitement of holidays, the presence of unsavory immigrants, and the weather were to blame. For the most part the natives and tourists alike failed to realize that other very real reasons existed for misdeeds of all types. They failed, for example, to consider the poverty and the poor education of the great mass of landless whites. They gave little thought to such mental derangements as kleptomania or sexual perversion. Finally, they ignored the fact that convictions of criminals by petit juries were all too rare; that pardons for those who were convicted were too numerous; and that police methods were too often ineffective.

The Criminal Type

Whatever caused their crimes, the criminals themselves were a diverse collection of citizenry, male and female. They ranged in age from childhood to near-senility, in education from illiteracy to college graduate, in basic intelligence from insane to brilliant, and in economic status from the very poor to the reasonably rich. Some were men or women of eminent social background. Most were not. Some were criminals by profession and desire, others as the result of emotional unbalance. When caught in their crimes, some were remorseful, some sullen, and some indifferent. As a rule they defied a general classification. This came as a shock to observers who had placed too great an emphasis on an assumed correlation between social status and obedience to law; and the shock gave rise in some cases to a pessimistic illusion that the criminal was the rule and the honest man an exception to it. "In reading and writing history," declared a chronicler of life and politics in ante-bellum Edgefield, "I often pause and ask myself whether men are not already devils, and this world a bit of hell set apart for their temporary residence and habitation."[53]

A few of those who committed crimes of one sort or another were children—boys, usually, of ten to sixteen years. In this connection, the tragedy was not the number of boy criminals, which was never great, but the fact that as many as one-half of the indictments against children were for murder or attempted murder. Such unhappy occurrences as the killing by fourteen year old Evander Jackson of his twelve year old cousin; the shooting of one of State Senator William Rice's political foes by the senator's young son; and the murders, on different occasions, of two Columbia townsmen by college students are examples. In addition, a number of boys fought duels, some of them with fatal results. Two Charleston youngsters in 1839 exchanged shots at twelve paces, each wounding the other; and a duel between two college boys at Columbia in 1833 resulted in the death of one and the later insanity of the other.[54]

Crimes of violence were not, of course, the sole misdeeds of youth. Children were involved, then as now, in petty theft and juvenile vandalism, and, at times, in rioting. One "beautiful boy" in Charleston was indicted in 1852 on three separate counts of forgery; and a Greenville youth was tried and convicted in 1841 of passing counterfeit money. "He will no doubt be pardoned," wrote Benjamin F. Perry, who defended him, "as he was seduced by drink & is of respectable parents."[55]

Much of the theft and vandalism perpetrated by youth was not crime according to juvenile definition. College students in Columbia, for example, who "borrowed the birds" from citizens' turkey coops, or broke windows in private homes, considered their antics as being amusing pranks. They would "never forgive you if you doubted their honor," wrote college President Thomas Cooper in 1822, and "every student in college holds himself bound to conceal any offence against the Laws of the Land. . . . The robbing of henroosts, the nightly prowling about to steal Turkies from all the houses in the neighborhood are common practices."[56]

The townspeople did not share the students' idea that all this was good clean fun. They complained at length. Such criticism was reprinted and voiced elsewhere within the State, and the college youth collectively got something of a bad reputation as a result. Attorney William J. Grayson's opinion of them and of their evil influence on still younger boys is an example of bad publicity from a respected source. "Collegiate provisions for imparting or preserving good morals are . . . remarkable," he wrote. "The raw freshman is subjected to the influence of companions a little older than himself. . . . He makes rapid advances in smoking, chewing, playing billiards; concocting sherry cobblers, gin slings and mint juleps, becomes an adept at whist and 'Old Sledge' . . . to say nothing of more questionable matters."[57]

More typical, perhaps, was the spring presentment of the Chesterfield grand jury in 1828. College misbehavior impressed this group as being evidence that the younger generation was "growing up in idleness & dissipation almost invariably." Essentially the same charge was made thirty-two years later when the editor of the Laurensville *Herald*, taking note of the discharge from school of twelve college students on charges of bad conduct, told his readers that "Young America is running mad!" But a gloomy attitude of the older toward the younger generation is not, it will be agreed, a state of mind peculiar to the ante-bellum decades.

South Carolina criminal statutes did not provide special punishments for child offenders. Juries were charged to base their verdicts on a delinquent's "understanding and judgment" rather than his age, and solicitors were informed that no child under seven years should be indicted for a capital crime while no boy under fourteen years might be tried for rape.[58] Whatever the law or the judge's charge, petit juries tended to acquit, lightly punish, or recommend to full pardon the youthful criminals. Perry's observation concerning the young counterfeiter, "He will no doubt be pardoned," was based on past experience in such cases. The usual verdict found against the boy or girl included such a statement as he or she "is young in years and we believe young in transgression, therefore we recommend to mercy."

Some critics deplored this liberal attitude. A Yorkville citizen, for example, demanded that a boy on trial there for serious assault and battery be punished "as severe as the nature of the law will admit. If he has commenced thus early to commit crimes, his future life would not be unmarked with others of a deeper die."[59] The recommendation was not followed in this case, and for the most part young men and women were generally forgiven their crimes both by the courts and by the public at large. It could and supposedly did happen that a South Carolina boy might be expelled from college for fighting; be readmitted to finish with his class; then become involved in a shooting scrape; be freed, then spend two months in jail for still a third offense; and upon his release be elected a member of the State legislature. Such a possibility amazed the visiting stranger. "What a state of society this requires and must produce!" declared the learned Francis Lieber, who recounted the incident.[60]

In contrast with the boy criminals were the old men who broke the laws. Unlike the youth, the elderly malefactors were rarely guilty of acts caused by such a factor as hot-headed exuberance. Rather they were men who had long records of crime or those whose mental powers had deserted them. The aged horse thief, Gibson Foote, "a man long unwhipt of justice," had no need for an animal. He simply found it difficult, from force of long habit, to pass up the opportunity to ride him off. And seventy-three year old Dempsey Hinds was not a malicious murderer by nature; he was an insane man.[61]

As one might expect, aged criminals were relatively few. Elderly people were not so large a proportion of the population as they are today. In addition, a man's declining years were not a period for lawless indiscretion. As they had been with the boys, jurors were tolerant of the old men who appeared before them. "We say guilty," the jury foreman might announce, "but recommend mercy from his extreme old age."

Equivalent tolerance and sympathy were not generally extended to women who found themselves defendants in sessions courts. Whatever the time-honored theory of chivalry toward women might have been, it did not extend to those who engaged in any of the forms of larceny, who were parties to assaults and batteries, or, who, "to the very great annoyance of the neighborhood," sold themselves in prostitution to "lewd men of little respectability." In the aggregate women criminals were involved in about fifteen per cent of the South Carolina sessions courts' indictments, and juries found them guilty in about the same proportion as men.

Their punishments were also similar to those given the men, being different only in degree of severity. Whereas a male convicted of receiving stolen goods was usually sentenced to thirty-nine or fifty lashes "on his bare back, well laid on," a woman guilty of the same offense received from one to ten, "moderately" applied. And while a man normally served a thirty day jail sentence for assault and battery with intent to kill, a woman's term was rarely more than twelve. Fines, on the other hand, were generally the same; and women guilty of capital crimes were sentenced to death about as quickly as men. For the crime of prostitution, women were most often punished by banishment.[62]

Many women hailed to sessions courts were accused of assault and battery. Some apparently were as ready to engage in public fisticuffs or club and knife fights as were any of their male counterparts. Seven indictments against female combatants were found by the Union grand jury in 1821-22, seven by the Darlington jury in 1846-47, and four by the Barnwell jury in 1830. Equivalent figures might be cited for other districts.

As a rule the women fought each other. Such court cases as those made against Sarah Bradley and Bridget McKinney, and Mary Bagget and Charlotte Ratcliffe, are examples. In the first instance the two women came to blows when Sarah accused Bridget of husband stealing. Sarah lost the fight, being "hit over the head several times with a shovel and [receiving] a blow on her side—4 or 5 blows on the head, [and] several on the arm." The second case cited resulted in a complete vindication of one participant and a heavy sentence against the other who was jailed for one month and then forced to post a two hundred dollar peace bond as insurance that she would "be of good behaviour towards all the Citizens of this State and especially towards Charlotte Ratcliffe."[63]

Some of the assault and battery indictments represented fights between women and men; and on occasion the jury deemed the woman the instigator. Two cases of this nature were Mary Craddock *versus* Shadrack Jenkins, of Barnwell, and Eleanor Moore *versus* Samuel Hillon, of Lancaster. The court adjudged Mary Craddock guilty in her fight, ordered her husband to pay the fine, and set her male opponent free. Both parties were fined in the Moore-Hillon case, but costs assessed the woman were fifty dollars while the man's were but half that amount.[64]

According to Judge O'Neall, one ante-bellum Carolina woman gained a reputation as a fighter par excellence. She took on all comers, male or female, and was known, affectionately or otherwise, as "Big Sall" or "Fighting Sall." Her prowess with fist and club reputedly won her on one occasion the unheralded honor of receiving a two-month term in jail. If true, this was one of the longest such sentences recorded in the State prior to 1858 for a member of the gentle sex.[65]

In addition to brawling, women were also charged with such crimes as petit and grand larceny, counterfeiting, arson, stealing animals, bootlegging whisky, and premeditated murder. Of these, the last naturally created greatest interest. The most celebrated woman murderer in South Carolina was Lavinia Fisher of Charleston, who in partnership with her husband robbed and killed a number of men at a tavern near the city. Lavinia was hanged in public ceremony, and her conduct at the gallows proved that her courage was equal to her ruthlessness.[66]

Other women killed their husbands or lovers; and a few women, unwed usually, were indicted for the distressing crime of infanticide. An example, typical in some ways, of the latter crime was the case of an Up Country school teacher who murdered her illegitimate child. Benjamin F. Perry defended her, and as the result of an impassioned speech to the jury in which he pointed out the erstwhile excellent character of the woman and described her inability to resist the temptation which had beset her, gained a not-guilty verdict. Other unmarried infanticides were less fortunate, and at least one South Carolina woman during the ante-bellum decades was sentenced to be hanged for having killed her infant.[67]

Infanticide cases, in common with other sex-connected transgressions, were handled gingerly if they involved ladies of high social rank. The defendant was not always forced to attend the public hearing, her lawyer giving word-of-mouth assurance of her whereabouts; and newspapers did not often print her name. The following statement from the Edgefield *Advertiser* in June, 1837, is illustrative: "The female is said to have previously sustained an excellent character, and her name is withheld to avoid adding a pang to the already lacerated feelings of her unhappy relatives, many of whom are very respectable."

But most women criminals were not of the favored social classes. This was equally true of the men and is not, in either instance, an unexpected observation. The average criminal in ante-bellum South Carolina was a man possessing little money or property, little formal education, and little social status. Courts' journals, coroners' inquest books, and recorded contemporary opinions all substantiate this conclusion; and it seems not unlikely that the low estate of the criminal group was a major factor in the consistent severity of the penal codes. The laws were written and enacted by one group to apply to a less acceptable group, and those responsible for the legislation neither admired nor had a friendly interest in those toward whom the statutes were aimed. It was the conclusion of one writer that the "people of quality" were so devoid of compassion that they "thanked God and took heart when one poor-white killed another."[68]

The foregoing is not meant to imply that no "respectable citizens" were involved in crime. As earlier noted, boys of good parentage and women of lofty social position now and then appeared in criminal courts as defendants. Men of high standing in their communities were likewise at times listed on court dockets. They might be indicted for such misdemeanors as assault and battery and they were, although infrequently, parties to murder, grand larceny, and the various categories of swindle.

Public brawling was the misdeed of most high ranking men who were hailed to sessions courts. Such men as Lewis T. Wigfall, the Edgefield attorney who moved to Texas and became a national Senator from that state; John Mackey, editor of a Charleston newspaper; John S. Preston, mid-state planter and legislator; Elias Marks, Columbia physician and educator; and J. L. Reynolds, Columbia theologian, serve as examples of prominent South Carolina citizens who so far forgot their status as gentlemen as to engage in street fighting. The courts very often tried and fined such men, regardless of their social importance. This was the case because to most minds a favored position in society was in part dependent on public conduct; hence street fighting, an activity considered beneath the dignity of gentlemen, amounted to at least a temporary forfeiture of rank.[69]

For that matter the petit jurors may have enjoyed bringing in misdemeanor verdicts against the favored group. At any rate they sometimes demanded that the judge show no favoritism. For example, in an assault and battery case involving a Barnwell property owner the jury added the following pointed statement to its verdict of guilty:

"The respectability of his standing does not [in our opinion] render him the less suitable object of punishment."[70]

Nonetheless, social reputation was a valuable asset to the defendants in trials for murder and in those concerning such serious offenses as grand larceny and forgery. Juries were seemingly reluctant to punish to the extreme letter of the law the prominent men or women who committed such crimes. Thus it was that Henry Shultz, a founder of Hamburg, South Carolina, was given a complete pardon after having assisted in the murder of a young boy; and William L. Yancey, the famed orator and politician, was set free by the governor after being found guilty on a manslaughter indictment.

The consensus of jurors concerning such men was adequately expressed by the reporter of a Spartanburg case in which pardon was requested for one of two defendants found guilty as partners in a grand larceny. Both men were deemed equally wrong, but one of them, Jordan Carden, was recommended to executive mercy. "The reasons which induced the Jury to . . . [make this recommendation]," wrote the recorder, "were . . . on account of his good character before the offense was committed and on account of his family connections."[71]

Essentially the same idea was expressed, it was said, by Judge Burke when on one occasion he ordered a petit jury to return a verdict of not guilty in the case of a hog-stealer who was a member of the State legislature. Asked why he demanded such a verdict, considering the fact that the culprit had admitted his crime and put himself on the mercy of the court, the venerable judge reputedly answered that he did it "for the honor of the country,—It was more important that so foul a stain should be kept off the character of the district, than that a hog thief should be punished."[72] Fortunately, perhaps, for Judge Burke and for the prestige of the State bench as a whole, few such undemocratic decisions had to be made. The majority of malfeasants who paraded before the sessions courts were too devoid of status of any sort to arouse fears that their punishment would disgrace either the State or the district wherein they resided.

The bulk of South Carolina's indicted criminals were illiterate. Inquest books and sessions records are filled with entries indicating that culprits could neither read nor write; and verbatim testimony, when made a part of the journals, is bluntly suggestive that some criminals were hardly able to speak the English language in an understandable fashion. How much of this was due to a lack of formal education and how much to simple weakmindedness is not clear. The latter attribute was apparently little understood. Unless positively identifiable as outright insanity, which was evident in only a few instances, it was rarely a factor in judicial proceedings.[73]

Distinguished observers such as Colonel Robert Barnwell and Francis Lieber recognized a clear relationship between education and crime, and both these men urged corrective action. But a host of reasons, not the least being insufficient funds, prevented the establishment in the State of any such modern development as compulsory education. A portion of Barnwell's speech to the legislature on the subjects of crime and education, as remembered by one who heard it, is worthy of repetition. "You talk much of the importance of having courts of justice established in all parts of your land, that crimes may be *punished*," Barnwell said, "Why not strike out the root of the evil by extending the means of education, that your children may learn to read the Bible and be instructed in the great principles of morality, and thus crimes be prevented?"[74]

A positive correlation between crime and poverty also existed. "The defs are poor" was a frequent entry in sessions courts' minutes; and statements to the effect that the court, as a consequence of the poverty of the accused, was forced to appoint an attorney for him were equally numerous. The situation did not materially improve during the ante-bellum years, and it was the opinion of an Horry grand jury as late as 1851 that so many defendants were then penniless as to make punishment by fine "a perfect mockery."

The existence of considerable poverty in the State was admitted by some observers as a definite cause of crimes, especially of petit and grand larceny. William Gregg, the textile manufacturer, wrote in 1845 that "thousands" in South Carolina were starving and were becoming thieves as a result; and ex-Governor James H. Hammond, five years later, estimated that as many as fifty thousand white people then had no gainful employment and were forced either to beg or to steal in order to live.[75]

A contemporary jingle pictured the economic situation of one area in these words:

> Barnwell District, Aiken town;
> O Lord in mercy do look down!
> The land is poor, the people too;
> If they don't steal what will they do?"[76]

They could do little, apparently, and certainly little was done for them. As long as a slave-worked system of one-crop agriculture remained the chief industry, the poor white (using the term literally) had little chance to improve his station. The abject nature of his poverty was shocking to observers inside and outside the State. Such English travelers as Margaret Hall, outspoken wife of the navy officer, and lecturer James S. Buckingham put his plight in print; and one acrimonious American writer penned a fictional description of a destitute South Carolina criminal which, while exaggerated in particulars, adequately sums up the quality if not the quantity of his poverty. The man described was a thief, serving his time in the Charleston jail. He was, declared the critic,

> a forlorn, dejected-looking creature. . . . His face was . . . so completely matted with dirt and made fiendish by the tufts of hair that hung over his forehead that a thrill of horror invaded our feelings. He had no shoes on his feet; and a pair of ragged pantaloons, and the shreds of a striped shirt without sleeves, secured around the waist with a string, made his only clothing. In truth, he had scarce enough on to cover his nakedness, and that so filthy and swarming with vermin, that he kept his shoulders and hands busily employed; while his skin was so encrusted with dirt as to leave no trace of its original complexion.[77]

Such a man, it was argued with considerable truth, need not be expected to remain honest.

Whether this particular wretch was a professional criminal or an amateur at the business of law-breaking is not stated. Evidence indicates that a considerable number of repeaters, "Old Offenders," and practiced experts in crime were at work within the State. The bulk of criminals, however, and especially those outside Charleston, were rank amateurs.

Professionals operated both in groups and singly, though most seemed inclined to "go it alone." As a rule the solitary professionals were either swindlers or larceners. The swindlers, as previously noted, were usually drifters with some education, who posed as physicians, jewelers, teachers, or the like. They were limited in number owing to the skill and audacity which their calling required, but they were eminently successful in South Carolina. The repeaters in larceny were a more varied lot than the swindlers. Typical of the larceny addicts were John Thomas, an incurable pickpocket; James Wilson, a waterfront thief who might be publicly whipped on Monday and found back at his petty pilfering on Tuesday; and Charles Bradley, "a bird of passage" who boasted that he had been in and out of thirty-eight jails in fewer than thirty-eight years.[78] Punishment made no apparent impression on these men. Crime was their habit, the only life they knew.

Such men were rarely dangerous. They were nuisances, but generally harmless to life and limb. On the other hand, a few criminals of the repeater type committed serious offenses, including the killing or maiming of their fellowmen. "Big Luke" Manning, of Lexington and Edgefield districts, was such a person. Prior to his being beaten and banished from the area by an angry citizen mob, he had murdered three men—gaining his freedom on each occasion at the hands of over-liberal juries. William Gaffney of Columbia had something of a similar record; except that he confined his brutal talents to the killing of Negroes. He was known to have shot or knifed two blacks by 1847. Like Manning, he finally went too far and was driven from the State by an irate citizenry. A third man with qualities of wild bestiality was William Steel of Lancaster, if the wording of that felon's arrest warrant is to be believed. According to this document, Steel was charged by the grand jury with "the murders of Sella, Bess and many more."[79]

Such homicidal maniacs as Manning, Gaffney, and Steel apparently found sadistic pleasure in killing; and Manning, at least, took a great pride in it. Some of the Manning-Gaffney-Steel type claimed self-defense in mitigation, but others could not offer the slightest pretext of a motive. A ruffian named Price, who beat to death a helpless old gentleman near Columbia simply because he could find no one else about "to vent his rage upon"; and two Charleston white men who, for the thrill of it, set their hunting dogs after an innocent Negro, and having caught him, reputedly cut him up with knives and fed him to the animals, typify those who killed wholly without reason.[80]

According to newspaper description, the usual South Carolina criminal, whether murderer, brawler, or petty thief, was twenty to twenty-five years of age, about five feet eight inches in height, of "sallow complexion," and endowed invariably with "a downcast look." He was most often an "ordinary-looking" person, but he might have such interesting physical features as projecting front teeth, a missing ear, scars on his face, a branded thumb or cheek, or perhaps a noteworthy birthmark such as a "remarkable large mole above his left eye brow" or "a flesh mark on one side of his neck, approaching a claret color." In addition, he might have noticeable

personality traits or educational deficiencies which could help lead
to his detection. Murderer James Roy, for instance, was said to be
"very talkative, but quite destitute of information, often using words
very improperly (as 'intencked' for 'attacked,' 'indolent' for 'impu-
dent,' &c.)."[81]

Many of the professionals made use of one or more aliases; and
some were best known to friend and foe by their nicknames. The
Charleston trouble-maker Joseph Williams was indicted by his title,
"Tarborough Joe," and his companion in lawless activity, Charles
Farrelly, by the name "Handsome Charlie." Much less endearing was
the descriptive surname "Big-Mouth" which was used in appellate
court records to identify James Brown, a noted stealer of Negro
slaves.[82]

On occasion the professional criminals organized themselves in
gangs. A number of these operated throughout South Carolina during
the pre-Civil War years. Rumors circulated periodically that members
of the famed John A. Murrell company of Negro and horse stealers
were working in the State, especially in the border areas of the Up
Country, but these were never proved. The Palmetto State gangs, it
would appear, were far less spectacular than that headed by the
"land pirate" of the Gulf states, whose exploits were the subject of
such atrocious South Carolina balladry as the following:

> John A Murrel is my name
> A man of renown;
> And my match in this country
> Is hard to be fown.[83]

The usual South Carolina gang was a small assemblage of miscreants, banded together for protection and convenience, and engaged in rustling cattle, robbing wayfarers, or burglarizing business
houses and residences. A Kershaw grand jury in October, 1825, complained that such a group was operating within their district and
similar reports came at intervals from Charleston, Columbia, and
other of the larger towns. Often these small groups contained members of the same family. Fathers might have their sons working with
them, as was the case with an Edgefield gang in 1849; or a man and
his wife might serve as the nucleus of a gang, as was true in 1804
of James and Mildred Carver of the Spartanburg area.[84]

Gangs were especially active in the 1840s and 1850s. A series of
robberies throughout the Up Country in 1840 and 1841 gave strong

evidence of gang operation and caused considerable loose talk about "daring North Carolina scoundrels." A small robber band was broken up by Charleston police after good detective work in 1854. This gang, four members of which were captured, confessed to activities extending from Columbia to the coast. During the same decade a group of counterfeiters and one of cattle rustlers met similar fates. A small band of highly skilled pickpockets in the Charleston area was more fortunate. This organization, which worked the railroad stations and such public events as slave sales and court days, had a woman confederate whose task was to engage the victim in conversation, holding his attention while one of her colleagues systematically rifled his pockets.[85]

No one of these criminal groups had a long existence, and none gained a wide notoriety. For that matter, no individual criminal in ante-bellum South Carolina was able to win much of a lasting reputation. The scapegrace who came nearest to capturing and holding the public attention was a forger and swindler deluxe, one David T. Hines, alias Colonel J. P. Floyd, alias the Rev. Mr. Bowman, and at least a dozen other cognomens. Beginning his one-man crime wave in Charleston in the late 1820s, he remained active until 1854 when he died in a Louisiana jail. During the quarter century he robbed numerous women, children, and elderly persons; forged notes on various banks and well-known individuals; and stole horses, watches, silverware, and clothing. He broke jail at least twice, bribed a police officer, served two light prison sentences, jumped bail once, and was banished from several communities. At least two state governors offered rewards for his capture. Ruthless, vain, utterly without moral conscience, he took considerable pride in his lawless successes and as early as 1840 wrote and had published a crude, egocentric biographical sketch of himself.[86]

South Carolina claimed Hines, but he worked at his profession in Georgia, Alabama, Mississippi, Louisiana, and Texas. Newspapers in each of those states kept track of him and by the date of his death his name was rather widely known throughout the lower South. "This notorious man is second only to Murrell," declared one South Carolina editor, "and as a literary man, [he is] far superior to the great land pirate. Few men possess as fine talents as the swindler in question, which in many instances places him beyond suspicion, and furnishes him capital to operate upon when in a tight place."[87]

David Hines was in a class by himself. For the most part South Carolina's criminals were ignorant and unimpressive. They were numerous—enough so to create anxiety throughout the State, especially in Charleston and the larger towns. Their crimes were occasioned, their contemporaries thought, by a variety of problems ranging from the free use of hard liquor to an inherited quickness of temper. They were, as they will always be, in South Carolina and elsewhere, an expensive, troublesome minority whose impact on social history was and is noteworthy.

II. The Types of Crime

CRIMINAL ACTS IN ANTE-BELLUM SOUTH CAROLINA WERE GROUPED much as today, into three main categories: crimes against the person, crimes against property, and crimes against public morals. The first consisted essentially of such misdeeds as assault and battery, mayhem, murder, manslaughter, and rape. In the aggregate these represent the numerical bulk of lawless acts committed by nineteenth century South Carolinians.

Crimes against the Person

As noted previously, assault and battery was the crime which occasioned more than half of all sessions courts' indictments. Ranging in variety from fights between husband and wife to attempts at murder, street brawls, and small scale riots, assault and battery points up a quality of pugnaciousness in ante-bellum society which in the twentieth century has been somewhat subdued. In 1950, for instance, it accounted for only fifteen per cent of South Carolina criminal indictments.

The high assault and battery rate was not a matter of public concern in the State. As long as property was not destroyed or "persons of quality" involved, the average citizen accepted the "Irish discussions with sticks" as natural outlets for over-agitated emotions. Grand juries which mentioned assault and battery seemed concerned less with the crime than with the fact that too much court time had to be devoted to it. Thus a Laurens jury in 1820 urged that judges be given the power to punish the offenders summarily; and a Chester jury in 1825 pled that assault and battery cases be placed under the exclusive jurisdiction of the less important magistrates' and freeholders' courts.[1] Nothing came of these and similar presentments, but they had some merit. The minor cases crowded sessions calendars; and although they were rushed through the courts with impatient haste, too often they forced the postponement of more serious business.[2]

A few newspapers carried notices condemning the superfluity of assault and battery but the bulk of such incidents, if reported at all by the press, received cursory treatment. Such an account as the following from the Charleston *Courier* is typical: "A fracas occurred, we understand, on Monday night . . . between William Nelson and Joseph Williams, during which the former was shot and the latter severely cut. . . . We refrain from entering into particulars."[3] Newspaper editors did become interested if the "sett-toos" involved numerous defendants. About five per cent of assault and battery cases listed three or more defendants and these were considered newsworthy. As a rule the law which applied to these multi-participant fights was the "riot code," and punishment was naturally more severe than for simple assault and battery.[4]

Such significant criticism as was made of either rioting or petty brawling came from interested citizens outside the circle of governmental officialdom. An angered resident of Anderson, for instance, wrote that he believed the toughs in his village ought to be driven from town by a volunteer posse. The ruffians were dedicated, he said, "to proving that men are descended from monkeys," and to that end they had "set themselves to work in scratching, biting, and otherwise mal-treating each others faces."

"How long shall these doggeries abuse our patience and corrupt our negroes?" he asked.[5]

In a lighter vein, Margaret Tinsley of Newberry also expressed her opinion of the "rougher element" in the district. Engaged in conversation with Peter Moon, a theologian who was instructing her in the wonders of judgment day, she said:

"You tell me, Doctor, that everybody will be there?"

"Yes."

"Will that lying Vines Dailey be there?"

"Yes."

"And that big bullying Bill Turner?"

"Yes."

"And that big fighting Billy McGlamery?"

"Yes."

"Then it is sure to be a great day of rioting. Doctor, give in my excuse; I will be there the day after."[6]

In their outspoken opposition both Widow Tinsley and the irate Andersonian represented a minority. Fights and brawls were not only accepted by most citizens as events akin to spectator sports, but were considered in some quarters as bordering on the necessary. "Of course to knock a man down is never good manners," wrote one editor, but "there are cases in society when it is quite incumbent on you to [do so]." . . . However, he continued, a certain graciousness should always be observed: "viz, whether you can command your temper or not, never show it, except by the blow. Never . . . use such expressions as 'take that' &c."[7]

Assault and battery in South Carolina was usually some non-crippling variation of "the game of knock-down and drag-out." On occasion it sank to the low level of eye-gouging or some other form of mayhem. These practices were not accepted with the tolerance accorded less desperate fighting and as early as 1786 any defendant found guilty of premeditated mayhem was legally subject to the death penalty. According to this harsh law, mayhem was "violently depriving" another person of a member of his body, the ears and nose excepted. The ears and nose were excepted, it was explained, because the loss of these only disfigured and did not physically weaken the victim. Thus to chew off an opponent's index finger was to take a chance on being hanged in public ceremony; but to snap off his nose was merely to invite a five dollar fine, or perhaps a turn at the whipping post.[8] Obviously it paid to bite in accordance with the statutes.

Perhaps because of the severity of the law, mayhem indictments were rare in ante-bellum South Carolina. Nonetheless, contemporary observers remembered it as a noteworthy crime. Benjamin F. Perry recalled meeting a number of Up Country men who had been blinded or half-blinded in gouging contests; and he wrote that Judge Aedanus Burke, while holding court at Cambridge circuit, was so appalled by the number of one-eyed men as to admonish his grand jurors: "Before God, gentlemen of the jury, I never saw such a thing before in the world! There is a plaintiff with an eye out! A juror with an eye out! And two witnesses with an eye out! What a state of society you must have in this part of the country!"[9]

Another South Carolina judge, Elihu H. Bay, was said to have had before him in the same court a defendant who was missing a portion of his upper lip and another who had lost an ear. Bay sentenced the men to equal terms in a common jail cell, saying "[now] you may *bite one another as much as you please.*"[10]

Mayhem, unlike assault and battery, aroused considerable public interest, but the populace rightly considered murder and rape the more serious crimes against the person. Of these, rape was the least important statistically, amounting to less than one-half of one per cent of sessions courts' indictments sampled. This figure is only slightly lower than that for 1950, and considering the fact that indictments of Negroes for rape are not included in pre-Civil War sessions courts records, the crime appears to have increased little, if any, with the passing of years.[11] In other words, the chivalric position supposedly accorded white women in ante-bellum years apparently was no more effective than present day attitudes in preventing such violations.

Possibly the fact that almost no publicity was given to rape cases accounts for the notion in some quarters that the crime was practically unheard of in nineteenth century society. Newspaper editors usually treated rape as a taboo subject, acting on the supposition, perhaps, that a raped woman and her relatives ought not to suffer the added embarrassment of publicity. This would seem somewhat futile, however, since the trial of a white rapist was held in open court.

Then as now in South Carolina there existed a strong belief that Negroes were more apt than whites to instigate rapes. Accounts of unsolved rapes which found their way into grand jury presentments frequently suggested that all local Negroes be carefully questioned. Such opinions could be found as well in the rare newspaper accounts of rapes. The Cheraw *Gazette,* for instance, had the following to say concerning an 1836 case: "Suspicion immediately fixed on a negro man . . . [who] had been seen lurking about the road during that day."[12]

Murder in ante-bellum South Carolina accounted for four per cent of all criminal indictments; but judging from newspaper accounts of unsolved crimes and from the number of questionable deaths reported by unskilled coroners' juries as "accidental drownings" or "Visitations of God," the indictment figure represents not more than half the number of murders actually committed.

The drownings especially illustrate this point. Almost without exception a drowned man or woman was declared a suicide. Bruises on the bloated bodies were said to have been self-afflicted; crowbars and other weights "securely lashed" to such bodies were said to have been affixed by the dead persons. In one noteworthy instance concerning a man found in a millstream, a coroner's jury returned a verdict of suicide despite the fact that the victim's "feet were tied together . . . and his hands were confined in the same manner."[13]

Whatever the actual murder figure, the indictment percentage alone is more than double that of white citizens for the same crime in present day South Carolina. The inference seems clear that the ante-bellum citizen shot or stabbed on slight provocation and that his generation had neither a high moral regard for human life nor a healthy respect for the laws concerning it.

One result of the high murder rate was a seeming callousness toward the crime on the part of people who might have been expected to react otherwise. Some voices were raised but they had little unity of purpose. Newspapers often headlined murder stories with such banners as "Appalling Intelligence," "Shocking Occurrence," "Melancholy Recontre," or "Horrid Affair," but more often than not disapproval ended with the title. In general it would appear that English traveler James Stirling was near the truth when he wrote from Charleston in 1857: "When Herr von Hinckeldey, the Prussian Minister of Police, was shot last year . . . the whole of Europe rang with indignant denunciation; while here, citizens murder each other . . . and the fact is recorded as coolly as the . . . variation of a cent a pound in the price of cotton."[14]

This general inclination of the citizenry stoically to accept homicide is not meant to imply that they paid it no attention. Like all people of all times and places the Carolinians had a morbid curiosity about killings and killers. Murder trials were the high points of court proceedings in any district, and murder tales, written or verbal, were popular. Such novels as *The Life of Johnson the Murderer,* published by S. Babcock and Company, and *The Devil in Petticoats,* written by Mason L. Weems, were widely advertised and doubtlessly sold well. In addition, bizarre incidents such as the slaying of several wayfarers by tavern keeper Lavinia Fisher and her husband became legends. Indeed, the amazon Lavinia, who was supposed to have shouted to the mob gathered at her gallows, "If you have a message you want to send to hell, give it to me, I'll carry it," became in the public mind something of a heroine.[15]

In type and character, murder in South Carolina was not essentially different from what it was elsewhere. Even so, certain observations are noteworthy. Murder was rarely committed for financial gain. Rather it came in answer to an insult, real or assumed, or as the result of the mixture of argument and whisky, or in connection with some minor affray which, in a later period, would probably have resulted in a bare knuckle fight.

Most murdering was done with a knife or club instead of a gun. In Horry District, for example, stabbing led shooting by a five-to-three ratio; and in Edgefield, murder capital of the State, twenty-four of thirty-seven consecutive murders were committed by weapons other than firearms.[16] This suggests that among the common folk, at least, pistols and rifles were not widely owned. Knives, rocks, clubs, axes, and an array of poisons were typical murder implements. Not so typical, but also used, were a sharpened stick, a horse's skull, a metal-bound Bible, and the "tip of a umbrellar."

Of all weapons, poison created the highest public horror and dread. This fearsome attitude toward poison stemmed from the idea that Negro slaves and free Negroes were skilled in its use, and any death by arsenic or similar chemical was given wide publicity. Such publicity, in turn, influenced the State legislature, and a special law was early enacted specifying the death penalty not only for actual poisoning but for any attempt at it.[17]

Murder totals would reach a higher peak, certainly, if deaths by duelling and the killing of Negroes were included. Legally both should be. According to the letter of the law, a man killed in a duel on "the field of honor" was, after 1812, deemed to have been murdered and his antagonist, whether the challenger or the challenged, a murder-er.[18] Similarly, the killing of a Negro, which prior to 1821 was defined by the courts as "the highest species of misdemeanor known in our laws," was thereafter declared to be murder. That is to say, it was murder unless the defendant could prove to the satisfaction of a jury that he had killed the Negro "in suddent heat and passion." If this could be done, the crime was again classified a misdemeanor and punished by a fine. This legal loophole was intentionally large and only a few white men were executed during the ante-bellum years for murdering blacks.[19] An English consul, stationed at Charleston during the 1850s, wrote with some truth that it was "literally no more to kill a slave than to shoot a dog."[20]

The number of slaves and free Negroes killed by white people before 1860 is not a matter of record outside of coroners' books. Most of these records, unfortunately, are not extant, but one of the few which has been preserved lists sixty-five murders, sixteen of which were Negroes killed by whites. Fourteen of these were Negro men, two were women, and all were slaves. Other available sources indicate similar statistics.[21]

Now and then, as might be expected, the procedure was reversed and Negroes killed whites. Such cases were heard by magistrates and freeholders summoned for the purpose and only those convictions which were successfully appealed by slave masters or other interested white men came into the regular sessions court system. Some whites hired or forced Negroes to kill for them, and at least one wife rid herself of an unwanted husband by this method.[22]

The duelling laws, unlike those concerning the killing of slaves, had no obvious loopholes. They needed none, for they simply were not enforced. The duel was too much a factor in the social system of the ante-bellum South Carolina upper classes for statute law to bring about its decline. Public opinion refused to regard duelling as criminal; and this conflict of law and sentiment was not resolved until the duel, like many Southern social institutions, became a casualty of the Civil War.

It is not known how many South Carolinians were killed or injured in formal duels. Affairs of honor, as they were called, did not always make newspaper columns and no official public record was kept of them. There are, nonetheless, sufficient sources of various types to indicate the excessive frequency of the "Gentlemen's altercations." William L. King, for example, lists in his contemporary survey of the Charleston press sixty-three duels fought by citizens of that city between 1806 and 1839; and the editor of the Camden *Gazette* apparently attached no special importance to a matter-of-fact announcement in 1817 that three duels had occurred in a single week near his town. One had taken place on Sunday, he said, another on Monday, and a third on Wednesday.[23]

Such foreign travelers to South Carolina as William Faux and James S. Buckingham may be cited in support of the thesis that Charleston and South Carolina generally held records for duelling episodes in America. Faux, writing from the port city, insisted that he had been introduced to thirteen men, eleven of whom "had killed their man each" in duels. They met, he said "as gay proud birds of a feather." Buckingham, an especially accurate English observer, was shocked by the number of duels in the State during the 1840s and declared that the citizenry shrugged off such affairs, even those which ended in death, as "manifestations of manly spirit."[24]

The avowed purpose of the duel was to provide a remedy for slander, insinuation, and personal slight. Defenders of the code declared that the courts were powerless to defend against insults and that gentlemen could not be expected to engage in fisticuffs. Hence the duel, carried out in accordance with written rules of procedure and protocol,[25] was regarded in some circles as a necessity. Whatever the merits of the argument, a challenge to a duel could not easily be turned down. One who refused was publicly posted as a coward and such a fate was considered far worse than being tried for murder under a duelling indictment.

Actually there was little danger of conviction in being so tried. Despite a growing opposition to duelling, led by ministers, judges, editors, and educators, and expressed through the mediums of "anti-duelling" societies, juries rarely found a duellist guilty of any crime. A few men were tried and a small percentage fined, but no duellist was tried and convicted of murder. Statute law held that homicide might be either "felonious, justifiable, or excusable," and South Carolina jurors invariably found one of the two latter limitations applicable to the duellist.

Indeed the failure of juries to bring in verdicts of guilty was not restricted to those murder cases which resulted from good aim on the field of honor. The bulk of all homicide defendants were either acquitted or found guilty of manslaughter, which did not carry the death penalty. Juries had full authority to return manslaughter verdicts,[26] despite the wording of the original indictment, and they did so with amazing regularity. A typical source which illustrates this laxness of juries concerning murder is the 1844-1858 volume of sessions court minutes for Edgefield District. During those years thirty-three men were tried on murder indictments. Of these, eighteen were acquitted, ten were deemed guilty of manslaughter, and only five were convicted of murder.

Some murder cases were never brought to court. Coroners' juries decided among themselves at times that certain murderers had killed their victims with "good cause" and should not suffer a trial. These jurors then worded their reports so as to exclude court action. Whether their decisions were morally correct or not, such an attitude hardly contributed to a respect for law or the judicial system. This tendency to punish lightly the most serious of crimes—to refuse to indict the "gentleman murderer," to return a "no bill" against the duellist, to acquit the killer of the Negro, and to "soften" the verdict against the common assassin—doubtlessly had much to do with the high homicide rate. In addition, it serves to illustrate the somewhat lackadaisical and resigned attitude of many South Carolina citizens toward all crimes against the person.

Crimes Against Property

The misdeeds calling forth the highest public wrath in ante-bellum South Carolina were crimes against property. Rioting and brawling might be passed off as "exercising hot blood," and murder might be excused as necessary or reasonable; but the social code called for personal honesty, and deviations from that principle were met with thorough disapprobation. The penal statutes illustrate this attitude. According to the law, grand larceny was to be punished by hanging, and petit larceny by a fine, jail sentence, public lashing, branding, or any combination of any of the four. Stealing anything with a value of four dollars or more was generally termed grand larceny; but even this illiberal distinction was not a rigid one and jurors were allowed to use their own initiative regardless of the nature or amount of the theft. It could and did happen that the same jury which would change a murderer's indictment to manslaughter would condemn a common thief to the gallows without hesitation.[27]

Perhaps it was well that thievery and associated varieties of larceny were so rudely accepted. For even with that deterrent seventeen per cent of all criminal indictments sampled concerned stolen property, and as previously noted the majority of thieves were not caught. The temptation to rob was a strong one in South Carolina where police were too few and poor communication facilities made escape relatively easy. Petty larceny, especially, was an ever-present evil in the towns and along the roads, and newspapers printed an endless series of advertisements of articles pilfered.

Stage roads which linked the villages and towns were favored by many thieves as areas of operation. The highways entering Charleston and the main road leading to Camden appear to have been particularly dangerous for the wayfarer. Now and then stages and trains were stopped by brigands who gave the mail bags and the luggage of the travelers their special attention, but a preferred procedure was to waylay the lone horseback rider. Nelson Alexander, of Fairfield District, was a victim of such an attack in 1837, and his case offers an example of the brutality which might be expected of highwaymen. Traveling toward Edgefield he was halted by three men who forced him to dismount. Then, "filling his eyes and mouth with a substance . . . of a poisonous nature," they dragged him to the woods where they beat him, robbed him, and left him for dead.[28]

But most thievery of personal goods took place in the towns. There desirable articles of prey were such items as "red morocco" pocketbooks, beaver hats, "drape cloth" overcoats, silver mugs, gold watches, dinner tableware, and soup ladles. The last named item must have been especially valuable. Newspapers mentioned them time and again as having been stolen. Such notices as the following were typical: "W. B." reports the loss of two costly soup spoons and a soup ladle; "J.P." offers a large reward for the capture of the thief who made off with eleven spoons; and "G. H." declares that a "heartless wretch" had taken from his home on King Street—one soup ladle.[29]

These large spoons were not the only unusual objects to attract the attention of the "light fingered gentry." A Yorkville barber reported the loss of his hone ("Borrowed without my Concent," he wrote); tourist Anne N. Royall had her travel-worn and well-filled notebook stolen from a bench in Charleston (police managed to return it to her); the body of a dead man was removed from its grave in Newberry (two local physicians were guilty); and at Lancaster the local newspaper office was rifled. "On Friday night last," reported the editor, "some poor devil entered the 'Ledger Office,' and took . . . several articles belonging to our foreman. He must have been . . . grossly ignorant of this world, or he would never have entered a Printing-office for plunder."[30]

Charleston in particular was plagued with petty thieves. There and in Columbia, Sumter, Hamburg, and other of the larger towns, professional pickpockets had to be reckoned with. Several of these scamps were caught, jailed, and exiled, but they seemed nonetheless not to decrease in number. Their crime eventually reached such proportions that it was made a felony, and newspapers printed special pickpocket warnings. *"Citizens Be On Your Guard!"* a Charleston paper warned in 1824; and as late as 1851, Sumter residents and visitors were told to "Beware of those who . . . press[ed] upon them" at public gatherings or at the railroad depot.[31]

Pickpockets who worked in pairs sometimes made use of the following *modus operandi*: one of the two, holding a pocketbook, would approach a stranger and ask, "Didn't you lose this?" The unwary gentleman would then pat his pocket, thus disclosing the location of his own wallet; and in due time the second rogue would relieve him of it. This trick, it was said, worked well with elderly victims.[32]

Street robbers, less gifted than pickpockets, depended on more direct physical contact for their success. They might, in rare cases, chloroform a man by pressing a doused cloth to his face, and rob him at leisure. Or two ruffians might steal a citizen's pocketbook and watch in this manner: one would throw his arms about the victim, the other would give the hapless prisoner a few sharp, quick blows to the stomach; and the robbery would proceed. J. B. Holmes, a Charleston physician, experienced this rough treatment and could vouch for its success.[33]

Town and city thieves did not devote their full attention to the waylaying and robbing of individuals. Homes, banks, places of business, and even ships in port were visited with discouraging frequency by "midnight marauders."

These criminals were rightfully considered more dangerous than pickpockets, and house burglars in particular were treated without sympathy by juries. Despite this unrelenting attitude concerning them, the house burglars were always at work. Toward the close of the ante-bellum period they became exceedingly active. A Charleston critic in 1854 declared that the city was infested with "night gangs" which brazenly broke into dwellings while the residents slept; and a Columbia citizen, a year later, made essentially the same charge with reference to his town. Similarly, during the 1840s and 1850s, house burglars were presenting Sumter and Edgefield town authorities with problems of major proportions.[34]

Those years also witnessed an increase in the plundering of business establishments. Unlike private dwellings, however, stores and shops had long been considered by the criminal fraternity as worthy of their notice, and newspaper accounts such as the following (usually more literate) were much in evidence from the early 1800s:

LOOK OUT FOR ROGUES

On Wednesday night, a Shop in Tradd-street was broken open and robbed. A white man was seen standing near with one shutter missing but not suspected at the time.[35]

House burglars and store robbers made use of a variety of tools in their work. A Pendleton robber in 1842 gained entrance into a general store with "a screw auger"; and a Charleston burglar some years later, who in his haste left his tools at the scene of the crime, had employed "brace, bit, screw-drivers, chisel, &c." A Sumter robber caught pursuing his odious profession in 1854 possessed not only a "bag of jimmy tools," but a "ring of skeleton keys" and a "vial of chloroform."[36]

Skeleton keys were often the only mechanical aids the thief needed. This was pointed out in 1857 by an Edgefield homeowner, who composed the following advertisement:

SURREPTITIOUSLY ABDUCTED

Last Saturday night, some petty felon introduced himself into our smoke-house and helped himself to three pieces of corned-beef and a . . . middling of bacon. There is someone about with a bunch of accomodating keys. Look to your locks, and load up the old blunderbuss as we have done.[37]

One species of property attractive to thieves in town and country was the domestic animal. More than twenty-five per cent of all larceny indictments dealt with stolen horses, cattle, hogs, and poultry. Of these, horses were the most important while hogs were the most numerous.

Until 1830 horse stealing in South Carolina was classified as a capital crime. Thereafter to 1860 the law specified the death penalty for second offenders only, punishing first convictions with a fine, a jail sentence, and from fifty to 119 lashes at a public whipping post.[38]

This promise of harsh treatment if caught did not, it would seem, deter the thief. From his point of view the chance of being apprehended was not very great. Horses were readily accessible to the night prowler, they could be ridden swiftly away from the scene of the theft, and they were salable everywhere. Many horse thieves were captured but it is clear, considering the number of animals reported stolen, that many escaped.[39]

The hog stealer and cattle thief apparently held similar views concerning their chances of being caught, and were equally active. Their punishment, if caught and convicted, was not so drastic as that given horse thieves. Generally the hog and cattle rustlers were fined twenty to forty dollars, or forced to suffer thirty-nine to fifty lashes for each offense.[40]

Court records indicate that more hogs were stolen than any other animal. Especially in the Low Country, unfenced swine must have been considered by many residents as nothing less than a species of common property. In Horry District, for instance, swine stealing cases over a forty-two year period made up eight per cent of sessions courts' indictments; and in Darlington District they were seven per cent for thirty-five years. In view of the fact that many hog stealers were never apprehended, such thievery in those districts must have been a crime of amazing proportions.

In that connection, an Horry case brought to light probably the champion of all ante-bellum animal thieves. At the fall session of court in 1835, John Rabon was tried on one count of horse stealing, one of hog stealing, one of bull stealing, and one of stealing bee hives. A lenient and perhaps admiring jury turned in a verdict fining him but one hundred dollars and sentencing him to only a year in jail.[41]

Any listing of property stolen from ante-bellum South Carolinians must include Negro slaves. As might be expected, kidnapping a slave was a serious offense and from 1754 carried the death sentence as a penalty.[42] Further, sessions courts' juries were rarely given to consideration of extenuating circumstances in arriving at their verdicts against slave stealers. Now and then a jury would recommend mercy, but such cases were few. A Darlington jury in 1816 recommended clemency for a kidnapper on the grounds that "the crime of stealing a negro is not more deserving of death than the murdering which only subjects to fine and imprisonment"; but the usual pronouncement stated, "WE say . . . [that he] is guilty and we say . . . [he] shd be hung at once."[43]

The rigorous enforcement of the death penalty in this connection probably points out the influence of the slave owner class over the jurors and agencies of justice generally. At any rate, no other South Carolina criminal was so consistently punished to the extreme letter of the law as was the stealer of slaves. The kidnapper of Negroes was "the anarchist of Southern serfdom" and as such could not be lightly treated.

Actual figures on slave stealing are impossible to obtain. Slaves were stolen but they also absconded of their own free will. In a doubtful case who could say which had happened? This fact was recognized by the slave owner, and most newspaper notices were headed: "RUN AWAY OR STOLEN."

Whatever the actual number of Negroes stolen, few kidnappers were brought to court. Of ten thousand indictments sampled, only 111 were for the crime. As pointed out by Professor Howell M. Henry in his Police Control of the Slave in South Carolina, slave stealing was for the glib criminal a singularly easy misdeed in which to deny participation. If caught with a Negro, one had only to say that he had come across the black, who appeared to be a runaway, and was escorting him to the nearest authority. Slave testimony to the contrary was not acceptable in court.[44]

The various categories of larceny constituted the bulk of crimes against property, but three additional species of lawlessness—arson, counterfeiting, and swindling—were listed in the same grouping. These three, while of comparatively little consequence in sessions courts' records, ranked high in public interest. All were considered felonies and one of them, arson, was a criminal act much feared by South Carolinians.

Indeed, the occurrence in a given area of any series of fires was a fact sufficient to put the citizens in a state of semi-hysteria. This was especially true of the towns. The presence of a multitude of flimsy wooden buildings, the general belief that Negroes were pyromaniacal, and the knowledge that fire fighting equipment was woefully inadequate were factors explaining the dread and hatred of arsonists.

The notion that Negroes were prone to use fire as a weapon of revenge was apparently little short of an obsession. Any fire, it appears, was followed by a fast moving rumor that a Negro or Negroes were responsible. In Charleston, as early as 1796-1798, slaves were arrested, tried, and some found guilty on the sheerest of hearsay evidence that they had formed conspiracies "to fire the city." Similar arrests took place in Camden in 1816, and these occasioned the observation from a frightened resident, that "our gaol is filled with negroes. They are stretched on their backs on the bare floor and scarcely move their heads. . . . This is really a dreadful situation to be in—I think it is time for us to leave a country where we cannot go to bed in safety."[45]

This situation worsened as the years passed, and from 1830 forward a burning house, barn, or cotton gin was the signal for increased patrol activity and for immediate "close examination" of all Negroes found in the vicinity of the fire.[46]

It seems reasonably clear, however, that the extreme fear of arsonists was not justified in terms of their number. Firebugs existed, and Negro slaves doubtlessly made some use of fire as an instrument of vengeance, but South Carolina citizens who considered all unexplained blazes to have been set by incendiaries were not being realistic. The fact that only a few arsonists were caught made little difference in this attitude of the people and newspapers rarely told of any conflagration, major or minor, without concluding the account with such a sentence as "Undoubtedly started by an evil disposed person," or *"Supposed to be the work of an incendiary!"*[47]

Private dwellings, general stores, paint shops, turpentine warehouses, manufacturing plants, gin buildings, even entire towns were listed, without proof, as targets hit by the firebrand. The disastrous Charleston fires of 1825, 1838, and 1849 were commonly supposed to have been set by such criminals, as were the Columbia fires of 1804 and 1854. A number of small blazes in Sumter in 1853 were declared to be evidence of attempts at large scale arson, and the discovery in 1837 of burning cotton bales on the Hamburg river front was said to represent an effort to destroy that new railroad town.[48]

At least one South Carolina editor, noting this mass of unproved charges, wrote in 1845 that despite the positive statements of his fellow journalists, he was beginning to believe less in incendiaries and more in "carelessness and dry atmosphere."[49] But his was a minority voice.

A sufficient number of actual arson episodes presented themselves to make the exaggerated fear of the crime somewhat understandable. Such events as the destruction of the *Courier* and *Mercury* offices in Charleston by a pyromaniacal journeyman, the burning of the Camden jail by an inmate, and the firing of the Sumter courthouse by "a person unknown" are cases in point.[50]

The police generally believed, with some reason, that thieves might try arson to cloak their activities. Similarly it was recognized that some store or home owners might be guilty of burning their own establishments in order to collect insurance.[51] Most proved arson cases, however, were deemed acts of "pusillanimous revenge," and in the absence of definite facts to the contrary were assumed to be the deeds of dissatisfied blacks. The intensification of the abolition movement in the 1840s and 1850s made such conclusions seem the more plausible.

The most successful criminals in ante-bellum South Carolina were not arsonists but counterfeiters. Few of them were caught, yet the appearance in newspapers from 1800 to 1860 of entire columns listing and describing counterfeit money makes it clear that they were numerous; or, if not numerous, a hard working and fast moving few.

In the 1820s newspapers reported that large quantities of fake half-dollar coins and equally worthless one-dollar, twenty-dollar, and fifty-dollar bills were flooding the State. Counterfeit half-dimes were said to be in wide circulation in the 1840s, and an issue of eight-dollar notes printed by the Bank of Charleston in 1847 had to be hurriedly recalled because it proved too easily copied. Fraudulent bank notes of every denomination from one to five hundred dollars were described in newspaper advertisements in the 1850s; and in 1855 the attention of citizens was called to the fact that gold dollars "made of pure brass, gilt" were being passed from hand to hand in Columbia. By 1853 counterfeit coins and bills became so numerous that a lecturer, John Vane, toured the State, teaching interested audiences how to recognize bad money at sight; and in 1858 *Peterson's Counterfeit Detector,* a monthly magazine, made its appearance in South Carolina.[52]

As early as 1787 counterfeiting was classified as a felony and carried the death sentence. This act remained on the statute books until 1845. In that year, despite an apparent increase of the crime, the death penalty was abolished and thirty-nine lashes, a fine, and one to seven years imprisonment substituted for it.[53]

One reason why counterfeiters were not often caught was their skillful mobility. They moved into a town, bought whatever they could with their bogus currency, and hastily departed. For example, one caravan of ten "coupon passers," captured near Columbia in 1852, had earlier disposed of bad bills in Charleston, and before that had operated with success in Georgia, Kentucky, Tennessee, and Louisiana.[54]

Counterfeiters were among the elite of the criminal class. They dressed well and made a good general appearance. Sometimes they operated singly, in the guise of teachers, physicians, or ministers. Again, they worked in groups, posing as traders or tourists. Whatever the mode, most of them were experienced in their criminal profession.

The manufacturer of fake money was simply a highly technical swindler. The 1845 law put him on a legal par with other dealers in fraud and malicious misrepresentation and from that date the counterfeiter, forger, professional gambler, and ordinary swindler were viewed alike by judge and jury.

In common with the counterfeiters, their cousins in crime, the forgers and sharpers generally were professional scamps. Like the counterfeiters they worked fast and made good use of such tools as an honest face, a glib tongue, and well-tailored clothing. Again like the counterfeiters, they were apparently more numerous than sessions courts' indictments suggest. They plied South Carolina during the ante-bellum years, fleecing the citizenry with schemes which ranged from marked faro cards and forged land deeds to complicated frauds; and apparently most of them escaped capture and punishment.

The South Carolina law against swindlers was not harsh by comparison with other criminal statutes of the State. Most varieties of swindle were punishable by fine or imprisonment, the court being authorized to determine by rules of its own choosing the amount of either. Usually a swindler was fined double the sum he had gained, plus an amount to be paid the informer, should there be one. If a jail term was substituted for the fine it most often ranged from six months to one year.

The single species of swindle which was not so treated was forgery. After 1801 the punishment for this misdeed was death on the gallows. Forgery was usually the signing of a man's name to a promissory note; and owing to the highly negotiable nature of such instruments this was essentially a counterfeit.[55]

Forgers were given little sympathy. To misuse a gentleman's name was a violation of the unwritten as well as the written codes, and it was rare that an indicted forger gained his freedom. Benjamin F. Perry was quite properly well pleased with his ability as a criminal lawyer when he wrote his wife in 1838 that he had spent the day "defending a poor fellow who was tried for his life on a charge of forgery, and succeeded in getting him acquitted."[56] Such success was uncommon.

The swindler most prevalent in ante-bellum South Carolina was not the forger but the professional gambler. "Of all the vices to which men are liable," wrote one critic, "that of gambling is the most hurtful. Oh, it is shocking! Abominable! Dammable! It corrodes the heart, it destroys all the finer feelings of man." Another declared that "The finished gambler has no heart. . . . The club with which he herds would meet though all its members were in mourning. They would meet though the place of rendezvous was the chamber of the dying; they would meet though it were an apartment in the charnel house. Not even the death of kindred can effect [sic] the gambler. He would play upon his father's sepulchre."[57]

Most complaints were not directed at gambling itself but to the thievery and murder which it allegedly caused. Gaming ruins the character, wrote one editor, but worse, it makes a man covet his neighbor's goods. It is "calculated to debase the human mind," said another. Gambling snares the young man, declared a third, and drives him, "from a sense of his degradation . . . [to] take the life of his fellowman." "If Tertullian wrote now," asked a fourth, "what would he say of those professing Christians who to make money build . . . Gaming establishments, and such like places? Would he not say that he who doeth such things is . . . implicated in the guilt incurred by the promotion of such drunkenness, vice, and murder?" In substance, whether or not gambling as such was considered wrong, it allegedly created robbers from honest men and killers from erstwhile peaceful citizens. It was for this reason, wrote "a citizen from the sandhills," that gamblers must be driven out of the State. "A few startling examples must be made," he insisted.[58]

But the startling examples were not made. Several city ordinances were enacted against open gambling, but regardless of these a substantial percentage of the male population refused to consider their "faro-faro," "rowley-powley," or "snap-and-rattle" as anything but wholesome recreation and exciting amusement with a possibility for profit. Hence police officers paid little attention to gambling. About two per cent of sessions courts' indictments were for gaming, but at least seventy per cent of such indictments failed to come to trial. Those gamblers found guilty were, almost invariably, itinerant professionals. The situation was perhaps accurately expressed by the editor of a Columbia newspaper in 1845. "The . . . [gamblers] are well known," he wrote, "and yet they are permitted to remain unmolested. The petty thief is zealously hunted and severely punished, but the *black legs,* the wholesale plunderers, the tempters and destroyers of our youth, are permitted to roam at large."[59]

In Charleston and Columbia especially the skilled gambler had an easy time of it. Despite the laws forbidding gaming houses and declaring the keepers to be vagrants, such establishments flourished from the turn of the nineteenth century. One traveler wrote that refugees from San Domingo had introduced "all the new French games" to Charleston gaming parlors, and that "aristocracy and sans culottes mix in friendly intercourse and indiscriminately surround the tables. It is asserted that they play very high."[60]

Two of the better known Charleston gambling houses were located on Legaré Street and on Society Street. The Legaré street establishment was run by Miss Polly Rupel, and there "the elite of society . . . risked their hearts and small change at cribbage."[61] But small change was not the issue at the Society Street house. According to an irate citizen, writing in 1835, "a young man from Sumter District was decoyed into . . . [this place] and a notorious individual, after getting him intoxicated, *'eased'* him out of *One Hundred and Seventy-five Dollars*. I called on the young man the morning after, and found him . . . resolved to commit *Suicide*. . . . Can we not scour these *demons out* of our city? Christians, I call upon you to answer this question."[62] Such episodes and worse continued to occur in Charleston throughout the ante-bellum decades. As late as April, 1851, a grand jury there declared that gambling, led by professionals, was an evil of "fearful magnitude," and demanded its "instant suppression."

Only in Columbia did requests for action against gamblers meet with any noteworthy success. Because of the presence of the college youth in the town, authorities made a strong effort to enforce anti-gaming legislation; but if the presence of the college boys was conducive to such a public attitude, it also made Columbia unusually attractive to the gamblers—for who would be more apt to bet his money than an impetuous young aristocrat, away from the restraining influence of his home? The gamblers took their chances and brought their "tables covered with green cloth" into the capital city.[63]

The favored games of chance in Columbia were chuck-a-luck and E-O. The latter, which apparently was a forerunner of present day poker, was made the subject of a special prohibitive town ordinance in 1817.[64] The former, a banking game played with three dice, was remembered by one Columbian as follows:

> All young men disposed to gamble,
> Chuckaluck's a game that's easy to handle;
> The more you put down, less you take up,
> And that's the game they call Chuckaluck.[65]

Either game could be costly to the participants. Philip Pearson, for example, recalled that on one occasion he had to go to the assistance of a prospective brother-in-law who had lost in one of the games not only his money but also his trousers.[66]

Professional gamblers usually operated singly and when criticism of their activity became too strong they quickly changed their base. On occasion they worked in pairs, using various signals to aid each other. Such a couple, it was said, won card games by the following procedure: One of the gamblers would while playing, sing the following ditty:

> There was a man, he had a cow,
> And nothing for to feed her;
> He slapped his hand upon her rump,
> And said, Consider, cow, consider.

It was finally decided by opponents that the singer's partner based his leads and bets on information given by the tune. "Look here," said one of the players, "don't tell that cow to consider any more. . . . When you lay stress on 'consider,' you mean one thing; and when you lay it on *slap,* you mean another. . . . I insist on your playing the game without bringing up that darned old cow."[67]

In addition to operating card games, professional gamblers took bets on horse races and cockfights. A few made quick fortunes through the skillful manipulation of a bean under three thimbles— a practice not unknown today. Others instigated illegal lotteries, selling the tickets and pocketing the profits.

The lottery was perhaps the most popular single form of gambling in the State. From Colonial times Charleston had been a lottery center in the United States, and ante-bellum city newspapers are filled with lottery advertisements. Chances were sold on all manner of items and sums. Money purses of as much as thirty thousand dollars were not unknown. The number of lotteries available at a given time to an interested citizen is well illustrated by the January-April, 1835, accounts of Edward Broughton. During those four months he purchased eighteen chances in ten different contests.[68]

Lotteries were heavily taxed by the legislatures of 1839 and 1846; however, these tax laws did not apply to "raffles," and thereafter the word "lottery" gave way to this less offensive term. Whatever its name, it remained popular. As a young lady wrote her mother, "7 of june today is a joyous one we take chances in a raffle it begins on friday I wish it were today."[69]

The "take-in gentry," as professional gamblers were often called, were usually swindlers; but at least they made little effort to disguise their purpose. Prevailing sentiment held that a man who lost funds to gamblers was not especially deserving of sympathy, and that the gambler himself was not in all cases detestable. But this was not true concerning other types of swindlers who pretended to be one thing and were another, who pirated on a man's honor and trust. These villains were heatedly disliked. Such swindlers had no set pattern and operated according to no single describable pattern. They were individualists, having in common only the desire to make a dishonest dollar. The ingenuity of their projects was indicative of high criminal cunning.

A favorite scheme of swindlers was to masquerade as professional men. Numerous "sharpers," as they were generally known, posed as physicians. The Barnwell grand jury in October, 1817, declared that so many false doctors were then abroad that the lives of the people were actually in danger. All classes of society, these jurors said, were "an indiscriminate sacrifice in the hands of these jugglers in Science, pretenders in medicine."

C. C. McKenzie, an army deserter, was such a fraudulent physician. He blandly advertised himself as both surgeon and general practitioner and worked his way west from the Low Country. The damage that he did was inestimable, but the people of Pendleton and Pickens, at least, were forewarned of his lack of skill.[70]

Other swindlers posed as ministers. The colorful and expert forger, David T. Hines, used this disguise at times, with varying success. The garb of the pastor was especially suited, Hines declared, to allay suspicions of women, young or aged.[71] Charles W. Appleton, who came to Charleston in the 1840s, was another who gained social acceptance on the basis of counterfeit theological credentials. His sudden and unannounced departure from the city became the subject of letters directed to other towns, warning their citizens not to accept the man. He was, one of the correspondents stated, "a daring imposter," a "wolf in sheep's clothing [who] should have a mark set upon his forehead, by which all mankind should know and avoid his pestilential presence."[72]

Two "artful dodgers" who arrived in Charleston late in 1858 represented themselves as Berlin professors, experts in the manufacture of optical lenses. They rented a shop near the center of town and for a time did a brisk business selling worthless glass spectacles. They left town before they were exposed.[73]

An even more daring scoundrel went to Laurensville in 1851. For a full day he obtained merchandise on credit by declaring himself to be a son, just returned from some years abroad, of "an esteemed fellow-citizen, Col. Parks." He was not caught and the editor of the Laurensville *Herald* pled with his readers elsewhere in the State to "look out for the scamp."[74]

During the same decade Lancaster merchants were victimized by two visitors who pictured themselves as sons of Alabama gentry, and said they had come to Lancaster to attend a nearby academy. A local girl who became amorously involved with them warned that they were departing without settling their accounts, but they nonetheless managed to evade capture. A citizen posse pursued them as far as the French Broad River in North Carolina before giving up the chase.[75]

A man and woman calling themselves Peter Stein and wife teamed up in 1854 to defraud Pendleton's unsuspecting folk. Announcing that they were skilled jewelers, the pair spent several days collecting watches and rings for repair, then disappeared with the valuable items. They were not again seen in South Carolina and were assumed to have "Gone North."[76]

Other noteworthy fraudulent masquerades were reported from various points. In Columbia a man named Dick Walters dyed himself brown and had a colleague sell him as a mulatto slave. The idea behind this was simple enough: he would escape, wash off the dye, and repeat the process. He was not notably successful. In Camden a fake real estate dealer sold numerous lots which he did not own. In Sumter two reputedly wealthy traders left a large box containing "a confused mass of waste-paper" as security for their hotel bills. And throughout the Low Country a quick-talking man named Howard had a gay time of it buying on credit food, clothing, and general merchandise which he said would be paid for by a circus soon to arrive, for which he was advance agent. The circus arrived; but according to its manager no Mr. Howard was or had been in its employ.[77]

The circus itself brought a "full quota of humbugs" to town and newspaper editors advised "our cousins from the country" to beware of the loquacious strangers and their "strolling shows." An advertisement concerning one of the latter is indicative of the entertainment they might offer:

THE LEARNED PIG

To be seen at the CITY HOTEL, *from 9 o'clock in the morning, until 9 in the evening.* As the extraordinary sagacity of this ANIMAL is too well known to need a vain, puffing advertisement, the Proprietor will only state what the PIG actually performs, as follows:—He reads printing or writing; spells; tells the time of day . . . the date of the year . . . distinguishes colours; how many persons there are present, gentlemen or ladies; and, to the astonishment of every spectator, will add, subtract, multiply and divide; and . . . any gentlemen may draw a card from the pack, and keep it concealed, and the PIG . . . will discover the card when drawn from another pack. Admittance 50 CENTS. N.B.— the PIG is for sale.[78]

This effort to dispose of the PIG points up the wide diversity in the character of crimes against property, as compared with those in other categories. Murderers killed and street-fighters slugged away at each other; but thieves had repertories of lawless acts which ranged from picking pockets to selling worthless goods at premium prices. Such disparity made crimes against property the greatest challenge to ante-bellum law enforcement officers.

Crimes Against Public Morals

The pattern of crime in ante-bellum South Carolina renders it both convenient and desirable to treat offenses against public morals as distinct from other categories, and to include with them such relatively minor misdemeanors as swearing and Sabbath-breaking. The crimes against public morals constitute the least important listing; yet one of the group, bastardy, is perhaps as illustrative of the moral temper of the plain folk as any illegal action described in this study. Bastardy indictments accounted for more than two per cent of session courts' cases reviewed. By way of informal comparison, such cases are now a negligible percentage of the total. The introduction into present day society of contraceptive devices may account for the difference in indictment percentage; but the conclusion seems inescapable that ante-bellum life had its full share of sexual promiscuousness.

To say that as many as two per cent of indictments were for bastardy means that practically every semi-annual meeting of court during the ante-bellum decades had at least one such case on its docket. Yet bastardy excited little comment of any sort, and was rarely mentioned even by the grand juries. Unlike murder or larceny, it was not a crime considered especially dangerous to the community at large and was not a subject lending itself to public notice. Thus the appearance of four bastardy cases on the Chester spring court calendar of 1817, of eight on the Greenville calendar in April of 1821, or of fourteen in five years at the Fairfield court were not events calling forth the wrath of any public agency. Grand juries complained of adultery, but rarely of bastardy; perhaps they felt that to condemn the former was by direct implication to condemn the latter.

It seems certain that a number of bastardy indictments were in reality cases of non-support. Many of the plain folk of the State were married according to common law and had dispensed with legal ceremony. The female half of such an informal arrangement who wished to force funds from her errant spouse found it necessary to sue on the criminal grounds of bastardy. Such must have been the circumstances, for example, in the three Horry District cases against John McCormick, all instigated by the same woman and concerning children whose ages were four, six, and eight. Similar conditions probably brought about the arrests of William Mackay, who was tried on two bastardy counts at a Fairfield court, and of Jeremiah Bobo, who was twice convicted by a Spartanburg jury.[79]

The content of courts' records makes it clear, nonetheless, that many cases were not of such an origin. For example, the indictments brought against Jesse Holloway by Mary Gandy, Vincent Brown by Sarah Platts, or William Bradley by Temperance Ivey, were worded so as to leave no doubt that the charge was bastardy, as such. Court testimony also made positive the nature of the assumed crime in the case against James Lowry, who pled not guilty and called thirteen character witnesses to his defense. Similar evidence was presented in the trial of Barton Abbott of Pickens District. Abbott, his lawyer told the jury, had not

> been granted by nature either in person or in manner with those seductive charms which are calculated to endanger the virtue or innocence of the fair Sex . . . the Prosecutrix lives & did at the time of her misfortune on a public road leading over the Mountains and much travelled by persons being in North Carolina; that he thinks it is possible that some gay Lothario living in that state & not liable to be prosecuted . . . is the father of the Child.[80]

In addition, the several accounts of infanticide by unwed mothers stand as mute evidence of the prevalence of bastardy. These cases were frequent, especially during the early decades of the ante-bellum period. The arrest of Mary McCarna in 1828 on a charge of killing her infant gave rise to the following paragraph in the Yorkville *Pioneer*: "This appears to have become a fashionable crime; and we have no doubt a rigorous enforcement of the law would at once put a check to it."[81]

Until 1847 the bastardy law in South Carolina forced the convicted father to pay about twenty-five dollars each year toward the upkeep of the child. The payments were to go to the mother and were to continue until the child had reached legal maturity. Should the father be unable to pay he was to be sold at public auction as an indentured servant to the highest bidder and his wages were then to go to the child. According to this statute a man might not be sold into servitude for more than four years; but this provision of the law was repeatedly ignored and in one case a guilty father was bound out for a ten year period.[82] After 1847 a man was no longer sold, but jailed. This left the child, as was pointed out when the new law was first introduced, "to be supported by the parish and the state [to] pay the expense of the suit."[83]

The 1847 law was not seriously contested. It represented on the one hand a general attitude that the selling of a white man into semi-slavery was not a proper punishment, and on the other a recognition that bastardy was decreasing; for bastardy indictments after 1845 were on the decline.

To be indicted for bastardy, whether before or after 1847, was practically to be convicted. More than seventy-five per cent of men so indicted were found guilty, a figure more than double that for most ante-bellum crimes. Jurors generally were forced to base their verdicts on nothing more tangible than conflicting oral testimony, and under such circumstances the woman usually had the best of it. In one case, at least, it was discovered that an innocent man had been convicted. The woman had actually given birth to a mulatto, but for exhibition at the trial she offered a white infant which she had borrowed from a willing neighbor. Her duplicity was not brought to light for several years.[84]

Added to bastardy as sex crimes against public morals were two infrequent and dissimilar misdeeds, buggery and bigamy, and two annoying and persistent misdemeanors, adultery and professional prostitution. Such sexual deviations as incest, contribution to the delinquency of a minor, and cohabitation with a Negro were also known, but numerically were of little consequence. Only one incest case was found in the sources consulted, that involving Abel Allman and his half-sister Lucy,[85] and few men, apparently, attempted liaison with children under sixteen years, the legal age of female maturity. Only two such cases were noted in the court records sampled.

Miscegenation and "general intimacy with the negur girls" were subjects of interest to some travelers and citizens, and were claimed by many people to be common practices. For instance, one ante-bellum South Carolinian declared that the gratification of lust with black women was the factor which kept the number of professional prostitutes as low as he believed it to be.[86]

If miscegenation was a common practice it was rarely treated as an indictable crime. A man guilty of it might "lose caste," but for the most part it became serious only when the white offender took up permanent residence with his black concubine. Now and then a white girl became enamored of a Negro male, but such cases were heard by magistrates and freeholders and were rarely made public.[87]

Although most sex disturbances not involving physical violence were treated as misdemeanors, buggery and bigamy were not. The penalty for either of these offenses was death. For that very reason, perhaps, convictions were hard to obtain. Buggery, or sodomy, was understandably a rarity in court records, amounting to only eight cases of the ten thousand studied. On occasion during the ante-bellum years a buggery scandal made the rounds. One of these, it was said, concerned a "well known lawyer."[88] But such rumors were rare. Bigamy was a better known departure from the social norm, and while formal indictments were few, grand juries, at least, believed the crime a prevalent one. An Horry jury, for instance, presented at one sitting in 1831 five men as being bigamists. One of the five, Alexander Waller, was reputed to have married two sisters, Margaret and Mary Singleton.[89]

Many cases which might otherwise have been designated as bigamy were, due to the severity of the punishment for that offense, treated by the sessions courts as simple adultery. Adultery in one form or another was, in fact, a prevailing vice. The district grand juries vied with each other, it would seem, in reporting cases and probable cases. Their presentments, taken in the mass, are a severe indictment of ante-bellum morals. Especially in the earlier years of the nineteenth century the jurors minced no words in making their public accusations. The complaint directed against John Sloan, "for creeping to bed with Elizabeth Alexander in the night time in a disorderly manner" is an example of a blunt one. The following announcement of a Barnwell jury in 1808 is another: "We further present . . . Joseph Sandiford . . . [who] lives in adultery with . . . [Jesse Bagget] and keeps her from her husband whom is anxious to receive her."[90] As late as 1830 the Barnwell jurors were still naming names. At the fall session of court that year they wrote:

> We . . . do present that . . . Edward Ramsey and Nancy Grubs, Thomas Wosdon & Polly Grubs, and Bolan Grubs, and a free negro woman are living in a state of lewdness and fornification to the great annoyance of the good people of the . . . upper part

of the said District. . . . We believe that the process of this Court ought to issue against the said parties for the verry corrupt and abandoned conduct.

But more numerous than the presentments which specified individuals were those which generalized. "We regret the necessity which impels us to report as a grievance men and women living in adultery and no law against it," wrote one jury. "Open adultery has of late become so common and notorious," reported another, "as to render social order insecure, to dispense with the ancient and honorable institutions of Matrimony, and load our Country with indigent orphans and prostitutes." A third group complained that not only were men leaving their wives for other women, but that the wives "thus abandoned" were living "in adultery with other men." A fourth pled for an end to the "evil tendency" of citizens to "destroy marriage, the pure fountain of domestic bliss, by living in a criminal way"; and a fifth wrote: "Whilst we would shrink from making a public disclosure of information disgraceful to society which we have received from members of this Jury, our duty imposed on us the necessity of calling the attention of the Honorable Court to it. It is stated that many married and some unmarried men have practically deserted their wives and children and . . . have entered into . . . bonds with the other sex, without the pales of matrimony."[91]

So far as the State legislature was concerned, such presentments fell on deaf ears. A bill making adultery and cohabitation serious offenses was introduced in the House of Representatives in 1844 by George W. Williams, but failed of passage. A similar bill met a like fate in 1856, and up to 1860 no change of importance was made in the existing laws which treated adultery as a nuisance and thus as a simple misdemeanor. Living "in a disorderly way . . . and bedding together" were, to the lawmakers, insignificant foibles.[92]

Prostitution was similarly viewed by the legislators. As in the instance of adulterers, grand juries insisted that prostitutes were "an increasing influence," and periodically called the women of ill-repute by first and last name. An example is the presentment of the Greenville jury in 1858. This group demanded that Polly McClennan, Emily Bishop, and Mary Graham and her daughter be arrested as residents of "a house of prostitution which men frequent night and day and are guilty of gross indecences."[93] Such presentments had little helpful effect, it would seem, and may indeed have served as a sort of advertising.

Most prostitutes, it was said, were found in Charleston and Columbia. Charleston was thought especially attractive to harlots.
Numerous Charleston juries protested the "number of houses of ill
fame or brothels throughout the city, which are an annoyance generally to the good citizens." The presence of the State college students in Columbia reputedly made that town also a favorite for the
"sisters of riotous sensuality." Complaints were printed in various
South Carolina newspapers that Columbia was a "perfect haven" for
these women. In 1835, M. C. Shaffer, captain of the town guard,
answered one such letter. Such tales were exaggerated, he wrote to
the editor of the Charleston *Mercury*. All towns everywhere had
bawdy houses, and Columbia had no more than its share. At any
rate, he concluded, recent insinuations that the college professors
were visiting city prostitutes, thus setting a bad example for students,
were "indeed false."[94]

After 1836 prostitutes were classed as vagrants and that removed
them from sessions courts' jurisdiction. The keepers of bawdy houses,
however, continued to be tried by judge and jury, and such people,
if deemed guilty, were forced to post two thousand dollar bonds as
security for their future good conduct. A second conviction not only
forfeited the bond but brought a one year jail term and often a heavy
fine.[95] About two per cent of court indictments throughout the ante-
bellum years were for "committing a nuisance," and the bulk of
these concerned "disorderly houses." Such houses were prostitutes'
billets, for gaming halls and like establishments were referred to by
their proper titles in indictments against their owners.

The 1836 act which classified harlots as vagrants was simply a
clarification of the law in that respect. By legal definition vagrants
in South Carolina were those people who "wandered from place to
place," who had no "visible means of honest livelihood," who were
"suspicious" Negro traders, horse traders or horse racers from "foreign parts," fortune tellers, "sturdy beggars," and those who led
"idle and disorderly lives." They were tried by magistrates and freeholders and, until 1847, were sold as indentured servants if found
guilty. Should there be no buyer, a substitute punishment of thirty-
nine lashes and immediate banishment from the area was meted
out.[96] Until 1860 whipping and banishment remained the standard
penalty for vagrancy, despite several grand jury calls for a more
stringent corrective.

Vagrancy was one of a class of minor nuisances which attracted scant attention in ante-bellum South Carolina. Grouped with it were such items as public swearing, which was punished by whipping or by a fine of forty-four cents to one dollar per offense, and "working or sporting" on the Sabbath, which could result in a fine of twenty-one cents for each conviction.[97] These minor offenses were more the worry of the church, apparently, than of the court system. The church often punished such offenders by reading them out of membership.

The listing of South Carolina crimes makes it clear that the ante-bellum criminal was no less versatile than his modern counterpart. Of the three categories of crimes, those against the person were the most spectacular, and owing to the large number of assault and battery cases, the most numerous. Crimes against property elicited the most denunciation; and those against public morals were the least numerous and the least noticed. These factors concerning crime classification suggest that South Carolina was something of a frontier state. This is neither a new nor necessarily an unexpected observation. As late as 1850 only twelve per cent of South Carolinians resided in towns populated by as many as five hundred people; and this rural atmosphere, in an age of poor communication and transportation, obviously made for frontier-like conditions. Such a careful nineteenth century observer as Frederick Law Olmstead noted the similarity of the South and the West in this regard, and such excellent twentieth century historians as Ulrich B. Phillips and Charles S. Sydnor have made similar observations.[98]

III. Catching the Criminal

SOUTH CAROLINA'S METHODS OF DISCOVERING AND ARRESTING criminals indicated remarkable resourcefulness on the part of its ante-bellum citizenry and also were rather significant for their frontier characteristics. Naturally, the percentage of criminals caught to crimes committed is impossible to discover, but as session courts' calendars were always crowded, it is safe to conclude that South Carolina was not a place of refuge for either its own lawbreakers or those from other places.

Legally hired or appointed police officials were few outside the Charleston area, and usually consisted of a sheriff and one or two deputies, along with varying numbers of constables for each district. Additionally, several of the larger towns employed policemen on either a permanent or a seasonal basis.

These town and district officers generally performed with zeal and commendable courage, and their achievements often were impressive. The search for criminals, however, did not depend entirely on the bravery, skill, or good fortune of the police. Individual citizens readily took the initiative in chasing wrongdoers, citizen posses were used whenever deemed needful, and every magistrate had authority to call forth the militiamen within his jurisdiction for tracking down and arresting "evil-disposed persons." Militiamen and volunteer citizen groups were not well trained in police science, but at times they could be notably effective.

Numerous criminals, especially those guilty of larceny, were caught through the medium of newspaper advertising. Headlined by such challenging eye-catchers as "BEWARE THE THIEF," "CATCH THE ROBBER," or "THERE GOES A SEDUCER," the typical advertisement announced a reward, explained in some detail the character of the misdeed, described the criminal, if at all possible, and ended with a personal plea for vigilance on the part of all readers. Many of these newspaper notices, particularly those penned by local sub-

scribers, were printed free of charge by the editors as a public service. Similarly, many editors added to such announcements requests that other newspapers copy the items.[1]

When printed at the order of police or other official agencies, the
notices were blunt and to the point. When written by and inserted
at the request of private citizens they were often colorful and expres-
sive screeds, calling forth the wrath of God on the "black-hearted
wretch" or beseeching the villain to give himself up and hope thereby
for divine pardon and mercy.

These last mentioned notices were not always as helpful as they
should have been. Criminals were described, for instance, in such
vague terms as "ordinary looking" or "well appearing." Many of
the advertisements simply stated that the fugitive had "the outward
appearance of a gentlemen." One unfortunate citizen, announcing
the theft of his horse, his money, and his wife, contented himself
with an attempt at description of the latter. She was, he wrote, a
woman with "large dark eyes, her nose rather larger than common
. . . and when in a good humor, very good looking."[2]

Not a few of the newspaper advertisements were as much for the
purpose of publicizing the criminal as for catching him. This was
especially true of accounts concerning swindlers and seducers. W. K.
Shaver, to cite an example, hoped that his notice pertaining to P. C.
Harper might forewarn others of that gentleman's dishonorable
amorous intentions. He wrote;

> I have understood since . . . [Harper's] flight that mine is not
> the only family whose hopes he has blighted—that mine is not
> the only child his filthy love has polluted; I therefore feel it my
> duty, in this public manner, to give that warning to others
> which unfortunately I did not receive in time myself. Oh! for
> a scourge in every honest hand, to whip the rascal naked through
> the world.[3]

Newspaper advertising was not necessary in early nineteenth century Charleston. There, for a nominal fee, the city guards at intervals during the day read aloud the reports of articles stolen and
other crimes committed.[4]

One common device of vocal announcements and newspaper advertisements aimed at catching lawbreakers was the offer of a reward. These financial inducements ranged from the legal minimum of
eight dollars and fifty cents, paid by the State to any citizen who
apprehended a felon, to a high of at least one thousand dollars, which

was offered in 1844 by the city council of Charleston for the capture
and conviction of a murderer. The larger rewards were generally
offered by the State under the signature of the governor, or by town
councils. Typical examples, in addition to that cited, are the rewards
of two hundred and fifty dollars offered by Governor James H.
Adams in 1855 for a murderer, and five hundred dollars offered by
the mayor of Columbia in 1824 for a suspected arsonist.[5]

Now and then a district grand jury instructed its clerk of court to
petition the legislature to provide money for awards to citizen police,
and on occasion groups of citizens raised purses for the same purpose. Whatever the source, the promise of hard cash, despite the
administrative difficulty sometimes encountered in collecting it, doubtlessly served to keep the public on the alert for wanted rogues. "Look
out boys," wrote the editor of the Lancaster *Ledger,* announcing a
governor's proclamation of reward, "$300 is quite a lift these days."[6]

Another important aid toward apprehending criminals was the
work of the informer. In early South Carolina he was not held in such
low esteem as today, and was clearly recognized by law. Any citizen
who turned in a felon was due both a reward and one-half of any
fine assessed the wrongdoer. Further, court solicitors were authorized
to make similar offers to minor criminals who would turn State's
evidence against their erstwhile colleagues. All citizens were urged
to act the part of informers, and it was pointed out that concealing
knowledge of a misdeed or its perpetrator was illegal. In cases of
capital crime an accessory before the fact or after the fact was himself liable to the death penalty.[7]

Much informing was done through the machinery of the district
grand juries. The presentments of these bodies were filled with reports of criminal activity "brought to our consideration by a good
citizen." This type of informing was directed more against nuisances
and moral breaches than major crimes, but in sum all species of lawlessness were included. These grand jury crime reports, which often
gave names and were bluntly descriptive, were not indictments but
requests for executive investigation and possible arrest. Their form,
which varied little throughout the ante-bellum decades, is indicated
by the following samples: "We present by the information of Gavin
Jones . . . Sabria Baxley for the murder of a child"; "We present upon information duly made . . . that Charles Spiers & the Widow Sharp
are living in a state of open adultery"; and, "We present that during
the last summer a regular Cock Pit was established in this Town on

a lot owned by John Williams . . . to the very great annoyance of the citizens."[8]

Informing now and then came as the result of a heavy conscience rather than the promise of pecuniary gain. Such was the case in Pendleton in 1829 where, it was said, a young lady at a protracted camp meeting had allowed the angels of the Lord to enter and chase the devil from her; and had as a result of this conversion tattled on the whereabouts of a male acquaintance who was wanted for murder. He was forthwith arrested.[9]

Then as now, informing might be a dangerous business. More than a few of the assault and battery cases which crowded the courts had their origin in informing. Harriet Martineau, who visited South Carolina in the 1830s, wrote that one of her Southern hosts had "carried loaded pistols for a fortnight . . . knowing that he was lain in wait for by persons against whose illegal practices he had given information."[10]

South Carolina citizens at times were not content to act as mere informers and took upon themselves the full duties of police. Unlike the informers, these self-appointed agents of law and order were not often well paid, if paid at all, for their efforts.[11] Nonetheless, criminals were frequently captured by individual citizen action, or by posses or vigilance groups.

The citizens who, acting alone, chased and captured law-breakers were not necessarily without legal sanction. A statute carried over from pre-Revolution codes required any bystander who witnessed a crime to arrest the party or parties thereto, and levied a fine against him if he did not. Further, this law was occasionally enforced. A majority of citizen police, however, acted as such because they were themselves the victims of the criminal's attack. Particularly was this true concerning pickpockets and common thieves, and these were the scamps most often caught by the volunteers. In Charleston, especially, the streets on occasion echoed to the cry, "STOP THE ROGUE," as some angry native gave hot chase to a "member of the light-fingered gentry" who had lifted his pocketbook.[12]

Most citizen police operated not as individual patrolmen, but as organized groups. Known as posses, these bands were vital cogs in the machinery for law and order in South Carolina. Their interest did not always stop with the arrest of the criminal. At times they became also court, jury, and punishing medium. This happened rarely, and when it did the posse was stepping from legal to illegal ground.

Except under conditions described above, posses were clearly distinguished from undisciplined mobs. The posse was based generally on the old English common law principle of "Hue and Cry," and, in the eyes of most contemporary observers, performed needful and important services. The consensus of critics, foreign and local, was perhaps expressed by English traveler James Stuart. "In an extensive district," he wrote, "where the expense of a police establishment cannot be borne by a few inhabitants, scattered at considerable distances from each other, no better scheme . . . can be devised."[13]

Posses were of two types: those organized by legally appointed police officers or magistrates, and those which came together on citizen call. The police-sponsored bands were the more frequent. Any ante-bellum police officer was authorized to call a "Posse Comitatus" to his aid, and constables of the rural areas were quick to do so. The men making up such a posse were in effect acting as deputy police. The chase and capture by a sixty member posse of a father and son who had escaped from the Walterboro jail in 1827 is an example of this type of organization. The hiring of a posse and bloodhounds by Constable Elly Godbold to chase a Marion District robber is another.[14]

Two special kinds of posse organizations which had police sponsorship were the patrol and the militia unit. The former was a citizen squad instituted for the task of regulating slaves and apprehending Negroes who violated the curfew laws. The patrol doubtlessly would have captured any white lawbreakers it came across; but it made the controlling of Negroes its main business. Established by State law, the patrol operated until after the Civil War and was an adjunct of the militia system. It had the power to try and punish as well as to apprehend and arrest, and as abolitionists increased their activities it increased its own.[15]

Militia units serving as policemen did so as part of their regular duty. After 1743 all South Carolina males, once they attained legal age, were subject to militia duty; and it was understood that this might include the tracking down of criminals. Indeed, when planter Samuel Porcher was elected a militia captain, he described himself to a relative as being then "a sort of chief of police in the parish."[16] Actually Porcher was taking an exaggerated view of his responsibilities. The militia units were used less often than he apparently believed. Posses were needed quickly if at all, and it was usually speedier to gather up the men nearby, without regard for their military standing, than to go through the formality of summoning the organized unit. Only where much travel was involved, or where immediate action was not deemed imperative, was the use of the militia unit really feasible.[17]

The extra-legal or citizen-organized posse was the most newsworthy type, and contemporary accounts indicate that it was at least as effective as officially constituted patrol or militia groups. Differing from mobs in that they were respected, well-planned, and kept under careful control by prominent leaders, the extra-legal posses were unofficial in name only. In such documents as courts' journals and inquest books they were afforded recognition as proper instruments of law enforcement.

The murder of Chester Sheriff Elijah Nunn in the early 1800s brought out a typical extra-legal posse. The news of his death quickly made the rounds. Men gathered at the court house. One or two local leaders gave out orders and laid plans; and the posse moved to its task. In this case it was successful, and arrested the killer. "By the exertions of the citizens . . . turning out to hunt the murderer," wrote the editor of a Charleston paper reporting the event, "[the killer] is now in Chester gaol. Poor satisfaction for the life of such a worthy man!"[18]

A similar posse with a pack of hounds gave chase in 1842 to an Edgefield counterfeiter. A newspaperman announcing it to his readers reported, "When last seen he was going ahead, well covered with mud, and several dogs in pursuit."[19]

Posses sometimes gathered to eradicate long-standing public nuisances. Charleston citizens in 1819, for instance, became aroused over reports that a nearby inn, "the Five-Mile House," was harboring thieves, gamblers, and prostitutes. Forming a posse, the citizens rode to the establishment, gave the inmates fifteen minutes to vacate the area, then burned the building to the ground. A similar group also gathered near Charleston in 1823 and chased and killed four "negro banditti." These escaped slaves, it was said, had "long infested the neighborhood of Nelson's Ferry, and had murdered a Mr. Ford."[20]

In Newberry, on one occasion, a posse was called together before any crime took place. Citizen Alexander ("Big Andy") Bartholomew issued the call for the group to meet with him on the opening day of court season. The posse would be named the "Croting Club," Big Andy said, and would have as its objective the running down and arresting of all thieves and troublemakers who might commit misdeeds during the judicial proceedings. Whether or not Big Andy's well-intentioned club met with success is not known.[21]

Now and then posses found themselves in gunfights with their quarry. One such episode was reported by a posse which had surrounded a robber in his hide-out near Aiken. Vowing that he would never be taken alive, the larcener shot it out with his pursuers and was critically wounded. He had committed so many crimes within the Edgefield area, he said before he died, that he knew surrender meant eventual death at the end of a rope.[22]

As might be expected, posses of any type were less numerous as the ante-bellum period drew to a close and the regular police force became stronger and more efficient. The police establishments were from their beginning the most used agencies for capturing wrongdoers. In addition, notwithstanding their sparsity in numbers and the rather crude training they had for their tasks, they were probably the most successful.

South Carolina's ante-bellum police forces were organized as two distinct groups, the rural constables and the city guards. The first was headed by the various district magistrates and by the sheriffs, but was under the general supervision of the district sessions courts. The city guards, on the other hand, were administered by the mayors and city councils or "intendants." The constables were far and away the more important since Columbia and Charleston were the only towns large enough to boast of much in the way of city guards. Thus the constables actually served the villages as well as the open country; and while the term "rural" was officially applied to these officers, it is apt, without qualification, to be misleading.

On paper the district constables were headed by the sheriff, but in reality he exercised only a loose control over them, in common with the justices of the peace or magistrates. He offered direction, issued arrest warrants, and received prisoners for detention. But constables were rarely hired or fired by the sheriff, and they made their reports to and requested their pay and allowances from the State legislature.[23] Magistrates and judges hired them, the General Assembly paid them, and the sheriff was expected to manage them.

From the sheriff's point of view the question of jurisdiction over the constables demanded clarification; on the other hand, the sheriff was accustomed to being made something of a square peg in a round hole, insofar as the capturing of criminals was concerned. He had the arresting power, but rarely the opportunity to use it. His work seemingly overlapped with that of constable, jailer, and court-crier. In some districts he personally punished all criminals, in others he acted as hangman only, leaving the lesser punishments to the constables and jailers. In some districts he headed the posses. In others he apparently took no official action concerning them. As an elected, bonded official, he received prisoners for detention, took bail when it was authorized by magistrates, collected (or tried to collect) the fines levied by the judge, ordered coroners' inquests, executed the *habeas corpus* act, called jurors and witnesses to court, and carried out the orders of the judge and the solicitors.

Black frocked, with cocked-hat and sword, the sheriff was an imposing figure as he led the biannual procession to court and as he attended the judge to and from his lodgings. But his duties were many and at times ill-defined, his pay was too little and that hard to obtain, and his critics were numerous and exceedingly vocal. As warrant-server, jail custodian, and court official he performed important services; but as policeman he gave way to the constable, and thus he lacked the luster of his counterpart in the Western states.[24]

South Carolina constables were appointed to their positions for four-year terms. Their duties, like those of the sheriff, might be numerous and varied, but essentially the constables chased and arrested lawbreakers. The execution of court orders, the delivery of magistrates' warrants, the punishment of Negroes, the granting of bail in petty cases, and the attendance on the magistrates' and freeholders courts were all incidental to their main task.

The constables took their appointments seriously, as a rule, and vowed to do their best. Several even put notices in local newspapers announcing that they fully intended to earn their pay. That of a Pendleton officer in 1807 is typical. He wrote: "As I long have viewed, with pain and displeasure, the conduct of some of the Citizens of this village and its Vicinity; it has induced me to drop a few hints, by way of caution. . . . In the execution of my office [I] am determined for the future to put the law in force against every offender, without distinction, and hope that my friends and fellow citizens will take the friendly caution and admonition, from one who wishes them well."[25]

Rural constables were too few, considering the job they had to do. Complete statistics for the State apparently are not extant, but figures do exist for several districts, and these show during the ante-bellum years an average ratio of one constable for each one thousand citizens. No district, after 1822, had fewer than eighteen rural policemen, a minimum set by State law.[26] On the face of it, this one-to-one thousand ratio appears adequate even by modern standards. But the figure is misleading and is subject to one important qualification: the rural constable served both village and country, and his territory or "beat" was extensive. His problems were not so compact, geographically, as were those of the town or city policeman. As he viewed it, the issue was not the ratio of constables to citizens, but constables to square miles.

For the most part, the constable's work was routine. During any average month he probably would arrest a few men accused of assault and battery; take custody of several Negroes caught at night without passes and a few others turned over to him by their masters for punishment; and conduct investigation into one or more cases of petty larceny, trading without a license, or professional gambling. He would probably summon at least one magistrates' and freeholders' court for hearing Negro cases, and he would serve a limited number of warrants at the request of the sheriff of his district. On rare occasions he might be commissioned to travel into another state to return a criminal whose extradition had been authorized.[27]

Pendleton Constable Richard Blackstock's activities during November, 1808, may be considered typical. He broke up a small-scale riot; arrested nine people on assault and battery charges; captured a cattle rustler; chased unsuccessfully an escaped felon for twenty-two miles; and arrested four men on sheriff's warrants. Not so busy, however, was Abbeville Constable Thomas Bigbie, whose December, 1828, report reads as follows:[28]

> For servin Seven warants 53cts 6m each — 3 71
> For whipin Eight negro slaives 53 6m each — 4 24
> for mileg in on seven warants 5 miles each — 1 75
> for Somes three free holders — 63

Now and then the constables were able to capitalize on their free time by accepting work as private detectives. Such duty was not especially lucrative, paying but fifty cents to one dollar for each day of service, and usually consisted of conducting a special search for lost goods. A group of Barnwell citizens hired such an officer, from the

Charleston city police force, in 1860. They believed a number of men in their midst were coming together as a gang to rob houses and shops at night. The officer managed to gain the confidence of the suspected men, discovered where and when they planned next to strike, and reported these facts to his employers. A citizen's posse then waited on the robbers and captured them all.[29]

Highlights of adventure sometimes enlivened the constable's day-by-day labors. On occasion he had to prove to the fullest measure his courage. The unnamed Barnwell officer who brought in maddened and dangerous Alex Davis following his "refusal to be taken," and Lexington Constable Jacob Rall, who arrested Daniel Wingard despite the fact that Wingard stood in the town's main street armed with a musket and shouting that he would kill whoever came after him, are examples of bravery among the rural police.[30]

In that connection, the number of constables who were shot or shot at while in the discharge of their official duties was large enough to make it clear that their profession was not one for the faint of heart. Newspapers carried many stories of constables involved in violence, and it was rare that a sessions court in South Carolina failed to include on its calendar at least one case of "assaulting a constable," "shooting at a constable with intent to kill," or "murdering a constable." Most cases, happily, were based on the first two of these three charges. Examples of officers who met with serious trouble in the line of duty were Constable Thomas Sanders, who was shot while trying to arrest Thomas Messer, near York village; Constable Charles Boyles, who very nearly met death at the hands of a prisoner named John Gill; and a nameless constable who, having surprised thieves in a warehouse, was knocked senseless with a keg of lard.[31]

Most constables were able public servants. Those who were not had short careers. Constables were under the surveillance not only of sessions courts' officials, petty magistrates, and sheriffs, but of the citizens they served. The citizen critics, especially, were quick to point out shortcomings or instances of bad behavior, and constables were sometimes indicted by grand juries on the strength of such testimony.

The circuit-riding judges were authorized to discipline the constables. Their relentless proclivity to do so was sufficient, apparently, to insure honesty and good conduct on the part of the bulk of rural police. At any rate, the State constabulary was free of scandal. Some grand juries insisted that constables, like sheriffs, be bonded to the courts for good behavior, but there seems to have been little actual reason for the requests and they were not honored with action by the legislature.[32]

For that matter such presentments were not numerous and reflect no wholesale dislike for constables. Benjamin F. Perry, in an angry exaggeration, once wrote that "One half of the cases in which I am consulted originate in some complaint against a constable,"[33] but his seemingly thoughtless statement is not elsewhere substantiated. For the most part the rural officers were respected and appreciated. In direct contrast to the Perry statement are petitions and present-ments such as those from forty-four Claremont citizens in 1850, sixty-four Sumter citizens in 1854, and the Fairfield grand jury in 1834. Each of these groups went on record praising the work of the constables and insisting that the pay and allowances of the rural officers be raised. That, certainly, was a high compliment. Perhaps the one valid adverse criticism of the rural police was simply that they were poorly trained for their tasks. Such a complaint was offi-cially made, but nothing constructive came of it.[34]

As noted, the constables were early replaced in Columbia and Charleston by regular intra-city police forces. These were established by law, usually on the initiative of district grand juries. The bulk of such proposals passed without opposition, and by the late ante-bellum decades most of the larger towns, including Aiken, Greenville, Georgetown, Cheraw, Abbeville, Camden, Sumter, Yorkville, and Hamburg, had official police establishments.

Except in Columbia and Charleston these urban police have a history not dissimilar from that of the rural constables who preceded them. The essential difference between the constables and the town policemen was that the latter's jurisdiction was greatly restricted as to area. On occasion city police were authorized to go outside town limits to chase and arrest criminals, but as a rule they were restricted to those limits.[35]

Columbia's first "police force" was set up in 1808 and consisted of one marshal. His duty was to "parade" through the town once each morning and once each afternoon in order to "suppress any riotous or disorderly conduct." This assumed, apparently, that the troublemakers would choose to riot or be disorderly at the time of the marshal's parading. In cases of necessity, of course, he could call on nearby citizens for aid.

By 1824 the marshal had been replaced by a regular twenty-four hour guard, consisting of a captain, two sergeants, and seven privates. Until 1856 this ten man force was not increased. At that time the town had slightly more than six thousand population, and considering the fact that four of the ten policemen were on duty at all times, the ratio of police to people was one to 1500.[36]

In addition to their regular activities, Columbia police had the special task of keeping the easily excited and somewhat pampered college students in hand. Such duty could prove most troublesome and even dangerous. A town policeman named Beaufill bore witness to this distasteful attribute of policemanship in the capital city when, in 1846, he barely missed being tossed headlong from a three-story college dormitory by the students. In the words of one of the college youth:

> Several weeks have elapsed since this scene occurred. One of the town marshalls . . . came into the Campus and proceeded to enter one of the buildings, going up to the third story. The students discovered him and unanimously collected around him . . . howling and bawling, every one armed with a club as if they were going to meet a regiment. . . . I had not been there two minutes before the cry was raised to throw him over the railing which would by the fall have broken every bone in his body, but the demand was mitigated into the penalty of being pushed down the stairs by force. All hands threw in their mite to the accomplishment of this purpose, and the result was he was pulled down, hooted out of the Campus.[37]

More serious than the Beaufill incident was the "guard house riot" of February 17-18, 1856. This episode was occasioned by the arrest in town of an intoxicated and quarrelsome student. Upon receipt of this information, most of the college boys on the campus fused into a mob and proceeded to the guardhouse to rescue their inebriated colleague. Rebuffed after a brief scuffle they hurried back to the college, procured arms from the college arsenal, and on the following day again presented themselves before the police. Both groups quickly formed makeshift battle lines, the police being reinforced by armed citizens, and for a time the situation was tense. Gunfire and bloodshed was averted only by the arrival of Professor James H. Thornwell, whose influence was sufficiently strong to force the youths back into their college dormitories.[38]

In size and organization Columbia's police force ran a poor second to that of Charleston which, in the eyes of many visiting critics, was not only noteworthy but among the nation's best.[39] Until 1805 Charleston had no regular police establishment but made use of a city sheriff who held a loose sort of jurisdiction over a varying number of local constables. In that year this informal group was replaced by an elected constabulary of twenty-four members, each a resident of a city district, outside of which he had no power of arrest. These men received no pay, but were granted a percentage of the fines levied against the criminals they arrested. Each officer was authorized to wear a badge of authority and to carry with him a "stave" for protection. Each was on call at all hours, attended all fires and public meetings within his area, and was given power to deputize bystanders in time of need.

No person elected as a city constable might refuse his appointment unless he were a lawyer, preacher, teacher, physician, vessel master, or ship's pilot; but it was understood that no citizen might be forced to serve more than one year in five. In 1806 a city marshal was appointed at an annual salary of six hundred dollars to give some semblance of central direction to this involuntary police force.[40]

Before the year was out the system of an unpaid, ill-governed constabulary was deemed unworkable, and in October the two dozen officers were replaced by a salaried, uniformed guard of seventy-five men. This new force, organized in military fashion, was regularly increased as the city grew and by 1838, with a total of 120 on the police rolls, it had reached its ante-bellum peak.

Operating from a central guardhouse headquarters, these police made periodic armed patrols into the various sections of the city. Each patrol was equipped with a "rattle" which could be used to summon aid. Each sergeant was armed with a sword and each private with a musket and bayonet. Their pay was according to the following monthly scale: captains, sixty dollars; lieutenants, forty-five dollars; sergeants, twenty-seven to thirty dollars; and privates, twenty-three dollars. In the late 1830s these wages were raised an average of twenty dollars for each rank, and the arresting policemen were allowed to share in the fines charged their culprits.[41]

As something of a supplement to the patrolling guardsmen, a marshal was also appointed for each city ward. In common with other policemen, he possessed the power of arrest; but in addition he was expected to watch for fraud on sale days, check reports of all manner of hazards to the citizenry, investigate houses of reputed ill fame, and note carefully the arrival of all strangers who might be vagrants, gamblers, or persons of "a seditious nature." The ward marshal received a yearly wage of 250 dollars plus a share of fines assessed guilty miscreants. Whether needed or not, he continued as an offshoot component of the Charleston city guard until 1846.

After 1821 the elaborate process of platoon patrols was discontinued in favor of the "beat" system still used in most American cities, and from that date the Charleston city police began to resemble modern-day officers in organization and type. As the years passed the force was steadily improved in a number of ways. Mounted officers were used after 1826. A detective force was added to the permanent police rolls in 1846. In 1856 a system of card files was instituted to classify and index law violators within the city, and in the same year a collection of daguerreotypes of known criminals was begun.[42] Mayors' committees regularly visited other cities to study their police, and reports from these committees generally resulted in needful changes. Mayor William P. Miles in 1855 took a special interest in bettering the police, and in something of a testimonal to his efforts the force was known during his administration, and for some years afterward, as "Paddy Miles' Bulldogs."[43]

By 1857 the Charleston police force was costing the city's tax payers in excess of ninety thousand dollars yearly.[44] For that very reason, perhaps, Charleston citizens did not always look on their uniformed protectors with favor. Such an individual patrolman as Moses Levy, who captured thieves, gamblers, and pickpockets with great success, became something of a hero, as did those officers who were wounded or killed in the line of duty;[45] but the average policeman was sometimes criticized as incompetent, arrogant, overpaid, and possibly corrupt.

"It certainly appears strange," wrote one angry critic in a typical charge, "That the watchmen should, always, be out of the way, when . . . [robberies] occur." And "Republican," writing in 1833, declared that it was his observed opinion that brawls in the city streets were on an increase because the police stirred them up and took pleasure in them. A third detractor, who signed himself "Echo," wrote to his friends in Laurens in 1850 that "Our city is infested by a gang of lawless and reckless vagabonds . . . Our *Efficient* police are, of course, on the alert, invariably missing the fox and capturing a lamb. Methinks I hear you ask, where are the hundred and odd Guardsmen and their pampered and salaried officers . . .? Echo answers, where?"[46]

More serious than these attacks were periodic reports of outright corruption. The correspondent who wrote that the officers, in order to collect more fines, were arresting innocent persons in the hope that these victims would be found guilty on the basis of false police testimony, and the citizen who declared that he had heard an officer demand a pay-off from an illicit trader, were making complaints which led to a number of serious investigations of the constabulary force. After 1839 such investigations were undertaken annually by the city intendants. Prior to that date 119 police officers had been jailed, fined, or discharged for various causes, most of them petty.[47]

On the whole the Charleston police were proved honest. Each individual officer, before he was hired, posted a cash bond as insurance for his future good conduct. From 1846 the amount of this bond was five hundred dollars, and the fear of forfeiting such a sum certainly acted as a deterrent to any officers otherwise tempted toward dishonesty.[48]

A considerable portion of the total appropriations of funds by ante-bellum South Carolina legislatures went directly for law enforcement. In 1840, for example, the State expended $23,268.89 for upkeep of jails, payment of rewards and special claims, and the like; and in excess of $300,000 for wages and allowances of constables and other law enforcement officers. In 1860 these figures were $49,194.49 for the mechanical expenses and in excess of $400,000 for wages and allowances. The totals listed would be even higher if they included the costs of city police establishments. Charleston's $90,000 police account in 1847 was the largest of these, but the combined expenses of police in lesser towns was also an imposing figure in a day when money was not counted in billions.[49]

A review of police effectiveness and methodology in ante-bellum South Carolina indicates that the State, throughout the Pre-Civil War decades, made a strong, expensive, and reasonably successful effort to contain the problem of lawlessness. The rural, frontier nature of the State dictated the loosely knit constabulatory organization and made imperative the resort on frequent occasions to the posse, militia unit, or impromptu citizen group. As the State's population increased, the police forces were expanded and formalized. The sheriffs, constables, and city patrolmen (especially the latter) were subjects of some criticism—most of it trivial and baseless—but in the bulk they were, with good reason, respected and willingly supported.

IV. The Criminal and the Courts

HAVING BEEN CAUGHT, THE CRIMINAL WAS EVENTUALLY BROUGHT to trial. In South Carolina the judicial body which heard his defense was either a five man panel, consisting usually of two petty magistrates and three freeholders, or a judge and a twelve man jury. The first of these was a minor court which until 1846 tried all manner of inconsequential misdemeanors. After that date, however, it rarely handled anything of a criminal nature other than cases to which Negroes were a party or those involving vagrants and prostitutes. The second judicial group, which heard all remaining criminal causes, was for the ante-bellum period a regularly organized court of law.

By and large, the magistrates' and freeholders' courts played a minor role. Essentially agencies for trying slaves, they rarely kept full records, met whenever the sheriff or justice of the peace deemed it necessary, and in general held the status of a special and separate division of the State judiciary. Considered in the aggregate, such courts, like the patrol, are best described as an agency of the State slavery system.

The circuit sessions courts, on the other hand, were carefully organized, adhered closely to time-honored English tradition, and were headed by judges who were consistently capable. Formal in their procedures, these courts met at stated intervals in buildings specially constructed for that purpose[1] and they kept permanent, official records. They were rightly objects of interest to contemporaries and later historians.

As a rule, proceedings began with a procession of notables and plain folk to the courthouse. Led by the sheriff, wearing his cocked hat and long coat, and carrying his sword as though it were a mace, the group made its way to the "seat of justice" where it heard a lengthy sermon by a local parson. Following this theological discourse, the black-gowned judge took his seat; and at the cry of

"Oyez! Oyez! All manner of persons having business in this court . . . are required to give attendance, for this Honorable Court now sits," the main business of the week began.

At this point the trading, gambling, hand shaking, and sight-seeing were forgotten and those who could crowded into the courthouse. There were never seats for all, and even standing room was at a premium. In good weather knots of people gathered outside the windows.

The ladies came with the men, and on the occasion of an important trial they "turned out in great numbers." They were welcomed, and always the judge "caused the rougher sex to give way that they might be comfortably seated inside the bar." Murder cases, it was said, drew the ladies in largest numbers.[2]

The judges recognized the public appeal of criminal proceedings and gave the on-lookers as much liberty as possible. Order was enforced, however, and the jurists rarely allowed spectators to get out of hand. The proceedings in a Low Country case in 1856 illustrate this point. Here the audience resorted to prolonged applause. The judge rapped for silence. The hand-clapping continued and there ensued the following conversation between His Honor and the sheriff:

> *The Court*—(In a loud tone of voice)—"Order in Court!"
> *The Marshal*—(In a louder tone of voice)—"Order in Court!"
> *The Court*—(In a high tone of voice)—"Mr. Marshal, where are your deputies?"
> *The Marshal*—(In a mild tone of voice)—"They have left the Court-room, sir."
> *The Court*—(In a fierce tone of voice)—"Then, sir, you must get others. The Court will not suffer itself to be insulted in this manner!"
> And there was once more order in Court.[3]

If the situation required more positive action than a verbal warning "in a fierce tone of voice," the judge acted without hesitation. Court records indicate clearly that drunken or noisy onlookers were speedily fined or jailed. Such entries as "The Court then ordered James Kelly Senr. who made a riot and thereby disturbed the business of the Court be committed to Gaol," or "Hugh Allen behaved disorderly in the presence of the Court and could show no good cause why he did so, and the Court ordered that he be sent to prison" are a regular part of sessions' journals.[4]

But contempt proceedings were never numerous enough to discourage attendance and court time throughout the ante-bellum decades was also carnival time. South Carolinians respected their criminal courts but they also enjoyed them. Many a felon sentenced to death must have felt at least a vague satisfaction in the knowledge that he had been for a moment the actor on the center of the stage. Neither the social nor the mechanical aspects of this court system changed materially from 1800 to 1860.

Prior to 1785 the State was divided into seven judicial districts, but in that year thirty-four counties were organized in their place. A justice of the peace was appointed for each to hear criminal cases, with the right of appeal being to the few regular law judges, stationed in the Low Country. Several counties, especially those upstate, refused from the first to accept the original jurisdiction of minor magistrates. Owing to their opposition, which approached the level of mob action, the county court system failed in 1798. Reorganization was immediate, and thereafter all criminal cases except those involving Negroes and those of a petty misdemeanor nature were heard by judges regularly elected by the legislature for life or during good behavior.

In 1800 the judicial districts, then nine in number, were abolished, as were the thirty-four counties within the various districts. In their place twenty-five separate court areas, again termed districts, were laid out and allotted to the judges who rode circuit to serve them. This system appeased the growing Up Country, and with normal enlargement and slight procedural change it lasted until swept away in the 1860s by Civil War and Reconstruction. By 1860 the twenty-five districts had been increased to thirty-one; and special courts, such as the city court of Charleston, had been added to the system.[5]

The key figure in this new court arrangement was the judge. Well-trained, placed above politics by the life-appointment provision of the 1790 constitution, and few enough in number to be widely known, South Carolina judges were a respected and influential group. Few complaints of any sort were lodged against them. For a time in the 1830s, following their strong public stand against the principle of nullification, they were placed "under a social ban" but this disapproval was short-lived. In general, what lasting criticism the jurists received concerned their salary, their tenure, and the fact that they were obviously overworked.

A judge was paid from five hundred to eight hundred dollars for his year's work in 1790, but by 1839 this had been raised to three thousand and in a few cases to 3,500 dollars. Some critics believed this to be an exorbitant salary and said so. In addition, not a few citizens were opposed to any governmental servant holding office for life. Between 1824 and 1844 six futile attempts were made to reduce the tenure of the judges to as little as four years.

Similarly and incongruously, a number of complaints were directed at the judges' excessive work schedules. The jurists traveled too far, it was said, and "were in the harness" too long at each court. As a result, their deductions were at times illogical and their overall ability impaired. This adverse criticism, if such it may properly be termed, had no apparent effect and the judges' workday remained crowded.[6]

In seventy years only six judges were made objects of specific charges. Of these only two were convicted. Judges William D. James and William Dobein were removed from office through impeachment proceedings in 1828 and 1830; both were guilty of drinking liquor while on the bench. Four additional judges, John F. Grimké, Hasell Gibbes, Waddy Thompson, and James S. Richardson, were tried without success on such charges as "bodily and mental infirmity" or "rude and overbearing conduct."[7] No judge was ever seriously accused of outright corruption.

The influence of the judges on the over-all operation of the sessions courts was indisputably great. Legislators made judicial proposals and passed "court bills" in accordance with the judges' suggestions. In many cases grand juries worded their general presentments so as to incorporate almost word for word the judge's charge to them. More serious, petit juries not infrequently allowed the judge to direct their decisions. The Beaufort grand jury in 1838 bluntly declared that all its recommendations were based wholly on the pronouncements of "His Honor"; and it was said of Judge Andrew P. Butler that his influence over Edgefield petit juries was so great as to make him invariably the decisive authority in determining a defendant's guilt or innocence.[8] Essentially the same claims might have been made for such judges as Elihu H. Bay, Abraham Nott, Edward Frost, John Belton O'Neall, Robert Munroe, and Daniel E. Huger. Each had a large and devoted following.

While the judges as a group were paid an enviable homage, individual jurists were remembered by the people for a host of different reasons. Such a judge as Josiah J. Evans was famed for his impressive dignity on the bench, while Judge J. T. Withers was noted far and wide for his Solomon-like impartiality. Lewis C. Trezevant was reputed to have been the acme of efficiency and a presiding authority who demanded the strictest order in his courts. There was a day in 1802, it was remembered, when he had failed to try a single case from the calendar, but had publicly chastised a tardy juror, jailed a disorderly spectator, fired two inefficient constables, and fined a deputy clerk for improper work.[9]

John Belton O'Neall, perhaps the best known of all the ante-bellum South Carolina jurists, was famed for his blistering sermons to guilty felons, for his grandiose jury charges, and for the severity of the sentences he passed on petty miscreants. "Jove in all his fury was no match for Judge O'Neall," it was said, when he leaned back in his chair, looked with a cold eye on a rioter, and lectured him from ten to twenty minutes on the seriousness of his misdeed.[10]

Judge Thomas Waites was said to have hated delays, petty quibbling, and long arguments by lawyers. He especially disliked the necessity for hearing "mean causes" and pushed them with unseeming haste. He was reputed on one occasion to have paid the prosecution the cost of a stolen pig rather than hear the case concerning it.[11]

Richard Gantt was remembered for his eloquence and pathos when passing sentence on criminals, and for his keen sense of humor. Aedanus Burke had a similar reputation, and was the most quoted judge of the group. "Don't mind, my good fellow," Burke once said to a culprit he had just sentenced to death, "It's only what we've all got to come to."[12]

The list might well be enlarged. Rare was the South Carolina judge who served for any length of time without surrounding himself with a store of legend, truth and half truth.

Court was officially opened by the sheriff at the order of the judge; and the first order of business was the swearing in of jurors, grand and petit. The names of these men had been drawn at the preceding term of court and their summonses had been served by the sheriff and his constables. Thus they were on hand and the swearing-in process was quickly done. It consisted of taking an oath faithfully to try cases and to return verdicts according to the "laws of God and man."

The oath-taking was concluded by a kissing of the Bible. This act was "Bibliolatry," complained one critic. "I would rather kiss a pretty girl twice, and my wife three times, as that dirty leather once. It always reminds me of the poor deluded papist, having to kneel and kiss the Pope's great toe."[13]

From the criminal's point of view, the two juries, grand and petit, were equally important—although the petit had the final say concerning his case. The grand jury, consisting of twenty to twenty-four of "the most respectable and independent" names on the general jury list, passed upon the bills of indictment prepared by the circuit solicitor and endorsed each of them as either a "true bill" or a "no bill" according to their interpretation of available evidence. Many men accused of crimes were able thus, by obtaining a "no bill," to stop proceedings against them at that point.

Grand juries recorded and preserved their verdicts. A broad sampling of these indicates that ante-bellum juries returned true bills in only sixty-three per cent of the indictments laid before them. By way of comparison, true bills in South Carolina in 1950 amounted to ninety-seven per cent of the total.

Nevertheless the more than sixty per cent of solicitors' indictments deemed worthy of trial were sufficient in number to keep the petit juries busy. Indeed, had grand juries not summarily disposed of about one-third of the criminal indictments the situation would have been hopeless. As things stood there was a constant complaint that sessions dockets were too crowded, with juries overworked and justice ill-served as a result.

Jury foremen regularly announced that they viewed "with deep concern the crowded docket" and "the slender prospect" of disposing of it. Less official observers bore them out. "The Fall Term of our Court . . . is now being held," wrote one well-informed citizen, "and I question much if more than half of the calendar will be disposed of." Sessions courts' records make it clear that such critics were correctly stating their point. Court after court failed to complete its criminal business and carried over cases until the next term. This resulted in a pile-up of old and new business, and by the 1830s the average case of any importance required at least two full terms to travel the distance between "true bill" and "verdict of the court." Charleston District Solicitor David Johnson graphically illustrated the problem for his area when in 1827 he wrote to Waddy Thompson that "we now have on the docket . . . more than 200 causes & . . . our average progress is less than 20 pr week." [14]

A number of efforts were made to rectify this situation. The obvious solutions—to hold extra sessions or to lengthen the regular ones—were not workable since judges were not available in sufficient numbers for such work and funds were lacking for hiring additional ones. On occasion a judge would agree to an off-season court in his circuit, but he did not have the time for many extra events and they were burdens on the State financial system. Court costs for a single day's proceedings were estimated at five hundred dollars. At any rate, lengthening a court term beyond the legal maximum of ten days not only required the attention of the legislature but also threw off schedule the timetables of the remaining courts in the circuit.

Noting these sundry limitations, some citizens urged that the magistrates' and freeholders' courts be authorized to handle the assault and battery cases. On the face of it this was a workable suggestion but it was overruled by noisy and numerous voices expressing a strong opposition to granting magistrates the power of trial over any white men. This was to be expected. The judicial importance of the magistrates had steadily declined after 1790. During the Colonial period they had headed all inferior courts; and until 1846 they had been authorized to try petty misdemeanors and suits-at-law which involved money or property in value less than twenty dollars. But from that date they were considered essentially the judges of slaves and free black offenders. This duty, added to normal tasks of issuing general arrest orders, granting bail, administering the vagrancy laws, and registering such documents as wills and marriage licenses, was considered sufficient to keep magistrates busy.[15]

Two procedures which were widely used to speed up the handling of criminal cases were a twelve hour working day and the empaneling of two petit juries. The first of these was vigorously condemned. As early as 1804 one observer noted that court was being held well into the night and questioned the wisdom of it; and as late as 1850 another critic wrote:

> After the first day of the term, the Court is called at nine o'clock; the Judge rushes on with business until two, adjourns one hour for dinner, and then continues the labour of the Court, always until dark, and frequently until nine or ten o'clock at night. So that the bench, the bar, and the juries, are worked incessantly, from ten to twelve hours a day during the week. Is it at all astonishing that this rail-road speed of dispensing justice fails to give satisfaction?[16]

Jurors especially disliked the swift pace urged on them by the judge. Thomas J. Mackey, in a jocular mood, once declared, "I have just come from Union where I held court for twelve days and ten nights, and only four of the jurors died from fatigue,"[17] but the jurors themselves saw little levity in it. They were not given time for calm deliberation, they said, and in addition they felt a natural repugnance "as free men" against dictatorial treatment.

There were occasions, certainly, when they had ample reason for their complaints. One judge reputedly went so far as to force a hung jury to travel "in a *cart* round the circuit from Court House to Court House" until it reached a verdict concerning the case in question.[18] Other judges locked up jurymen and refused them food and drink until they came to agreement.

One angry juror wrote from Chester:

> This case was given to the Jury about 8 o'clock P. M. (before supper) and the constables were sworn not to allow them to have any meat, drink or fire (water and lights only excepted) until they had agreed on their verdict. It was a very cold and disagreeable night and the cruel barbarity of the law that requires a body of intelligent, free white men to be thus treated struck us with peculiar force . . . . What would the world think of a law which required the members of the Senate and House of Representatives . . . to be imprisoned without meat, drink or fire, until they were of the same mind? But thanks to the humanity of some of our good citizens the jury in this instance were not . . . allowed to suffer the severity of the cruel law in . . . full force, as they, despite the efforts of the Constabulatory to the contrary, were supplied from a back window with a small quantity of the good things usually found on a comfortable supper table. About five o'clock the next morning the jury agreed on their verdict.[19]

While this unhappy jury was deliberating in cold quarters, another was hearing an additional case; for almost every court in the State after the early 1800s made use of two petit juries. "Two setts of jurymen are kept in readiness," wrote lawyer-school teacher Edward Hooker in 1803, "so that as soon as one has retired . . . the other may begin to try a new cause."[20]

This system generally worked well. The procedure was to swear in forty-eight men, divided into two active juries of twelve each with an equal number of reserves standing by to replace any who might be challenged by the defense or who might for some reason fail to make an appearance after the opening day. This took the time of many men who probably needed to put it on their fields or their businesses, but it was a necessity if the courts were not to flounder in a morass of undecided cases.

The addition of an extra twenty-four men to the number legally required for the two juries seems excessive, but it resulted from the lenient laws of challenge and the understandable regulation forbidding near-relatives of the defendants to serve. Any defendant was authorized to challenge two would-be jurors without cause, and up to twenty if adequate reason could be given.

The workings of the challenge laws may be readily illustrated. John Mitchell, on trial in Chester for petit larceny, objected to eleven jurors in 1801. Daniel McLeod, being tried on a murder charge by a Darlington court in 1853 challenged eighteen. Jeremiah Benson of Horry District, accused in 1857 of a felony, disallowed fourteen. One court reporter, noting a case in which a large number of available jurors had been successfully challenged, wrote in his record that a not-guilty verdict "was reached by a jury selected by the prisoner."[21]

Despite loud grumbling from various officials, these liberal challenge laws were not extensively changed. "As every lawyer knows," declared Attorney General Isaac W. Hayne in 1852, the challenge is used "mainly to exclude character, intelligence, and impartiality from the jury, and practically seldom for any other purpose."[22]

The drawing of twenty-four grand jurors and forty-eight petit jurors for each session of a district court sometimes worked a special hardship on those who were eligible to serve. An act of 1798 made any male citizen of good character and reputation who paid as much as one dollar property tax a prospective juror; and by 1857 a reputable taxpayer of any amount was added to jury lists.[23] By no means were all men taxpayers; and of those who were, not all possessed the necessary "excellent character." Hence, while the average jury was a cross section of the State's white male population, a study of the court records shows a recurrence of the same names time and again. To cite examples, Jacob Epting of Newberry was a member of four grand juries and three petit juries in ten years; and Jacob Schirmir of Charleston was a member of four petit juries in eight years.[24]

Some of the repeaters doubtlessly enjoyed their jury service. It is certain that many did not. The consensus on this point is perhaps best expressed in the words of James B. Grimball, a prominent Charleston citizen, who wrote in his diary: "This evening the Sheriff called with a notice to me to serve as juror. . . . This is a disagreeable duty and if it were possible for me to avoid its performance without being fined I certainly should do so. . . . This sitting [on] the jury is disagreeable in the extreme and a duty which almost every man performs with reluctance."[25]

The widespread distaste for this duty is also indicated by the large number of jurors who failed to show up, or who slipped off from duty, hoping not to be missed, or who were excessively quarrelsome and obstreperous while serving. Indeed the failure of citizens to honor their jury summonses and the tendency of jurors to leave after a day or so of duty were evils so serious as to be a definite factor in the delay of trials. A juror who failed to appear was usually fined, the amount ranging from fifty cents to twenty dollars, but despite the fact that this law was rigidly enforced it failed to halt non-attendance. Thirteen Chester district citizens were fined for failure to answer a jury roll call in 1803; eleven Edgefield residents were fined for the same offense in 1810.[26] Elsewhere in the State throughout the antebellum decades the situation was similar.

Jurors who answered the roll call often were angry men and showed their ire by sulking, arguing, and being generally unpleasant. Some of them expressed their distaste by drinking on the job. The drunk jurors, indeed, presented a problem of interesting proportions. Such an entry in court records as "David B. McLeod . . . who after adjournment of the Court for dinner . . . returned to his jury box manifestly drunk and unfit for duty" was commonplace.[27]

Difficulties with petit jurymen, whether or not they arrived for court, may be illustrated by a survey of the Barnwell court for the fall of 1807. The Sessions Journal reveals that on the first day jurors John Cave and John Hall failed to answer roll call and were indicted for non-attendance. Three additional jurymen absented themselves the following morning. On the third day another pair of jurors managed to obtain permission to return to their homes. On the fifth day jurors William Weathersbe and Shadrack Stallings failed to appear. During the afternoon of the sixth day John Nelson was discovered to be too drunk to sit. His relief, Henry Ford, had apparently slipped out of court. Another drunk juror was removed from the box on the seventh day, and two more were missing the following morning. Juror Robert Bradley blandly refused to serve on the ninth day; and by the close of court the next afternoon six others had followed his lead. To sum up, in ten days twenty-one jurors had either failed to

appear, left with or without permission, refused to serve, or incapaci-
tated themselves. It is little wonder that the fines levied against such
recalcitrant jurymen became larger as the years passed.

For their part the jurors complained not only of long hours and
too-frequent appearance of their names on venires, but of poor pay
as well. Until 1844 they received but one dollar each day for their
services and they quite properly considered this too little. In the
angry words of one grand jury presentment:

> Grand Jurors Common Plea & Petit Jurors are dragged from
> their families and from the most remote parts of the district
> without one cent. . . . Many of the poorer class of the citizens
> who are compelled to attend the legal process of mandate of
> Court are probably without one Dollar to procure lodging or a
> meal at a tavern and some are driven to the woods for a pillow
> to relieve his weary head upon and then draw a biscuit from his
> napsack to satiate his hungry appetite.[28]

By 1844 such criticism resulted in a travel grant of ten cents for
each mile (one way only), and by 1858 in a general increase of
juror's pay to $1.50 daily. These changes were not sufficient to satisfy
the jurors.

The outstanding single characteristic of the petit jurors was their
leniency. Whatever the reason or reasons for it, whether the influence
of clever defense lawyers, a genuine sympathy for the criminal class,
or a disinclination to declare a man guilty due to the severity of the
penal codes, the twelve men good and true handed down guilty verdicts in only about thirty-nine per cent of the cases brought before
them. The figure for 1950, when guilty pleas are included, is more
than ninety per cent.

For that matter the leniency of ante-bellum South Carolina jurors
was not expressed alone in the apparently excessive number of acquit-
tals. As earlier noted, about half the defendants in murder cases were
found guilty not of that crime but of manslaughter, which carried a
lighter punishment. On occasion the same was true concerning grand
larceny indictments changed by juries to petit larceny. In addition,
numbers of guilty felons were extended mercy upon direct request
of the jurors hearing the cases. Judges were not legally bound to
honor such requests, but public opinion generally supported jury
verdicts and judges were willing to appease the public mind on such
matters.

Juries made use of a number of criteria in arriving at mercy recommendations. Youth, old age, social position, and presumed insanity were common ones. Now and then, as in the case of Abraham Champion, a Negro stealer, mercy was asked "on general principals of humanity." In other cases, such as that of larcener Milley Vaughan, mercy was recommended "from the disadvantage of her raising."[29]

This same wide range of common law reasoning influenced the not-guilty verdicts. "We view the Prisoner Justifiable in what he has done & we say he is not Guilty," was one jury's solution to the problem of statute law versus public sentiment.[30]

Rumor had it that several of the extra-legal not-guilty verdicts were returned by juries which did not bother to leave their seats. Judge John F. Grimké reputedly tried such a case. A defendant brought to trial before him entered an outright plea of guilty and threw himself on the mercy of the jury. Forthwith the jurymen put their heads together and announced a verdict of not guilty. "How could you return such a verdict, after his confession?" asked the judge. "Why," said the jury foreman, "he has always been such a liar that we could not believe him."[31]

But the situation was conducive to little humor. As the years passed criticism of jury leniency increased. State Attorney General Isaac Hayne made the futile suggestion as late as 1852 that each juror be forced to pledge before trial that he would not acquit solely on the ground of code severity; and a number of critics pointed out to the sympathy-smitten jurors that they were but turning felons back into society where they might commit additional crimes. Such admonitions were of negligible effect.[32]

Some critics believed that over-lenient juries were packed with bribed men or with friends of the defendant. These charges were difficult to prove and were not numerous enough to merit serious investigation. Benjamin F. Perry wrote in 1836 that one of his clients, guilty of manslaughter, had "got to" the jurors and won acquittal as a result. "There was a good deal of management on the part of Findley with the Jury," Perry noted in his diary; "he staid with five of them the night before the trial."[33]

Another allegation of bribery was printed in the Lancaster *Ledger* in 1855, based on "remarks overheard" by the editor; and at Charleston in 1859 a juror seen talking with a defendant was heatedly reprimanded by the judge who fined the deputy sheriff for allowing the conversation to take place.[34] These instances were serious enough, but they were apparently rare and no general charge that jurors were criminally dishonest was made by responsible authority. It was assumed correctly that the inclination of jurymen to set free many criminals and to mitigate the indictments of others was based on less tangible factors than bribery or similar corruption.

The Criminal's Defense

Perhaps the most noteworthy difference between nineteenth and twentieth century lower-court criminal cases in South Carolina is in the part played by the defense attorney. The twentieth century barrister is more a "case lawyer," more apt to gain his verdict on fine points of law and on careful presentation of evidence than on oratory or base appeal to the jury. Sensationalism and play on emotion are still of considerable moment in criminal jurisprudence; but in ante-bellum sessions courts the lawyer was much more a pleader, a showman, a player on the sympathies and provincialisms of his jurors.

In the opinions of pre-Civil War clients the lawyer was clearly the key figure. The prisoner acquitted of petty theft who thereupon declared he would never steal again, promised to remember the jurymen in his prayers, and said to his attorney, "you are indeed the criminal's benefactor," was merely echoing a widespread belief that whatever the misdeed, the "right sort" of lawyer could win a man his freedom. So it was that the forger who, having fraudulently signed a barrister's name to a promissory note, then attempted to employ the same lawyer as his defense attorney was but expressing his full measure of faith in skilled legal talent.[35]

A good criminal lawyer, it was said, was "bold, ready, regardless of respect to opposing counsel, witnesses, or clients, and unscrupulous as to the language in which he expresses his contempt; skilled in cajoling and bullying the judge; little sensitive as to his own feelings, and utterly without regard to the feelings of others. One purpose only seemed to govern him—the purpose to gain his case at all hazards."[36]

The point is well illustrated by a nonsensical anecdote which went the rounds concerning the talents of "Gov. S_____," an old-time pleader "who could talk a jury out of their seven senses." On one occasion he defended an accused horse thief, and in due course won acquittal for him. "Jim," the freed felon was later asked by a friend, "the danger is past; and now . . . didn't you steal that horse?" "Well, Tom," came the answer, "I've all along thought I took that horse, but since I've heard the Governor's speech, I don't believe I did."[37]

The notion that guilty criminals were often set free by the expert pleading and legal trickery of attorneys was supported by court-room evidence, oft-repeated fiction, and now and then by the bitter statements of lawyers and ex-lawyers themselves. Court-room evidence, it is true, was rare; but any one case was certain to assume exaggerated importance in the minds of those who wanted to believe the worst. Such a contest as that in which John C. Calhoun, as a young barrister, admitted his client to be a murderer—only to have a senior member of the bar step in and on a plea of extenuation gain acquittal for the guilty man—is an example of case evidence from a high source.[38]

Other incidents were admitted by Benjamin F. Perry. At least twice he used his superior legal talents to free acknowledged renegades. One of these, a forger of Negro passes, was so grateful that he later named a son after the successful lawyer. The other expressed his appreciation by paying his fee with a worthless note. He was remembered by the infuriated Perry in these words: "A greater scamp never escaped the gallows. He had been . . . [a counterfeiter] for several years & I think it very likely he is still at it."[39]

This proclivity of lawyers to defend the guilty was given by some men as their main reason for quitting the profession. Such well known names as John C. Calhoun, William Lowndes, and William J. Grayson are among them. Calhoun departed the active practice of law, states his most able biographer, because "He could not argue a case in which he did not believe, nor convince himself of the necessary righteousness of the side prepared to pay the larger fee." Lowndes, when asked his reason for dropping a lucrative practice, declared with what must have been considerable exaggeration that during his several years as a lawyer he "had but one case in which my conscience and my duty concurred."[40]

William Grayson, who admittedly had been a failure at law, delivered the most damning blow. Arguing that "Right, justice, truth, are secondary considerations or rather no consideration at all" with his erstwhile colleagues, he fired the following heavy salvo at them:

> The lawyer is mixed up with the bad passions of the Community and becomes their agent and supporter. He keeps the unjust; he sustains the vindictive; he protects the knave. He is

Lancaster County

Colleton County

JAILS IN USE BEFORE 1860

York County (shown as office building many years after its use as jail).

(Right)

Old jail at Pinckneyville, former seat of Union County, where prisoners were lowered into cells from the top.

(Left)

Union County. (Inset) Sheriff Gideon Long.

of some use, it is true. . . . There are lawyers who are not carried away by the evil influences of the profession. But they are
rare as snow at midsummer. . . . The life is not to be coveted
which ministers to the evil passions of a neighborhood; which
serves as a tool for its contentions; as a server for the passions
of the Community to gather in and be carried off.[41]

Newspaper editors and correspondents added to this series of
serious condemnations a steady outpouring of stories. Such tales were
ludicrous for the most part, rarely based on truth and often were
copied from out-of-state publications; nonetheless they were a factor
in bestowing on the South Carolina attorney something of an unsavory reputation.

One account told of a lawyer who defended a counterfeiter, and
with a great speech which wrung tears from the jurors' eyes, won his
case. Then turning to his client he was heard to say, "And now, you
old rascal, go about your business, and never let me catch you passing counterfeit money again." The jury, it was said, "stared in
wonder."[42]

Similar accounts dealt with "Shocko Jones," who could all but
hypnotize juries into doing his bidding; or "John Taylor: The Timon
of the Backwoods Bar and Pulpit," who divided his time between
the camp-meeting and the courthouse and whose legal speciality was
obtaining freedom for pretty girls who had been forced to shoot over-
anxious lovers.[43]

But most newspapermen chose not to take potshots at any specific,
albeit fictitious, practitioner. Rather they preferred scatter shots,
aimed in the general direction of the entire profession. "Show me a
lawyer with hair in the palm of his hand, then I'll believe he is an
honest man," was one of their pet impeachments. "Judge a man by
his actions—a poet by his eyes—an idler by his fingers—a lawyer
by his leer," was another.[44]

The reprinting of "remarks overheard" was also a favorite pastime
of the editors who were having fun at the lawyers' expense. Three
Negro children, for instance, had held this conversation, according
to a writer in the Camden *Gazette*:

> "You know me (said Joseph)—I great man—I captain—I
> gentleman."
> "I greater as him (said the other)—I gentleman too—but I
> bold peter."
> "I no gentleman [said the third]—I n-n-nothing but a
> lawyer.' "[45]

Again, a country man had engaged a barrister in the following discussion:

> "Squire, I called to see if you would like to take this boy, and make a lawyer out of him."
> "He is too young. . . . Have you no older boys?"
> "Oh, yes, sir I have several; but we have concluded to make farmers of the others."
> "But why do you think this boy so much better calculated for a lawyer than your other sons? What are his peculiar qualifications?"
> "Why, do you see, sir, he is just seven years old today. When he was only five, he would lie like the devil; When he got to be six, he was sassy and impudent . . . and now he will steal anything he can get his hands on."[46]

Added to these were gleeful accounts which told of lawyers who had met with defeat or misfortune of some sort. The fictional tale of three attorneys who were outwitted in their efforts to cheat an honest landlord was given space in the Edgefield *Advertiser*.[47] And a letter in the Laurensville *Herald* told how the law business there had fallen off. "Would that you could cast your optics upon the lean, lank, hungry cadaverous phizzes of these miserable bipeds, ycleped attorneys," wrote the happy correspondent. "Oh! It would make you weep. . . . However, what's one's poison, is another's meat. If the lawyers suffer, the people prosper."[48]

The bulk of such newspaper linage devoted to lawyers was admittedly facetious and presented to provoke laughter rather than ill will. But whatever the intent, it could have a deleterious effect. For example, it was no amused reader who, following the appearance of an anti-lawyer item in the Laurensville *Herald,* wrote the editor that if it were true that "the quibbles and technicalities" of barristers were "defeating the ends of justice," then drastic action ought to be taken at once.[49] Other subscribers, doubtlessly, were similarly impressed.

The editor of the Sumter *Banner* took note of this unfortunate situation when he wrote in 1848 that he feared the press attack on lawyers was causing far too many people to consider all lawyers as being "heartless and mercenary." It was his observation, he said, that no other profession in the State was held in such general low esteem as that of law. This must be corrected, he urged his readers, for most lawyers were honest, law abiding, and vital to the welfare of the community.[50]

By the 1850s a few additional papers began to print items, especially fiction, which portrayed lawyers in a favorable light. These never equalled in number those to the contrary, but they offered something, at least, in rebuttal. The presence of two favorable stories in a single issue of the Laurensville *Herald* is a case in point. These two, "A Piece of Legal Advice" and "The Accommodation Bill, or Experiences of a Barrister,"[51] must have been warmly welcomed by the legal fraternity.

Whatever the general opinion of South Carolina people concerning the lawyers, the legal profession did not suffer from membership as a result. In 1771 South Carolina had but twenty-four practicing attorneys, but by 1800 a French traveler wrote with good reason that the State seemed to have too many lawyers. This was the result, he believed, of an "absured vanity" attached to the profession by the members of the higher social stations.[52] Two hundred lawyers were registered in the state by 1820, 230 in 1840, 260 in 1850, and 315 in 1860. The *United States Lawyers' Directory* for 1850 listed by name the South Carolina attorneys in active practice at the beginning of that year and pointed out that these 260 had their offices in thirty-six villages, towns, and cities. Sixty-two of the total resided in Charleston; but the remainder were spread throughout the State.[53]

Most South Carolina lawyers were trained men, qualified by study and experience to practice their profession. On this point the adverse critics of the barristers were silent. Lawyers were licensed from 1785 by State judges, and the licensing process was regulated both by law and custom. The 1785 law forced the legal neophyte to complete at least three years of formal apprenticeship either in a law school or in a competent barrister's office, and following this to stand an oral examination on "his knowledge and character." The three-year clause was modified in 1801 and removed from the statute books in 1812; nonetheless, only a few men chose to begin their practice without considerable prior preparation. By the year 1854, for example, 382 graduates of the South Carolina College at Columbia had become attorneys. Other lawyers, such as John Siegling and Augustin Taveau, had studied at Harvard. A few men had attended the famed Tapping Reeves Law School in Litchfield, Connecticut, and others had gained legal background at the London Inns of Court. In addition, apprentices were reading law in the offices of many of the State's practicing attorneys.[54]

The examination before the judge was, as pointed out, the immediate step which led to the granting of a license to practice. Statistics
are not available on the number of applicants who failed their oral
questioning; but contemporary observers were generally agreed that
the examination was, as a rule, a mild event, informal, and leisurely
administered by jurists who had already made their decisions on the
fitness of the man facing them.

One critic believed that "a single perusal of Blackstone, the work
of a few weeks," was sufficient to pass the benign ordeal. Another
wrote, "The examination was not so formidable. . . . A letter from
. . . [the examiner's] brother had macadamized my way." A third
barrister declared that his bar examination had consisted solely of
the following exchange:

> "What will you charge a client for filing a bill?" asked the
> examiner . . . .
> "Fifty dollars," was the ready reply.
> "You are admitted," said the Chancellor. "You understand
> the science exactly and are fully prepared for practice."[55]

The prisoner at the bar did not, naturally enough, concern himself
so much with the lawyer's educational background as with his proved
ability to sway a jury. Such ability in ante-bellum South Carolina
depended more on a thorough understanding of local pride and local
customs than on Blackstone and Coke, and it was expressed more
effectively through moving oratory than cold legal reasoning or case
precedent. Criminal lawyers made use of fine points in the law and
of past decisions in their arguments, but they did so sparingly. It
was considered something of a compliment to be thought "not a
case lawyer."[56]

Any study of the ante-bellum criminal lawyer in action is essentially research in the use and influence of oratory. The judicious
selection of jurymen and witnesses, the ability to seek out flaws in
indictments, and the knowledge of accepted methods by which cases
might be postponed were all weapons in the criminal lawyer's arsenal,
but once the case was off the court calendars and the trial underway,
forensic excellence became more often than not the skill needed
beyond all others.

Attorneys and the general public alike attested to the importance
of a talent for oral persuasion. Traveler William Faux might refer
to the pleading of South Carolina lawyers as "jargon . . . little short
of nonsense," but in Benjamin F. Perry's more expert opinion,

oratorical ability was the positive secret of any barrister's success. "I have a very loud voice and a fluency of speech when animated," he wrote. "This pleases the crowd . . . [and they] think me a 'good lawyer.' "[57] In similar fashion, William J. Grayson blamed his inability to speak well for his failure at criminal law. "I had not the faculty of ready talk," he complained; "I was destitute of . . . the face of bronze and tongue of iron so indispensable at the bar."[58]

Often fluent address was indispensable. "Thrilling eloquence and withering rebuke" apparently won as many cases in South Carolina's ante-bellum sessions courts as any other single factor. The acquittal of Thomas Gayner in 1810 and of Jesse Adams in 1840 are cases in point. Both men were accused of murder and both admittedly were freed as a result of the powerful and touching arguments of their attorneys. Gayner's lawyer devoted his passionate appeal to a thesis that God and God alone demanded the right to sit in judgment of his client. The jurors were sufficiently impressed to return a verdict of innocence. Adams' lawyer gave a two-hour address which was reported by one witness as the most telling oration he had ever heard. He believed it was certain to carry conviction of its thesis to the minds of the jurors, and he was right.[59]

The effect of fine oratory on ante-bellum juries is also illustrated by the numerous reports of contemporary observers. A juryman who sat in judgment on Daniel Neu, charged with maintaining a public nuisance, reported the legal arguments in that case as follows:

> Lowyer Noble talked powerful strong; told us the law an' read it out of the books, the same as the gospel. Ever'-thing looked shore all right for Dan'el. Jeams L. wus seated down an' lissened an' sometimes hit the floor with his stick. He then looked out the door, an' 'is face wus so pitiful we felt sorry for him an' thought we wus shore beat. Bine-by Lowyer Noble gets through talkin'. Jeams L. get up. He bowed to the judge, an' he bowed to the jury an' ever'body very perlite. He didn't bring no books. He started easy like, an' said that his friend Lowyer Noble talked very nice, but all that he had read out of the books had nothin' to do with this case; an' before he had talked five minits he had Lowyer Nobel's argyment busted wide open. He then begin to talk better'n any preacher I ever hear.[60]

Fiction as well as fact was used to point out the power of the expert lawyer's plea to the jury. Indeed, the general notion that eloquence won cases must have gained a large measure of acceptance by the telling of such popular tales as that concerning a lawyer defending a pretty girl. As the story went:

> First of all three advocates spoke in succession for the prosecution. . . . They about equally partitioned their howling . . . betwixt the prisoner and her . . . counsel, as if in doubt which of the twain was then on trial. . . . [Finally the defense lawyer] sprang to his feet, crossed the bar, and took his position almost touching the jury. He . . . commenced in a whisper, but it was a whisper so wild, so clear, so unutterably ringing . . . as to fill the hall. . . . At the outset, he dealt in pure logic . . . till the whole mass of confused evidence looked transparent . . . and the jurors nodded to each other signs of thorough conviction . . . . He then changed his posture, so as to sweep the bar with his glance; and began to tear and rend his legal adversaries. His sallow face glowed as a heated furnace; his eyes resembled living coals; and his voice became the clangor of a trumpet. I have never, before or since, listened to such murderous denunciations. It was like Jove's eagle charging a flock of crows. . . . His features were livid as those of a corpse; his very hair appeared to stand on end; his nerves shook as with a palsy; he tossed his hands wildly toward heaven, each finger stretched apart and quivering. . . . His voice grew mournful as a funeral song, and his eyes filled with tears, as he traced a vivid picture of man's cruelties . . . [to] a poor and friendless woman . . . till a shout of stifled rage arose . . . and even some of the jury cried, "shame". . . . One half the audience wept like children. . . . The jury rendered a verdict of "Not Guilty," without leaving the box; and three cheers shook the old court-house.[61]

But there was more to legal oratory than the clever use of gestures and the studied change of tone. An expert criminal lawyer knew his judge and made it a point to know his jurors. Different judges had differing reputations for leniency or harshness. By obtaining a delay of a case a lawyer might be able to swap jurists. Attorney Perry, for instance, wrote in his diary, "Judge O'Neall is very severe in his sentences . . . & is no favorite with the Sessions folks. . . . Judge Gantt is the . . . [opposite] of O'Neall. We always make it a point to try criminal cases before Gantt if possible."[62]

Respecting the petit juries, a lawyer played on their prejudices, made capital of their religious convictions, and appealed to their local pride and patriotism. To cite examples, in a case involving a poor man and a rich man, the poor man's lawyer said, "It is difficult for a humble citizen like . . . [my client] to contend with a man of wealth and influence such as . . . [our opponent]." And a contest in which one party was from another state turned on the following statement: "Gentlemen, that may be law in Philadelphia, but it [is] not law in Coosawhatchie."[63]

Cases might also be won by diverting the attention of the jury from the accused to the accuser. James L. Petigru ruined one prosecutor's case by forcing from that hapless gentleman, while on the witness chair, a confession that he did not regularly attend church. An Up Country barrister gained a similar victory when, instead of attempting to prove the innocence of his client, he pointed out that the prosecutor was a betrayer, a "false friend" who had tattled on his neighbor, and hence was a man without honor. Less successful but not less resourceful was a Columbia lawyer who, hard-pressed in his efforts to defend a woman client, bravely attempted to persuade the jurors that the lady's "bald . . . pot-bellied and bandy-legged" adversary was in reality a "gallant, gay Lothario."[64]

On countless occasions lawyers resorted to religious appeals. One critic of the South Carolina barristers denounced the "frequent and unnecessary" references to the "Supreme Being" as a major evil of criminal pleading. Appeals made in the form of prayers, he wrote, "make clever rhetorical flourishes, and furnish a resting place for the mind of the juror"; nonetheless, the name of God "should never be pronounced but when necessary, and then only with reverence. Whatever amounts to more than this, is downright profanity."[65]

The lawyer paid little if any heed to such complaints. The Father, the Son, the Holy Ghost, and the Old and the New Testaments were called in as witnesses and character references in case after case. On at least one occasion a defense attorney went so far as to manufacture in his own mind a Biblical quotation which might serve to justify his client's activity. According to the lawyer who told the story, the accused was forthwith set free—but one of the jurymen reported some weeks later that he had been and was still searching his Bible for the citation which had been used.[66]

The matter of appealing to the jury, of pleading the case, took precedence in ante-bellum South Carolina over the process of cross-examining witnesses. But the latter aspect of legal procedure was not wholly overlooked. Then as now good witnesses won cases and poor witnesses lost them. It seemed to be the consensus of contemporaries that South Carolina lawyers considered any witness as fair game, to be threatened, ridiculed, bullied, or falsely accused of a wide variety of moral failings.

A favorite trick was to accuse the opposition witness of being a mulatto. Such persons were not allowed to testify against white people, and any witness charged with having Negro blood had to stand immediate examination by the court. This could be, to say the least, an embarrassing procedure.[67]

In one district the grand jury reported the impolite treatment of witnesses by attorneys as a grievance warranting legislative action. They deplored the "excesses of language by Members of the Bar towards . . . witnesses," and believed the practice served only to anger them and to "provoke apparent Contradiction in their testimony as well as to wound . . . [their] feelings & character."[68] Some years later a Lancaster correspondent added to this the charge that the rude treatment of witnesses was a sign that lawyers were, as a class, a crude and unprincipled lot. "The Bar profess to be gentlemen," he insisted; "now one of the elements of a gentleman is, to say or do nothing . . . that would mar the enjoyment of the innocent."[69]

Whatever the nature of the attacks on this aspect of their methodology, successful lawyers continued to examine witnesses with an eye toward winning the case and without considering the possibility of bruising tender sensibilities. For that matter, the lawyer who could consistently turn opposing testimony to his own use was respected and envied by the bulk of his colleagues. This made it easier to shrug off the attacks of the ill-wishers outside the legal circle.

Some lawyers may have used "professional" witnesses in a last-ditch effort to win their cases. This was suggested by the editor of the Lancaster *Ledger* in 1855. He had noted, he wrote, that one particular individual had appeared in court a number of times as witness for sundry defendants. "Why is this man witness, in so many cases?" he asked. "Is it the result of his officious and meddlesome habit? Or, is it, when a man wants anything proved in court, he knows where to find the witness?"[70]

If there were any large number of "Paid-off Witnesses" they were not indicted for perjury. Few such cases are recorded in sessions courts' journals. To be sure, there were numerous instances of conflicting testimony; but such conflicts were generally deemed not to be "willful lying."[71]

Viewed in retrospect, the life of the South Carolina ante-bellum criminal lawyer was not especially pleasant, nor was it always highly rewarding in terms of dollars and cents. "Irksome, perplexing & unprofitable" were the adjectives one member of the bar used to describe it,[72] and in a very real sense he was correct. The average South Carolina sessions court lawyer rode a lengthy circuit, traveling from court town to court town by horseback, in a stagecoach, or, after 1840, possibly by train. He argued from ten to thirty cases at each sessions term, most of them being the "mean causes"—the petit larceny and the assault and battery cases—which were of little importance either to his reputation or to his pocketbook. He had scant time to prepare his arguments, even those which were important; yet his several clients expected miracles from him. His work, in short, became routine and dull, and there was a considerable turnover in his profession as many of his coterie went as soon as they could from criminal law to politics or planting.

Circuit riding was a tiring necessity. Sessions courts were held but twice each year in each district and for financial reasons alone a lawyer had to attend as many as possible. A typical circuit was that traveled by Benjamin F. Perry in 1836. During the spring session he attended court in Greenville, then rode directly to Pickens. From that village he traveled to Anderson, and from there to Spartanburg. From Spartanburg he moved on to Laurens. At the conclusion of court there he returned home. It was his belief, he wrote, that a "young practitioner will acquire more legal knowledge on the circuit in one week than he can from books in a month"; nonetheless a year later he wrote the following: "I am sick and tired of a tavern. . . . The crowd & company annoy me very much—It is . . . painful in a very high degree to be always in company."[73]

Circuit riding was a group affair, with lawyers and perhaps judge traveling in a party from town to town. They drank, joked, brawled, and swapped tales, humorous and otherwise, as they rode. They shared the sundry problems of travel—the poor food, vermin infested beds, swollen streams, and bad roads,—and they became, many of them, fast friends as a result. This latter aspect of circuit riding was perhaps the greatest compensation it offered.[74]

But friendship was not allowed to interfere with law business. Once a lawyer group had arrived at a "seat of justice" it was every man for himself. At a sessions court each lawyer had first to obtain his share of clients, then win his share of cases, and competition was keen both outside and inside the court room. This competitive spirit sometimes so aroused the gentlemen involved that they exchanged blows; and now and then the local citizens were treated to the spectacle of lawyers themselves being tried for disturbing the peace.[75]

A young, inexperienced lawyer was naturally handicapped in his search for clients. Perry remembered that he obtained only nine of more than one hundred possible cases when he began his practice in the 1820s. By 1839, however, he had won an enviable reputation as a successful criminal lawyer, and in the spring of that year defended 130 clients. Most lawyers, after a few years' experience, got a fair share of available business. Sessions courts' dockets were usually crowded, spring and fall, and the best lawyers could not take all the cases offered them.[76]

Actually the problem was not that of getting clients, but of obtaining those able and willing to pay legal fees. Perry was speaking for many of his colleagues when he wrote, "The profession would be pleasant enough if the lawyer was always employed in important cases and *well paid*. But nothing can be more disheartening than to have a *mean case,* a *poor client,* and a *troublesome* one in the bargain." A few years later, he added, "The *law* is dull. I want money very much—My clients do not pay promptly."[77]

Perry kept records of his cases and of fees charged and collected, and his account books make it clear that his complaints concerning financial profit from the profession were generally justified.[78] He charged fees of five to twenty-five dollars for pleading cases of "little importance," and twenty-five to 150 dollars for defending clients accused of felonies. These charges were by no means excessive, by standards of the time,[79] but they would have provided Perry with an adequate income had he been able to collect them.

This he was never able to do. Between 1827 and 1834, for example, he averaged collecting about half the accounts due him; and not all of these were paid in legal tender. In 1836, to cite a noteworthy instance, he defended and gained acquittal for a gentleman on trial for horse theft. In lieu of the money fee, this man gave Perry a horse.[80]

Perry's cash income from law practice for his first fifteen years as a barrister averaged slightly more than five hundred dollars a year. Some South Carolina lawyers would have considered that sum rather an imposing figure. Attorney Joshua H. Hudson, for instance, reported as his law income in 1857 one hundred dollars—a portion of which was paid in shelled corn. He was, he said, and we can believe him, "then heavily in debt."[81]

But if law did not always pay well and if the work of the criminal lawyer was often monotonous and generally arduous, the barristers continued nonetheless in increasing numbers to argue their cases. As pointed out, law was a stepping stone to politics and public office. In addition, despite the low estimate held by many citizens of their profession, lawyers knew that they ranked well with the highest social classes. Such factors overshadowed less rewarding aspects of their labors.

Despite some revision in the defense lawyer's technique of pleading, the criminal court processes in South Carolina have undergone no great changes since the mid-decades of the nineteenth century. Basically the procedure was and is (1) indictment; (2) grand jury action; (3) examination of witnesses and presentation of evidence; (4) final appeals by lawyers; (5) petit jury verdict; and (6) sentencing by the judge. A seventh factor, the appeal of guilty verdicts, might also be noted, for appellate courts existed in the State after 1800 and some criminal cases were reviewed by their judges. The importance of appellate jurisdiction in criminal cases is, however, essentially a modern development. During the ante-bellum years the bulk of criminal cases began and ended in the lower courts.

V. Punishment

WHEN THE LAWYER HAD DONE HIS BEST AND FAILED HE GENerally wrote in his case book, "cause lost—no fee." The convicted miscreant, on the other hand, stood with fear in his face and possibly a prayer on his lips. If guilty of a felony, his punishment might well be death. If guilty of a misdemeanor, he might be fined, jailed, whipped, pilloried, or branded; or he might receive a sentence which was a combination of two or more of these punishments and might include expulsion from the State. To a large extent the severity of the punishment depended on such factors as the criminal's age, his "respectability," his prior record, and the inclination of the judge.

The sentences which aroused the greatest public interest were those of a corporal nature. Of these, the one which sent a thrill of horror throughout the court room was death by hanging. According to the State penal code, 165 crimes carried such a penalty in 1813; and although the number decreased to fifty-one in 1825, thirty-two in 1838, and twenty-two in 1850, South Carolina continuously led neighboring states in offenses punishable by hanging.[1]

The situation was not so bad as the figures imply. Viewing the large number of capital crimes, jurors and judges alike adopted a policy of extra-legal compassion. Thus convictions by jury were not easily obtained and death sentences from the bench were few. "While this state of things exists," declared a Chester grand jury in October, 1816, "prosectuors will be found to come forward with reluctance and jurors thru motives of humanity will sham to acquit even where severe punishment is demanded."

A correspondent to the Laurensville *Herald,* some twenty-five years later, made essentially the same complaint. The existence in the written law of so many capital misdeeds had "converted trial by jury into a mere thing of mockery," he said, and as a result robbers, arsonists, and counterfeiters alike were being "tried, convicted, and sentenced . . . to no more than a little incarceration and a few stripes laid on merely for the sake of exposure."[2]

The critics might have added that more than half of those who were sentenced to death escaped through a legal loophole known as "benefit of clergy." This meant simply that a felon who was a first offender might be branded or, after 1833, fined and jailed rather than hanged. Until the 1850s, benefit of clergy was widely granted in South Carolina. Especially was this true during the early decades of the ante-bellum period.

The reluctance of judge and jury to hand down death sentences and the existence of such a device as benefit of clergy did not by any means do away with capital punishment. They merely reduced the number of executions to a point where such events did not become commonplace.

The hanging of criminals in ante-bellum South Carolina was done publicly, at a cost to the taxpayers of about a hundred dollars each.[3] No spectacle presented to the people was better attended and none more vividly remembered. Public hangings were well advertised for weeks beforehand and on the appointed day people gathered, as if for race week or court time, from all parts of the district. They came on foot, on horseback, in wagons and stagecoaches, in private carriages, and when possible, in special trains. They brought or purchased box-lunches, obtained hastily written pamphlets which introduced the victim and described his crime, and thus armed they vied with their neighbors for a vantage spot near the gallows.

The hangings took place where as many as possible would be able to see. If available, a "low, flat place" bordered by high ground was selected for the erection of the gallows. Wooden platforms were sometimes built where the natural slope was not sufficient to allow the rearmost spectators a good view. No attempt was made to seat the audience and as a result all classes and ages stood together, rank and race forgotten. In the language of a modern writer, describing the 1820 hanging of murderess Lavinia Fisher:

> Staid merchants were there, inwardly surprised at themselves for coming, and with them were dandies with . . . extravagantly cut pantaloons; coonskin-capped wagoners; soldiers from the garrison at Fort Johnson; Dutch, French, and Spanish seamen; country cousins who had come to town for Race Week and neglected to go home again; free Negroes with their plump mulatto wives; slaves and white apprentice boys, all gathered around the gibbet. Little masters and misses broke from their nurses and . . . trudged to the hanging. Here and there were even fashionably clad women . . . . The keepers of grog shops and

sailor's boardinghouses in Bedon's Alley were there. The girls from the houses near the jail were there, on their best behavior.[4]

Such crowds were understandable enough in the city of Charleston, but the story was generally the same elsewhere. More than two thousand people, for example, witnessed a hanging at the small Up Country village of Pendleton in 1824. And four years later, another public execution at the same place occasioned the following newspaper comment:

> On Friday last . . . Uriah Sligh was executed at this place for the murder of Jehu Orr. As usual on such occasions, a large concourse of people assembled to witness the last pangs of a suffering fellow creature. It is certainly a strange curiosity which prompts people to attend the execution of a criminal, but it has so happened that the three occurrences of the kind which have unfortunately taken place here within two years, have severally collected together a more numerous assemblage than we have observed on any other occasion. The solemnity of the scene did not, in this instance, seem to produce a lasting impression on the beholders.[5]

People attended hangings for a variety of reasons. The most usual, of course, was morbid curiosity; but this was not always admitted. Many said they were fast friends of the culprit, and had come from a sense of duty to pay him final homage. Others claimed to be relatives. Some declared that they came in hope of obtaining a souvenir. A bit of the rope used in a hanging would, it was claimed, cure the worst sort of toothache; and others said it would prevent horses from balking and wives from nagging. Still others declared that it would, if used properly, ward off bad luck and evil spirits generally. If an inch or so of the rope were not obtainable, a chip of the gallows might be used in its stead. Even the bark off nearby trees was thought to possess special curative powers.[6]

Essentially the people came anticipating a spectacle, and they were rarely disappointed. There was always the view of the condemned being marched to the hanging-place, led by the sheriff, flanked by guards, and accompanied by a minister. And there was the last speech of the culprit—that alone was usually worth the trip. Finally there was the deep moment of hush and palpitation as the trap dropped and the body at the end of the rope jerked and twitched its last. This "swinging-off" was the climax. Here friends and relatives of the doomed man might seek to leave with him a final thought or word of advice. "Goodbye, Jim," called out a heartbroken acquaintance of a dangling Columbia felon, "take good care of your-self."[7]

Men met their public death with different attitudes. A few gloried in the attention they were receiving and died smiling and joking. Some quaked and prayed aloud or screamed and had to be dragged to the gallows. Some attempted to unnerve the hangman by calling on God to "strike dead" the man who "would take another's life." Some proclaimed their innocence to the last, and a number of these begged the onlookers to come to their rescue. Some, ungraciously, were wholly impassive.

A Pendleton murderer in 1828 entertained the multitude with a long speech in which he urged his listeners to go to church every Sunday and to take the temperance pledge at once. Following this he led them in a prayer for his soul. John and Lavinia Fisher, being hanged from the same platform, embraced each other at the insistence of the mob. A Newberry felon, David G. Sims, sat on the edge of the gallows platform, listened attentively, and added an occasional "Amen" while the Reverend Samuel P. Pressley preached his funeral discourse. And at Abbeville, a malefactor devoted the bulk of his final oration to an appeal that some one of the bystanders marry and care for his widow-to-be. "She is a good woman and handy and no mistake," he declared.[8]

Any man who met his death with courage was sure to gain the sympathy of many in the crowd and to die something of a martyr. This possibility occasioned much of the weak and ineffectual criticism which was voiced against public executions. "Much more of terror would be inspired," believed Governor John H. Means, "by the knowledge, that at the tolling of a bell . . . a human being, within the narrow compass of his cell, was launched into eternity, unsustained in his last dark moments by the sympathies of a surrounding multitude."[9]

But Governor Means was not speaking for a majority of South Carolina people. Criticism of public hanging was rare. A resolution aimed at prohibiting the open execution of white persons was introduced in the legislature in 1844 but died after a brief flurry of seeming success in the House.[10] The Newberry grand jury in the fall of 1852 requested without result that a private execution enclosure be built in their district for condemned felons; and in 1857, Governor R. F. W. Allston stated in his annual message that whenever he "had occasion to interfere at all with the sentence of the courts" he had directed the sheriff "to confine . . . execution to the precincts of the jail-yard, with the Clerk of the Court and some substantial citizens as witnesses."[11] But these were not backed strongly by other agencies of popular opinion. The demand for semi-private punishment did not crystallize until the post-Civil War period was well underway.

Nearly all criminal executions in ante-bellum South Carolina were by hanging. One Negro rapist was burned to death, legally, in 1825.[12] In addition, there was some talk of substituting "galvanism" for the hangman's rope;[13] but electricity as a means of dispatching criminals was apparently not tried in the State before the Civil War.

Court records indicate that perhaps ten per cent of criminals standing trial on felony indictments were sentenced to death. Of these, a considerable number were pardoned by the State executive. The exact number is difficult to determine for governors handled pardon appeals on an individual basis, and such records as were kept appear only as scattered notations in miscellaneous correspondence files.

Indications are that some governors pardoned freely. For example, Patrick Noble in 1839 requisitioned a supply of pardon forms with these words: "I have not one blank. . . . I beg you to forward as early as possible blank pardons in cases of white persons and also in case of negroes. . . . I have daily calls for such things."[14]

William Aiken, governor from 1844 through 1846, was the executive most criticized for having too liberal a pardon policy. Editors and grand jurors alike condemned his "free use" of that prerogative. One grand jury deemed his liberality "a mockery to our judicial decisions . . . and a *broad* encouragement to the commission of crime with the hope of impunity."[15] Such complaints, it would appear, did not sway Aiken toward a stricter policy.

The question of excessive numbers of pardons was still being debated in 1852. State Attorney General Isaac W. Hayne in that year urged the enactment of legislation which would prohibit any pardon not recommended by the judge and jury which had heard the case.[16] No such law was passed, and governors continued to pardon according to the dictates of their own consciences.

Pardons were not complicated documents and consisted of nothing more than blank forms filled out by the governor and sent directly to the sheriff having charge of the prisoner. The governor might, if he desired, write in any number of conditions pertaining to the pardon and this was sometimes done. A man might be pardoned, for instance,

OLD SOUTH CAROLINA
COURTHOUSES

Top to bottom:

    Chester County

    Camden

    Lancaster County

    Williamsburg County

Top to bottom:

Georgetown County

Colleton County

Marion County

Horry County

only at the conclusion of a stated jail term; or he might be pardoned on the promise that he would leave the State within a specified number of days. The usual blank, however, set the subject free without reservation.

Pardons were sometimes received by the sheriff at the last hour, which is not necessarily a noteworthy occurrence; but at times they were delivered before sentence had actually been passed. At least three such pardons are officially noted in sessions courts' records: one at Chester in 1801, a second at Edgefield in 1824, and a third at Barnwell in 1853. "On being asked if he had any Reason to Offer Why Sentence Should not Be pronounced against him," wrote the reporter of the Chester case, "he [Sam Barber] Produced the Governor's pardon."[17]

Some of the last minute pardons did not meet with public approval. A Newberry felon, for example, whose pardon was delivered to him by the sheriff while he stood on the scaffold with the rope about his neck, was severely whipped by a committee of the crowd. Men cursed, it was said, at being deprived of the show they had come to see.[18]

The procedures for obtaining pardons were as informal as the granting of them, and ranged from a simple request by the criminal's lawyer to a citizen petition. Defense lawyers regularly asked pardon for their guilty clients, noting such extenuating circumstances as were applicable.[19]

At least one pardon in the ante-bellum years was requested by the prosecution. "I think the conviction was righteous," wrote the conscience-stricken prosecutor, "but I should regret the execution of the poor old convict. . . . [He] is 73 years of age—has an aged wife, and a most pitiable family of idiot children."[20]

Citizen petitions for the pardon of criminals were usually circulated by the defense lawyers and often were appended to the barristers' own requests. Now and then they were mailed in as separate documents, and often, apparently, the defense lawyer had nothing to do with them. Ten friends of William Reagin petitioned for his release in 1834, and two condemned Negroes were pardoned by Governor William Aiken in 1845 as a direct result of citizen petitions.[21]

The citizen petitions were generally effective, but pardon was most likely if either the judge or the jury which heard the case applied for it. This sort of request was sometimes made by the judge, but more often by the twelve petit jurors. A typical jury verdict asking pardon is the following: "WE find the prisoner guilty, but from the good Character WE have had of him and his penitence, WE recommend him to the mercy of the executive of the State."[22]

As earlier noted, the governor might attach to his pardon a condition that the subject leave the State. Banishment was, in fact, both a substitute for and an addition to other types of punishment. Courts often made it the sentence or a part of the sentence given any petty miscreant who seemed to have a proclivity to repeat his misdeeds; and it was not uncommon for a judge to give such a criminal his choice between leaving the State at once or receiving a public lashing and a jail term. "He was suffered . . . [to] give leg bail . . . which he did in a hurry," wrote an Anderson citizen, referring to a persistent troublemaker.[23]

A criminal banished from the State might be sent out for life or for a certain number of years. In cases of life banishment the culprit could legally return only in consequence of an act of the legislature, and such bills were rarely passed. Those men who returned without such permission were subject at once to the full punishment called for by their original crime.[24]

Banishment became popular as a means of punishment after 1840 and was almost the standard penalty for persons convicted of illegal trading with Negroes, harboring slaves, handling "seditious literature," or being "of an abolitionist bent."

The ninety per cent of convicted felons who did not receive death sentences were punished approximately as follows: about fifty per cent were fined, twenty per cent jailed, and thirty per cent whipped, pilloried, or branded. These figures include many criminals who were punished by some combination of the five, usually by a fine and a lashing. Early in the ante-bellum period a few unfortunate wrongdoers, especially those guilty of grand larceny, suffered all five in sequence.

The three of these punishments under heaviest attack by the reformers were branding, pillory, and whipping. Branding and pillory in particular were targets for vehement and persistent attack and by 1833 both were legally abolished. This was anticlimactic, however; judges had by that date virtually ceased to sentence a man to such ordeals.

Standing in pillory was a common practice during the Colonial decades and until about 1810. Sessions courts made use of it not only as a part punishment for felons who had prayed benefit of

clergy but also as a full or part sentence for such criminals as petty
larceners, manslaughterers, and bigamists.

In South Carolina, standing in pillory was a tiresome but apparently a mild punishment, used for the purpose of exposing the victim to
public scorn or ridicule. To this end it was effective. A person thus
subjected to public gaze rarely remained in the area following his
release. In Anderson, for instance, a village drunkard and trouble-
maker was sentenced to pillory. He mounted the platform with a
wide grin; joked and laughed as his head and hands were being
adjusted; and called to the crowd to furnish him with a "chaw o'
backer" so that he might enjoy the stay. His spirits dropped, however,
as the jeering crowd gathered; and some time before the sheriff
released him he was "meek and quiet."[25]

A pillory, usually erected in the courtyard near the whipping post,
was a wooden frame having holes through which the offender's head
and arms were thrust and held fast. A person sentenced to pillory
usually stood for periods ranging from ten minutes to several hours.
Shortly after the turn of the nineteenth century the pillory gave way
to the whipping post and the former punishment became obsolete.

Branding, like standing in pillory, was something of a relic from
the pre-Revolution era, but it died a slower death. Branding was done
either by the sheriff or the jailer in the presence of the court. A typical
sentence was that recorded for Joseph Hodges of Darlington District,
who had been indicted for murder and found guilty of manslaughter.
"The Court Ordered," the record reads, "that the sheriff . . . do immediately brand the said Joseph Hodges on the brawn of the thumb
of the Right hand in open Court, which being done the Court Then
Ordered that the prisoner be discharged."[26]

Three letters, "T", "M", and "F", were used in South Carolina
brandings. These were burned into the victim's thumb, cheek, or in
rare cases, his forehead. The letter "M" was used exclusively for
malefactors guilty of murder or manslaughter. "T" marked the thief,
and "F" was used for the freymaker (rioter). The depth and severity
of the burn might well depend on the victim's quickness of speech,
for sentences sometimes required that the sheriff hold the hot iron in
place "until the words 'God save the State' could be pronounced
three times" by the unhappy culprit. A stutterer, needless to say, was
in an unenviable position.

Some brandings were punishments in name only. It happened on
occasion that a jury would convict a man of a crime which called

for a branding, and at the same time ask that he be granted mercy. In such cases the judge might order the sheriff to apply "a cold iron."

Brandings, like public hangings, were well attended. Since they took place in court not so many people could watch the proceedings, but crowds gathered nonetheless. In the words of the lawyer who defended Michael Toohey, a citizen branded in consequence of a manslaughter verdict: "To witness this *ridiculous ceremony,* an immense concourse of people thronged the court, and all the avenues leading to it. The prisoner was placed in an elevated frame, and his arm and hand pinioned to a projection adapted to the purpose. . . . But by the clumsy operation of the hangman, who officiated on this occasion, the impression was inverted—thus W."[27]

A far more common penalty than branding was public whipping. A specified number of lashes was, for instance, the most frequently authorized punishment for all crimes against property. A whipping post, "made of the best light-wood," was an adornment of every court yard or village square during most of the ante-bellum years, and the view of a pickpocket or a hog-stealer receiving his "dorsal application" was a common one.

Most whipping posts were simply a pair of poles connected by a cross beam to which a criminal's arms were tied. A single pole or a tree might adequately serve the same purpose. The most elaborate South Carolina whipping post was in Charleston and was used especially for punishing slaves. As described by a German traveler, "The machine consists of a sort of crane, on which a cord with two nooses runs over pullies; the nooses are made fast to the hands . . . [of the victim] and drawn up, while the feet are bound tight to a plank. The body is stretched out as much as possible, and thus the miserable creature receives the exact number of lashes counted off."[28]

The "exact number of lashes counted off" was usually thirty-nine, a carry-over from the Biblical code of Moses which called for "forty stripes save one." But sentences were handed down which varied greatly from the traditional thirty-nine. Ephraim Carter of Horry District, guilty of petty larceny, is an example of a misdemeanant who received a light sentence. In his case only two lashes were given. Similar sentences called for three, four, or five stripes; and in 1835 a Charleston white woman was sentenced to receive but one blow.[29]

The case of two Columbia horse thieves in 1852 illustrates the opposite extreme. Each was ordered to receive a total of 119 lashes. These were to be given in monthly installments of 39-20-20-20-20, and between whippings the men were to be jailed. Such a splitting up of harsh sentences was the usual procedure in cases of white persons. Horse stealers generally received the heaviest whipping penalties from South Carolina sessions courts. Rarely was such a criminal allotted fewer than fifty lashes.[30]

For some reason Negroes were thought to be able physically to stand heavier whipping sentences than white persons. Whereas a sentence of 119 lashes was considered unusually heavy for a white man, Negro slaves, men and women alike, were not infrequently given double that number. Some Negroes, of course, died as a result of such beatings.[31]

Light sentences were aimed at embarrassing a criminal and not at punishing his body. Public whipping was considered a particularly degrading form of chastisement, and it was said that "when a white man once had . . . [a public lashing] he disappeared and never turned up again." This was an exaggerated statement but it certainly applied on occasion. Governor John H. Means believed that criminals "degraded" by a public whipping lost thereby any "spark of will" to become worthwhile citizens later, and he deplored the punishment on that ground.[32]

Public whippings were administered by sheriffs or by jailers. Culprits were stripped to the waist, and while one official counted aloud another swung the leather thong. The blows were either "moderately laid on" or "well laid on," in accordance with the wording of the sentence. Where the judge did not specify, it may be assumed that the intent was the latter; but one capable critic declared that "our sentimental sheriffs, in the exercise of an uncontrolled discretion as to the manner of inflicting the *whipping,* have gone far to abolish that, as a physical punishment."[33]

During the early years of the ante-bellum period a considerable number of white women were sentenced to public lashings. Like the men, they were supposed to receive the blows at the hands of the sheriff on their bare backs. No white woman, it would appear, was sentenced to as many as thirty-nine lashes, the usual figure being ten or less. Few white women, for that matter, were ordered to the whipping post after 1812 and one such sentence in 1853 engendered so much public furor inside and outside the State that the governor immediately pardoned the woman.[34]

Whether for men or women, whipping was under strong attack in South Carolina after the 1830s. Governor John H. Means in

1852 adequately described the volume of criticism when he wrote that people were so opposed to whipping that "it is exceedingly difficult for the Executive to resist the earnest appeals and powerful influences brought to bear upon him, either to remit or change" sentences which called for such punishment.[35]

A Charleston grand jury in October, 1846, offered one noteworthy criticism of public whippings. These men wanted an end to such exhibitions, they said, because crowds of Negroes invariably gathered to watch a white man being whipped and these blacks, as a result, were being improperly led to consider some whites as on their own social level.

Beginning in 1852 a number of bills aimed at abolishing whipping as a punishment for white people were introduced in succeeding legislatures. These were hotly debated but none became law. However, they served to settle a cloud of disapproval over the whipping post, and public lashing of whites forthwith became less frequent. Slowly but surely "Tying to the Hickory" gave way to two less odious forms of retribution, fining and jailing.

Of these, the first was the more popular. From the earliest years of the ante-bellum period it had been the standard judgment afforded the man or woman found guilty of assault and battery. Levies for these affrays ranged from one cent to one hundred dollars, the average being ten dollars.

A seemingly large number of fines were stated at one cent, five cents, or twenty-five cents, but these do not necessarily represent the leniency they imply. For instance, one cent fines might be charged when a prisoner had more than a single misdemeanor indictment pending. Such a man was Benjamin Chambers of Chester District. At the 1816 spring meeting of court he was twice convicted on affray charges arising from a drunken spree. On the first count he was fined twenty dollars and on the second, one cent.[36]

Small fines in the amounts of ten cents to one dollar were quite often levied against defendants who were known to be poverty-stricken. Precisely why these people were fined instead of being given a jail sentence is not clear, nor was it clear to contemporary critics. Nonetheless, small fines were often preceded by such statements as "the defs are poor" or "he shd be severly punished . . . [but] is unable to pay much fine."[37]

Many small fines—perhaps most of them—were charged because the guilty parties had been unable to raise bail and had been in jail a considerable time prior to the meeting of court. This was true, to cite an instance, in the cases of Philomon and Baalam Grubs, two Barnwell residents who were fined one cent each.[38]

Bail was generally high, averaging as much as one hundred dollars for a misdemeanant and reaching as much as twenty thousand dollars for a Negro stealer, animal thief, or murderer. A poor man of unsavory reputation found it difficult, of course, to borrow the necessary funds. He was forced to "board at the sheriff's hotel" until court met, and a judge might reasonably conclude that this was of itself sufficient punishment.

Bail was high simply because there were so many bail-jumpers. It was not uncommon for court reporters to note that as many as ten criminals in a single session had forfeited their bond. One may only conjecture as to the number there might have been had bail been low. As things stood there was considerable criticism of the bail laws. One angry editor, reporting two "escapes of murderers through the fraternal sympathy of their bail," concluded his account with the following: "Can money dry the widow's tears or restore life? Can money sooth the mother's, sister's, brother's or orphan's heart? If so, then [the] law is just and correct. But look on the picture and melancholy is the scene."[39]

Such criticism did not result in a decrease of bail-taking; but it did aid in raising requirements. In addition, it made judges and magistrates bail-conscious—and they were careful to grant bail only in strict accordance with statute law.

Assault and battery, as noted, took the lead as the crime most often resulting in punishment by fining. Percentagewise, certain other misdeeds were not far behind. As early as 1790 such minor departures as "profane swearing" and "violations of the Sabbath" were punished by fines, with the proceeds going to the district poor funds; and throughout the pre-Civil War decades professional gamblers and swindlers were fined. The latter often paid large amounts and in many cases jail terms were added to their sentences.[40] Besides this, they were usually banished from the State.

The highest fines on record were assessed men guilty of manslaughter. After branding was declared illegal, fining became the standard punishment for man-slayers and they frequently paid levies in excess of one thousand dollars. The money, as often as not, was turned over by legislative action to the widow or nearest relative of the killer's victim.[41]

In substitution for or in addition to their fines, criminals might be obligated to post peace bonds. Indeed, most wrongdoers or suspected wrongdoers who were not destitute could be hailed to court and forced to deposit financial security for their future behavior. Any "person of sane mind" was entitled to request a sessions court to bond a fellow citizen, and records indicate that numerous South Carolinians exercised that prerogative. Wives, for example, sometimes obtained peace bonds against their husbands. A typical case of this sort was decided by a Barnwell court in 1854 against Thomas Brown. He was ordered to post a one thousand dollar bond as security for two years' good conduct toward his wife, Mary. She had charged that he treated her "with cruel indifference," spent "much of his time with lewd women," and that he "beat and put her about, abused her in most offensive terms and threatened her life."[42]

Not all peace bonds were for high figures, however. Magistrates frequently ordered bonds of less than twenty dollars. In one case, at least, a magistrate called for a bond in the sum of $1.43.[43]

The outstanding problem facing the ante-bellum South Carolina court which used fining as a means of punishment was that of collecting the money. In connection with the more serious misdemeanors, such as petit larceny, the solution was a sentence which promised a jail term or a public whipping if the fine was not paid within a certain time. In the "mean causes," however, many judges refused to do more than state the fine. Such sentences as "You stand committed until you pay" or "You shall stand committed if you do not pay" were too rare, and those stating, "The Court shall not say in what time you shall pay . . . but as soon as possible," were too frequent.[44] As late as fall, 1851, the Horry grand jury protested such a situation and insisted that jail sentences be made mandatory for those people who failed to pay within a reasonable time the amounts charged them.

The evasion of fines was a legal process in many cases. Any criminal told to pay any amount of money could by law declare himself insolvent. Having done so he was set free on the assumption that he would pay when able. But neither the courts' records nor the accounts of fines and forfeitures indicate that any large number of delinquent fines were paid or that any strong effort was made to collect them. The fines and forfeitures files are especially graphic in description of money due and money received. Name after name appears, followed by, first, a statement of the fine charged; and, second, the curt notation "Nothing Got." The Greenville files for October, 1817, serve as an excellent illustration. Twenty-one persons are listed as having been fined at the session of court just concluded, and only ten are marked paid.

Those people who did pay their fines sometimes persuaded the executive or the members of the legislature to return the money. Any person could legally request a "fine pardon" from either or both sources, and on occasion such a request was granted. The Horry District court, for example, wasted its time in 1814 when it fined Adam Jordan; as did the Abbeville court in 1818 when it fined Morris Thompson and Joseph Mosely. In each case the governor returned the money.[45]

According to the penal code any crime punishable by fine was also punishable by jailing; and jail sentences became a popular corrective after the 1820s. South Carolina's first legal jail of any consequence was established in Charleston in 1769. This "close, stincking" building, twelve feet square and designed to hold sixteen culprits, was the pattern for others and by the Revolution each judicial district had a somewhat similar detention chamber.[46] In view of this fact it is a matter of interest that confinement was so rarely used before 1825.

The answer appears to be a twofold one: first, a traditional idea carried over from Colonial times held that the purpose of a jail was to keep prisoners until their trials and no longer; second, and perhaps more realistic, most South Carolina jails prior to the 1830s were in such bad repair that the retaining of any number of unchained prisoners was simply an impossibility.

Concerning this latter point, grand juries penned presentment after presentment calling attention to the poor physical condition of their jails and the annual reports of the board of public works attested to the accuracy of such reports. In 1821, for instance, the board declared that of twenty-eight district jails, eight were being repaired, thirteen needed repairs, and six were incapable of being repaired. Only the Horry jail, the report concluded, was in an acceptable condition.[47]

The details were filled in by the grand juries. To cite examples, a Laurens jury in 1808 insisted that its jail was "entirely insecure," and a Kershaw jury in 1805 stated that its prison had "not a single room which would hold a criminal who was not chained." An Orangeburg jury in 1817 reported the jail there to be wholly beyond repair, and similar statements were made by a Chesterfield jury in 1816, a Beaufort jury in 1817, a Pendleton jury in 1818, an Abbeville jury in 1819, a Darlington jury in 1822, and a Colleton jury in 1825. Others complained that their jails had such specific defects as worthless locks, broken windows, sagging walls, leaking roofs, falling bricks, and rotted planking. "It is highly probable," wrote the Colleton jury in the fall of 1806 that "the roof [of the jail] will fall in and all . . . inhabitants perish." "We are under the impression," declared the Chester jurors in the spring of 1811, "that those who are or may be confined in sd. jail . . . are in eminent danger, for the walls thereof appear to us to be in a Situation of Tumbling."

The legislature duly noted such presentments, but was either unwilling or financially unable to repair the jails as fast as they deteriorated. For the most part the legislators answered the angry presentments with acts which required the transfer of inmates from an "unsafe gaol" to a "fast gaol" in another district. This was not only a gross injustice to the few districts having fair jails but was also expensive. The November, 1839, accounts of Spartanburg Sheriff A. C. Bomar, for instance, indicate that the total cost of transporting inmates from Spartanburg to the jail in Columbia was $420.36. These factors considered, it is not surprising that judges ordered other types of punishments.

The "wretched situation" of the jails was improved in 1827 when, in each district, a seven man committee was appointed and empowered to receive fines and levy special taxes for jail repairs. These local boards did not halt complaints of "decayed prisons" but they did lessen them; and from the inception of the boards the percentage of criminals sentenced to jail terms steadily increased. As the years passed new jails were constructed, the majority of them being two-story or three-story buildings of brick or stone, and by the 1850s South Carolina jails were generally adequate both in size and strength of construction.[48]

The usual jail sentence was less than three months. Sentences longer than three years were rarely given to any criminal and two weeks or thirty days were preferred by many judges. This emphasizes the point that the majority of jail residents were misdemeanants. Sentences of short confinement were thought to be too mild for felons.[49]

Such a consideration was not necessarily based on actuality. A stay of any duration in an average South Carolina jail was a heavy penalty if discomfort and dolorous annoyance were goals to be sought. Jails were cold in winter, hot and damp in the summer, dark and dirty always. And if some were worse than others, all were bad. The single South Carolina jail which impressed any number of travelers or interested citizens as being clean, healthy, and well administered was the Negro work-house in Charleston. The city's main prison, on the other hand, was remembered by an observer in the early 1850s as

> a sombre-looking building . . . surrounded by a high brick wall, and its windows . . . grated with double rows of bars. . . . Altogether its dark, gloomy appearance strikes those who approach it, with the thought and association of some ancient cruelty. You enter through an iron-barred door . . . ascend a narrow, crooked stairs and reach the second story; here are some eight or nine miserable cells—some large and some small—badly ventilated, and entirely destitute of any kind of furniture; and if they are badly ventilated for summer, they are equally badly provided with means to warm them in winter. In one of these rooms were nine or ten persons, when we visited it; and such was the morbid stench escaping from it, that we were compelled to put our handkerchiefs to our faces. This floor is appropriated for such crimes as assault and battery. . . . From this floor, another iron door opened, and a winding passage led into the third and upper story, where a third iron door opened into a vestibule, on the right and left of which were . . . dark gloomy cells. . . . In the floor of each of these cells was a large iron ring-bolt, doubtless intended to chain refractory prisoners to. The ominous name of this third story was "Mount Rascal." The floor of these cells bore evidence of very fine specimens of carving and flourish work, done with a knife. Among them was a well-executed crucifix, with the Redeemer, on Calvary.

A typical cell on either floor of this jail, according to this observer, was

> about twenty-six feet long and ten feet wide. The brick walls were plastered and colored with some kind of blue wash, which, however, was so nearly obliterated with dirt and the damp of a southern climate, as to leave but little to show what its original color was. The walls were covered with condensed moisture of the atmosphere, spiders hung their festooned network overhead, and cockroaches and ants, those domesticated pests of South Carolina, were running about the floor in swarms. . . . Two small apertures in the wall, about fourteen inches square, and double barred . . . served to admit the air. . . . There was not . . . even a bench to sit upon.[50]

The Charleston jail was one of the State's largest, but smaller prisons generally fitted the same depressing description. An official report concerning the Edgefield jail, for example, stated that it contained four cells, each with a tiny window about eight feet from the floor. "When entering these cells," declared the chairman of the investigating group, "the heat and stench about them were so great that I was obliged to decline entering. . . . Any confinement in this gaol, is an excessive punishment, and if long continued, must prove fatal."[51]

Collectively, South Carolina jails were obviously considered unhealthy places. The Board of Public Works in 1821 deemed them "the abode of wretchedness and disease" and a Barnwell grand jury in October, 1838, petitioned for the release of prisoner Charles Yaun on the grounds that "he is now sick & to be sick in a jail need not be remarked upon." Jails were excessively dirty, critics charged, and no serious effort was made to clean them. It was the dirt, they insisted, which caused the "intolerable affluvia arising." As early as 1821 the Board of Public Works brought this condition to the notice of the legislature and urged the appropriation of adequate funds for janitorial service. As things were, the Board said, jailers were understandably unwilling to expend any portion of their salary toward the hire of "sweepers and scourers," and white jailers were not, of course, expected to do this work themselves.[52]

Some jails were considered unhealthy because of their poor location. The Lexington and Coosawhatchie prisons are examples. Both were eventually moved to more suitable sites, but before that each had gained an evil reputation. The Lexington jail was rumored to be a haven for insect pests, and the district grand jury at the fall court in 1818 gave support to the rumor with an assertion that "the unfortunate whose lot is cast in [our] prison . . . [is] begoaded even unto death by the musquetoes, before his guilt can be made appear." Beaufort District's Coosawhatchie jail, built in a boggy area, was still more infamous. As lawyer William J. Grayson remembered, "It was unnecessary to try a criminal there charged with a capital offense. All that was required was to put him in jail in May to wait his turn at the November court. The State paid for a coffin, and saved the expenses of trial and execution. At night the jailer thought it unnecessary to remain in the jail. He locked his doors and went away to some healthier place until morning, confident that his prisoners had neither strength nor spirit to escape."[53]

In any jail prisoners who became sick were attended by local physicians at State expense. Thus while little attention was paid to removing the cause of ill health, some effort was made to cure the disease. Physicians' accounts and reports from 1809 forward indicate that the doctors were regular visitors at the jails. They "dressed blisters," administered "billious pills," "anadyne," "fever powders," "antilax drops," emetics, and castor oil, and they also drew teeth. Some visits were made "in the deep of the night."[54]

The physicians' reports indicate that there was considerable fighting and brawling among the prisoners. Dr. A. B. Arnold's accounts, covering a period of thirty-two months, requested payment for treating twenty wounds caused, apparently, by in-jail violence.[55]

Poor food doubtlessly had as much to do with the reputed bad health of prisoners as any other factor. "Hunger was the greatest grievance of which they complained," wrote one critic, speaking of the prisoners; "the allowance per day was a loaf of bad bread, weighing about nine ounces, and a pint of thin, repulsive soup . . . served in a dirty-looking tin pail, without even a spoon."[56]

This was very true, but considering the meager funds allowed sheriffs and jailers for dieting prisoners, the bread and soup was about the best fare possible. The daily money allowance for each white prisoner from 1805 to about 1830 was 37½ cents; and this was reduced in the 1830s to thirty cents. Sheriffs and grand juries alike pointed out that the South Carolina figure was from fourteen to twenty-five cents below that allowed by neighboring states, and that food cost no less, certainly, in South Carolina than elsewhere. "I humbly ask," wrote a Marlboro jailer to Governor Robert Y. Hayne in 1833, "what sheriff can feed a man on such small fee?"[57] His question received no public answer, and nothing was done by the legislature to rectify the situation.

An additional and not unimportant complaint aimed at jails was that their small size and bad architecture often required that all ages, classes, and, on occasion, both sexes of criminals be confined in common cells. The typical two-story jail devoted its first floor to quarters for the jailer and his family and to the debtors, who were not considered criminals in the elementary sense and hence were not locked with ordinary miscreants.[58] The second floor, sometimes divided into two, three, or four cells, but often merely one large room, served to retain the other inmates.

Early in the ante-bellum period it might happen that men and women were jailed together in the one-cell buildings. This was, in the words of a Richland grand jury, an "uncivilized situation" and was corrected as rapidly as possible.[59] On the other hand, despite frequent complaints, no concentrated effort was made to separate "the first offender from the hardened felon—the youth from the seasoned veteran." In 1856 Charleston's city fathers began the erection of a house of detention for juvenile lawbreakers but elsewhere criminals of all types and ages were packed into a common cell.[60] There was one noteworthy exception: the felons in the larger jails, awaiting the dates of their executions, were granted the doubtful privilege of living their last days to themselves.

A meliorating factor in the treatment of prisoners was the rather widespread practice of allowing "prison bounds." By legal definition this was granting to trusted prisoners the prerogative of going at large within a designated area surrounding the jail, returning to their cells only at night. Aimed originally at offering relief to debtors and others jailed as the result of civil processes, prison bounds privileges were by the early 1830s allowed to misdemeanants of many classes. For example, those criminals sentenced to both a jail term and a fine were generally given prison bounds in order that they might go about the business of earning the fines levied against them. In addition, workingmen jailed on such charges as assault and battery or drunken rioting were often authorized prison bounds on request of their employers.[61]

The granting of jail bounds in some districts became such a common practice that judges were forced to specify in their sentences which criminals the sheriff might or might not be allowed to free. Such a sentence as the following was used when the judge did not wish jail bounds to be allowed: "It is ordered that the Sheriff take the said prisoner into Custody and convey him to Gaol, there to be confined *within the four walls of said prison.*"

Such mandates insured that the granting of prison bounds would not reach such proportions in any district as to constitute a general jail delivery. Hence most prisoners were forced to spend the full term of their sentence in the jail cell, inactive, ill-fed, and bitterly protesting. The official who was the target of their complaints, and of those which came from most other critics of the prison system, was the jailer. Deservedly or not, he bore the brunt of such attacks throughout the ante-bellum decades.

As a group jailers ought neither to be praised nor condemned. There were bad ones and good ones. On the whole they seem to have done as capable a job as was possible under the circumstances. They had thankless tasks, were paid personal wages and fees which together rarely amounted to three hundred dollars yearly, and were forced to operate their unpopular establishments on insufficient appropriations. They were expected to live in the jail, to feed and clothe inmates, and to accept responsibility for the physical appearance of the building. In some districts the sheriff acted as jailer in addition to his regular duties, but in the larger districts he appointed the jailer and assumed jurisdiction over him.[62]

Jailers found guilty of corruption usually were those who took bribes in return for special privileges or those who sold whisky to jail inmates. In addition a few were tried on charges of neglecting their guard duty or maltreating prisoners. John Clarke, a Laurens jailer, was dismissed from office for subjecting prisoner Robert Turner to torture; Edgefield's jailer in 1845 was heavily fined for refusing medical attention to a sick felon; a Charleston jailer was branded for accepting a bribe to allow a murderer to escape; and Darlington's turnkey, Carma Parnell, was indicted for allowing drinking and gambling inside the jail.[63] Such examples were cited by the critics as evidence that the legislature and not the several sheriffs ought to appoint and control the prison keepers.

Much of the most heated criticism of jailers was directed at their oft-demonstrated inability to prevent escapes. Some custodians were charged with giving direct assistance to jail-breakers, and although few were proved guilty there was understandable suspicion when escapes became frequent.

This they did with embarassing regularity. Now and then, it was claimed, escapes were possible because the jailer was not on the premises as he should have been. Or perhaps he "left the keys lying about," or neglected to bolt the windows, or allowed himself to be overpowered by criminals. Whatever the circumstances surrounding the escape, the jailer was usually blamed. This had the effect, in some cases, of making them over-cautious and unnecessarily brutal. Some turnkeys, for example, resorted to the severe expediency of keeping prisoners, during the night at least, chained to the floors or walls.[64]

This "ironing" of prisoners was not sufficiently widespread to curtail escapes in large numbers and the notices of escaped prisoners are so numerous throughout the ante-bellum decades as to make the jail appear almost a ridiculous institution. To cite typical examples, chosen at random, four inmates escaped from the Charleston jail in 1805; five from the Edgefield jail in 1815; five from the Greenville jail in 1817; and three from the Spartanburg prison in 1823. Similar statistics could be cited for the Sumter, Lancaster, Marion, Darlington, Union, Columbia, and other jails. Further, the over-all situation did not noticeably improve with the passing of the years. As late as 1858 Governor R. F. W. Allston wrote that "Escapes have been more frequent the past year than I am willing to enumerate."[65]

Some prisoners displayed considerable ingenuity in effecting their escapes. A few sawed their way out of jail by using the main springs of watches, the handles of water buckets, and the like. Some tunneled through double-layer brick walls. One man cut his way with a small knife through two thicknesses of "nail studded logs." A Darlington prisoner smuggled an auger into the jail and bored his way to freedom. A Lancaster criminal exchanged clothing with his wife while she visited his cell, and veiling his face "as if crying," walked past the unsuspecting guard.[66] But far too many found it unnecessary to resort to such interesting originality. These simply forced their way through rotted or weakened ceilings, floors, or walls, and hurried off. The ease with which they broke jail and the frequency of their doing so were severe indictments of the State's poorly administered and inadequately supported prison system.

Extra-Legal Punishments

The punishments thus far delineated were those legally ordered and legally carried out by the judicial and executive branches of the State government. In addition to these were penalties of an extra-legal nature, inflicted on criminals and suspected criminals either by spontaneously gathered mobs or by organized and well led "vigilance societies." An undetermined but apparently small number of unpopular citizens and visitors fell into the hands of these groups, discovering forthwith that "justice" did not necessarily come at the order of judge and jury.

For the most part the story of lynch law in ante-bellum South Carolina is an addendum to the tragic history of slavery. It would appear that as many as ninety per cent of the lynch, or "club law," cases after 1840 concerned abolitionism and related activities. Prior to that date lynchings of any sort were so minor a factor in the criminal record of the State as to be negligible.

In sum, the usual varieties of malfeasants—the robbers, rioters, murderers, and swindlers—were left to the police and to the sessions courts, while the "abolition criminals" (a title given to the incitors of Negro riots and the spreaders of anti-slave propaganda) were dealt with by citizen groups outside the law.

This was true for a number of reasons other than the mass hysteria and fear generated by abolitionists. First, it seemed desirable to hasten the trial and punishment processes of those who "tampered with the negroes"; the regular court channels were too slow and legalistic to satisfy the clamor against such a thoroughly detested class of men. Second, it was thought necessary to "make public examples of a few of the itinerant fanatics" as a "caution to like offenders that may be disposed to come this way"; and no better example could be provided, certainly, than an action of lynch law. Third, many citizens urged punishment of the suspected strangers before they had actually committed any overt act; and it was recognized that the sessions courts could not be properly used for the accomplishment of such a purpose. Finally, the leaders of the proslaveholder vigilance societies recognized the basic fact that their groups served handily as a "powerful instrument in controlling public opinion"; that is, in keeping the people, especially those who possessed no slaves, militantly anti-abolition.[67]

Whatever its essential purpose, the "club-law" which was applied to the "interesting abolition strangers" differed markedly from the lynch law which sometimes, although infrequently, was the lot of ordinary criminals. Briefly stated, the difference was that club law was organized illegality while mob law was not; and whereas the former was popular with most white people of all classes, the latter was not so kindly accepted.[68] This was perhaps one reason why lynching was resorted to rarely.

Such events as the tarring and feathering of a thief near Charleston, the wrecking of a house of ill repute by a mob in Edgefield, and the hanging of a presumed horse stealer in Ninety Six by spectators who disagreed with a jury's not-guilty verdict, were episodes of wrath in the history of South Carolina crime and punishment; but they were uncommon events.[69] They were violent and emotional outbursts when they did occur. The case of the hanging of the legally acquitted horse thief is an example. Judge Aedanus Burke, who had been on the bench during the trial, stood helplessly aside as the determined mob took over. "Do something, do something," implored the wife of the victim. "Good woman," the judge said sadly, "before God, they will hang me if I attempt to interfere."[70]

"Club law," on the other hand, was generally less brutal than these mob excesses and was expressed through the medium of respected vigilance committees. These groups, found after 1854 in very nearly all the larger communities, were formally organized. They operated for the most part with fair efficiency. Many of them kept records of their membership and a considerable number saw to it that local newspapers printed full notices of their meetings and their projected and completed activities.[71]

In brief, the vigilance committees took pride in themselves, considered their purpose a patriotic and noble one, and felt they had the best wishes of the mass of citizenry. The consensus of critics was expressed by the editor of the Pendleton *Messenger* on June 20, 1849. Noting the organizational meeting of a fifty-three man vigilance group in the Pendleton-Pickens area the editor commended their desire to rid the section of the abolitionists, whose "polluted footprints" were "everywhere in the state." "This Committee cannot fail at this time to do much good," he said, and "they will be sustained in any course they take—every citizen should take a lively interest."

The editor of the Rock Hill *Ledger* expressed a more radical view in his two-column Amen to the formation of an extra-legal band in his area. Vigilance committees were needed in every South Carolina community, he wrote, because "It is time for our people to wake up, look out for these [abolitionist] scamps and hang them higher than Haman. It is the only effectual mode of protecting our homes and *our* institutions."[72]

Voices were raised against the growing power of the vigilance groups, but they were few and generally unpopular. One aspect of pro-vigilance society propaganda was to insist that critics of the movement were most likely those men who were tainted with abolitionism. As the fear of the abolitionists grew in the minds of Southern people, this unreasonable defense of lawlessness gained wide acceptance.

A typical anti-vigilance society item is an editorial in the Charleston *Observer* of August 2, 1835. The writer pled that "Clubs that take the law into their own hands" ought to be "crushed out." Refusing to distinguish between club law and mob law, he added the following: "The half way and tardy measures which have been adopted for quelling mobs have been found to be worth just nothing at all— or rather they have added fuel to the flames. It is not popular, we know, to advocate rigor in the exercise of authority; yet there is no alternative. . . . The career of Mobocracy must be arrested or we may soon prepare to sing the dirge of American Liberty."

Governor Robert F. W. Allston assumed the late ante-bellum leadership of forces opposed to club law in South Carolina. It was his firm belief, he told the legislature in 1858, that regular officers of the law were able, without the aid of citizen gangs, to punish criminals of every sort. The public acceptance of vigilance committees was making the police "a ridiculous and expensive pageant," the statute law a mockery, and constitutional justice a "mere pretence."[73] Neither the legislators nor any appreciable percentage of the State's residents heeded his words.

To a large degree the acceptance of the vigilance committees was based on the fact that they were led by respectable men, outstanding and wealthy citizens. This was recognized by the critics and they knew that their efforts to halt the spread of club law were doomed as a result. James L. Petigru touched the truth of this situation when he wrote in 1860 that "these things all are awful foreboding of what is to come . . . and the truth is our gentlemen are little distinguished in a mob from the rabble."[74]

The dates of the vigilance society movement are roughly 1840-1860, but citizen clubs for the extra-legal enforcement of law in South Carolina were older than that. During the decades 1760-1790, a loose federation of citizen posses had functioned both as police and as judiciary. In their heyday these clubs, collectively termed "the Regulation" and led by "respectable planters," arrested and punished malfeasants and suspected malfeasants in an area extending from the borders of the Charleston District to the Indian Country. They were occasioned by the sparsity of sessions courts, however, and were generally disbanded following the introduction of the circuit court system in 1769. Thus while they may have set an example for, they were not typical of the associations which rose outside the law and the courts to combat abolitionism.

Depending on one's point of view, vigilance societies were evil or good, benign or vicious. Robert Bunch, a British consul writing from Charleston in 1859, spoke for those who considered the groups pernicious and sadistic. He described the situation in the port city as being but little short of a "reign of terror" and insisted that "Persons are torn away from their residences and pursuits, sometimes 'tarred and feathered'; 'ridden upon rails,' or cruelly whipped." He was exaggerating the extent of vigilance club activities but he was picturing accurately their mediums for punishing. "Tarring and cottoning," rail-riding, whipping, and banishment from the State were the usual instruments of vigilance society justice.[75]

Brutal though the system was, few of its victims were killed. That in itself indicates the high level of vigilance society leadership. Threats of death were made but they were rarely followed up. "Our vigilant men will make a search for him, and if we find him, will return him to you dead or alive," wrote the Landsford society to friends in Lancaster;[76] but this was bluster and bluff. Should the subject of such a letter be captured he received at worst thirty-nine lashes, a coat of tar, and an order to "Go North." Even this amount of physical punishment was unusual. The standard penalty was only a lashing and on many occasions the individual concerned was punished corporally not at all but simply told to move along. Indeed, it sometimes happened that the committee made up a purse to purchase transportation for their prisoner; and members of the vigilance committee might ride with the deported person in order to insure that he did not leave the train or coach before it crossed the State line.[77]

Whatever the punishment, it was administered only after some semblance of a trial. A statement such as "We extended to him every lenity and justice" was a regular part of the published vigilance society proceedings. Even a hostile Englishman, writing from Columbia, was forced to admit that "the wildest excesses of Lynch law are perpetrated with a tragic-comic gravity . . . a punctilious observance of Newgate etiquette."[78] This insistence on some form of semi-legal nicety is, once again, an indication of the character of the vigilance society leadership. "Respected" citizens knew that they were taking the law into their own hands. To an extent they were conscience-stricken; and by cloaking their activities in a false legal dress they were seeking to minimize the seriousness of their action.

The majority of victims of vigilance society discipline were content to let well enough alone, to accept their punishment, leave town, and be thankful things had been no worse. A few insisted on hailing their tormentors into court. As a rule this was time and money wasted, for jurymen refused to do more than jokingly reprimand the accused persons. An early case concerning a citizen whose house had been destroyed by a society is typical. He brought suit against several of the admitted leaders of the vigilance group. Their sole defense was that he fellowshipped with Negroes and was thus "a great vagabond, with whom no white man associated." The judge charged the jury with a statement that had he been one of the defendants he "would have done as they had done." The twelve dispensers of justice heard the case through, retired from their box, and forthwith returned with a verdict for the plaintiff—in the amount of only one cent. Their decision was greeted with laughter and applause by the judge and the audience.[79]

Of the number of people who brought such suits, only one man, apparently, gained a full victory. This person, a "low yankee" who claimed he had been "abused and treated like a dog . . . [by] the gentry of St. Bartholomew's," was on one occasion brutally lashed in consequence of trumped-up charges of larceny. He engaged James L. Petigru as his lawyer and brought suit. Petigru carried the day in what must have been one of his greatest cases, and the innocent Northerner was awarded a verdict of $2,500.[80]

Except as it was an element of the vigilance society movement, mob law was an inconsequential aspect of the South Carolina criminal system. By 1790 both the constabulary and the sessions courts were formalized in organization and the usual varieties of criminals were turned over to these legal agencies for trial and retribution. The abolitionist, it will be agreed, was not an ordinary criminal. His platform in many instances was race rebellion. This does not excuse the vigilance mobs in their activities; but perhaps it does explain them.

Efforts at Penal Code Reform

Apologists for vigilance societies and for the infrequent mobs sometimes claimed that the extra-legal organizations existed because the penal statutes were too severe and because there was no central administration over the district jails. In these views they were joined by a number of critics who were anti-vigilance society as well. Strictly legal procedures failed on occasion, these people said, because jurors and judges time and again set hardened wrongdoers free on the ground that punishments necessitated by law were overly harsh. In fine, the law was too severe; hence the courts were inclined to be too liberal; and thus illegal citizen groups were required if criminals were to be punished at all. A reputed upswing in the number of criminals active in the 1830s and 1840s gave stature to this strained defense of lynch law, and it seems to have had something of a hold on the public mind.

To correct the conditions complained of in their indictments, the several critics formally proposed a revision of the penal code with the liberalizing and humanizing of the statutes as the essential objective. Specifically they urged that the punishment for crimes be jail sentences or fines to the complete exclusion of death penalties and corporal castigation, and that the jail sentences be served in State-owned, State-administered penitentiaries. It was believed that these improvements would result in a general decrease in crime, a lessening of jury sentimentality, a reduction in the number of pardons granted, and possibly a rehabilitation of criminals who, having served their terms in a well-run State penitentiary, would repent their evil ways and not return to them. It followed that once these results had been obtained there would be no need for such groups as mobs or vigilance committees.

Actually the movement for liberal revision of the penal code began in South Carolina as early as 1800. By that date appropriate writings of such foreign philosophers and reformers as Montesquieu, Beccaria, Voltaire, Hume, and Bentham were being read and discussed throughout the United States. Montesquieu's demand that crimes be classified according to their seriousness and that punishments then be made to fit was repeated in America. Cesare Beccaria's "God Exacts His Own Punishment" was a famed document in America as it had been in Europe since its publication about 1764. Jeremy Bentham, the great English humanitarian and author of Britain's 1832 Reform Bill, could count many followers in the United States.

For that matter, interested Americans did not have to read the books and pamphlets of reformers to turn their minds to the work of improving jails and liberalizing penal codes. Noteworthy examples of such activity were being set forth by many European heads of state. Midway in the eighteenth century Frederick of Prussia began the rewriting of his penal code with an eye to reducing the number of capital crimes. During the 1760s and 1770s, under the influence of Voltaire, similar efforts got under way in Sweden, Austria, and Russia. By 1800 the French people were following suit, although the bloody excesses of their revolution overshadowed their reforms and made them seem somewhat insignificant.

In the United States the impact of all this writing and acting on prisons and criminal codes was first felt in Pennsylvania and Virginia.

Legislation to bring about penal reforms was introduced and enacted there prior to the turn of the nineteenth century. Quaker influence in Pennsylvania brought about a revision of the penal code as early as 1787; and a committee headed by such illustrious personages as Thomas Jefferson, George Wythe, and George Mason rewrote the Virginia code in 1796. Northern states joined the parade, and by 1842 practically all those north of Maryland had redrawn their criminal statutes. Maine, Connecticut, and Vermont went so far as to outlaw all forms of capital punishment. Pennsylvania, New York, New Jersey, and Massachusetts stopped public executions and drastically cut the number of capital crimes. Only in Delaware and in Rhode Island was there a lagging of such reform measures.

In the South, Georgia led with the adoption of a new penal code in 1811 and another in 1816. Alabama followed, as did Kentucky and Tennessee.[81] These examples were pointed out many times by the South Carolina reformers, but to little avail. Penal reform in the Palmetto State was not to come until 1868.

Aside from their main plea for mitigating the severity of the statutes, the proponents of change in South Carolina argued their case on the ground that the criminal laws were antiquated in form. Charleston Sheriff Nathaniel G. Cleary spoke for the group on this point. "Our criminal Code stands before you a patched, rusty and uncouth edifice," he wrote in 1825. It is based on "sombrous ignorance," he continued, and its statutes "survive to us morbid, pernicious . . . impediments to the administration of justice, reprobated by the intelligence of the Bench and the Bar."[82]

An Edgefield grand jury in April, 1857, indicated that this same criticism stood at that late date. The code, according to the members of this body, needed immediate revision—chiefly for the simple reason that the citizens could not understand upon reading it "what is and what is not law."

Sheriff Cleary and the members of the Edgefield jury had in mind especially the carry-over into the South Carolina code of ancient English terminology. As they and others pointed out, some South Carolina criminal statutes were practically verbatim reprints of Colonial laws. As late as 1840 judges were being forced, in connection with a few of these laws, to translate English pounds into American dollars in order to arrive at legal limits for fines. "Our glorious young eagle in his transcendant career, should not be coupled with any foreign owl, however ancient," Sheriff Cleary declared, and such an appeal to provincialism did not fall on deaf ears. With respect to terminology at least, progress was made from 1840 to 1860. It was slow progress, however, and it was hindered by such ultra-conservatives as Governor David Johnson who, in 1843, told the legislature that he "would lay it down as a rule, that any attempt to change those great land marks [the criminal statutes carried over from Colonial days] . . . ought to be done with great care and circumspection."[83]

But modernization of language did little or nothing toward making the penal laws less severe and this was the great goal to be sought. Several grand juries, a few governors, and a small group of interested citizens led an unsuccessful philanthropic movement to this end.

An opening shot in the battle for humanizing the criminal laws was fired by a Laurens grand jury in the fall of 1800. Declaring that punishment ought always to bear positive and direct relationship to offense, this group urged the legislature to "study the temper, prejudices and passions of the people" and revise the code accordingly. Their presentment received no serious attention. For that matter, it was not favored with so much as a perfunctory answer. Not until 1817 was there sufficient grand jury criticism of code severity to merit genuine legislative interest. By that date the presentments on the subject were not only more numerous but were more direct and demanding. The attitude of these post-1817 juries is best illustrated, perhaps, by a citation from the York District jury presentment of 1818. The penal code then in use, these men insisted, must "have originated in the barbarous ages of the world and [is] only suited to the Views and ends of despotic and monarchial governments."[84]

Having been started off by the grand juries and pushed along by favorable endorsement from governors James B. Richardson, Paul Hamilton, Charles Pinckney, and Joseph Alston, the movement for code reform gained some minor headway by 1835. In 1838 it acquired a concerted, centralized leadership, and during the 1840's it stood its best chance of rolling to full success.[85]

The leadership which came in the late 1830s is typified by Francis Lieber, distinguished professor at the South Carolina College, and by Benjamin F. Perry. Lieber, whose liberal ideas had landed him in several European prisons and had brought about his expulsion from Germany in 1826, was well qualified to head a drive for penal reform. He arrived in South Carolina in 1836 and by 1838 had penned a long pamphlet urging "mild laws, firm judges, calm punishments."

His views were widely read and discussed and he won over Benjamin Perry, among others, to his thesis of solitary confinement as a replacement for other punishments. Perry drew up in 1838 a new code of criminal laws, embodying the Lieber suggestions, and submitted it to the legislature in the form of a report. No immediate action was taken by that body, but the consensus seemed to be favorable and it was apparently believed that the proposed code would be adopted at a later date.[86]

At this point, however, a non-legislative opposition to a changed code began to make itself heard, and the growing fear of abolitionism and Negro rebellion began to operate toward stopping liberalism in its tracks. The opponents of Perry's code and Lieber's idealism remain for the most part unknown, but they had a strong effect on the public mind. Their arguments, printed in newspapers and pamphlets ran from such a simple appeal as "Go Slow, Go Slow" to such a religious warning as "God calls for punishment in kind"; or to such suggestive doggerel as

> *Old Wood* to be burnt—
> *Old Books* to be learnt—
> *Old Wine* to be gusted—
> *Old Friends* to be trusted—
> *Old Laws* to rule us—
> *Old Judges* to school us.[87]

A correspondent to the Laurensville *Herald* on March 16, 1849, expressed the persistent temper of this opposition. He feared change, he insisted, on the fundamental ground that harsh punishment was more effective than mild. No real proof could be offered, he said, that mild codes had ever made for increased obedience to law. In his words,

> The new lights have lately discovered that we are a wondrously immoral people; that we have a code of laws with awfully ugly appurtenances. I am of that same opinion. There are some very ugly fixings [in our laws] for the special accommodation of criminals. There is nothing enticing in a gallows, it is true. . . . We don't want pleasant punishments . . . [but we are willing that] the gallows should be entwined with everblooming roses, and the culprit suspended by the heels in a hogshead of molasses.

Added to such violent outbursts were softer but equally telling impeachments presented by old-school conservatives. Among these was James H. Thornwell. Outstanding leader of the Presbyterian

Church in the State, and perhaps the most influential figure on the South Carolina College campus, his espousal of changelessness in moral matters was a heavy blow against any such progress as penal reform. Further, his persistent refusal to support Francis Lieber, whom he distrusted and disliked, did much to destroy what influence that German political scientist might otherwise have exerted.[88]

The intensification of abolitionism in the 1840s gave the kiss of death to both the Perry and the Lieber proposals. First, the fear and hatred of abolitionists worked to push the plea for a liberal penal code in the background and to offer in its place a call for blood. Secondly, the architects of a liberal code were, many of them, suspect as men of possible anti-slavery inclination.

Lieber was placed in such a position and, despite his several attempts to clear himself, his effectiveness as a leader of the penal reform movement was lost.[89] He and others who headed the fight for code revision were caught in the pre-Civil War vortex of public fear and their efforts were doomed forthwith. Governors James P. Richardson in 1841, William Aiken in 1846, and Whitemarsh B. Seabrook in 1849 and 1850 urged the acceptance of the Perry plan; and three legislators, Alexander Mazyck, James B. Perry, and J. M. Gadberry, introduced bills to that end in 1854 and 1856. All were futile attempts.[90]

Indeed, one who sought concrete results from the sound and fury concerning the reform efforts could find at best only four isolated advances: horse stealing was removed from the statute books as a felony in 1830; prison bounds privileges were extended in 1831; the branding of criminals was halted in 1833; and men convicted of bastardy were not sold as indentured servants after 1847. These four liberal steps were partially counteracted during the same years by an 1858 law declaring pickpockets to be grand larceners, and by an 1859 statute holding that any attempt to poison was to be punished by death.[91]

The ill-fated efforts to humanize the penal code were paralleled by appeals for the establishment of a State penitentiary system. These likewise met with failure, but their proponents were far more active and outspoken. Grand juries again led off, and once more Lieber and Benjamin Perry gave strong individual leadership.[92] Judges Daniel E. Huger and John Belton O'Neall were also converts to the proposal. O'Neall in particular rarely missed a chance to place his views on record. His support of the plan made it acceptable to many

citizens who venerated the judge and his opinions, but the legislature
as a whole was not impressed. "The judge is right," wrote one editor,
"the grand juries are right . . . and when the Legislature gets right
we will have it."[93]

A number of editors wondered aloud how legislature following
legislature could continue to thwart public opinion on the penitentiary
issue. This question has merit—for certainly the evidence indicates a general desire on the part of the people for the establishment
of a State prison. Not only did practically every grand jury in the
State, at some time between 1800 and 1856, recommend a centrally-
administered penitentiary, but spontaneous citizen petitions to that
end were offered to the various legislatures from 1802 until 1860.
Many of these documents were signed by more than fifty persons.[94]
In addition, numerous private citizens wrote long letters to newspapers demanding that some sort of force be applied to the stubborn
lawmakers. "Tyger" in 1849 called on the people to demand from
their representatives an answer as to why the penitentiary issue "was
always overlooked." The legislature treated any penitentiary proposal
as if it were "a many-headed monster," he said. "H" wrote during
the same year, that the law makers must be stupid; for everybody
else seemed to know that a penitentiary "would be an *engine* of
Justice for the *protection* of the *State;*—an *Haven* of *Mercy* for the
reformation of the guilty." "Humanity" in 1853 repeated all arguments favoring the penitentiary and concluded that the legislators
were either malicious or unreasonable.[95]

The failure of the General Assembly to build the State penitentiary
was publicly explained on the ground that funds were lacking for
the erection and annual support of such an establishment. Legislators
deemed this explanation sufficient, apparently. No other noteworthy
reason was offered for their failures in 1844 and 1849 to pass bills
aimed at setting up a penal system similar to those in such neighboring states as Georgia, Alabama, and Virginia. In this connection
Governor Whitemarsh B. Seabrook, a liberal by comparison with
many South Carolina ante-bellum executives, declared in 1849 that
although in normal times the State would be able to raise funds for
such a worthy project, all money was then needed "to put the State
in a proper condition of defense."[96] So it would appear that abolitionism and the expectation of civil war again operated to stifle a
liberal movement. South Carolina erected no State penitentiary until
1866. To that date, in common with North Carolia and Florida, she

continued to jail prisoners of all classes in hovels which ranged from exceedingly bad to tolerable.

Refusal of the legislatures of South Carolina to revise the criminal statutes and to erect a public penitentiary serves as a climactic illustration of the majority opinion of the leader class concerning punishments generally. The accepted thesis in South Carolina throughout the ante-bellum decades was to revere the old and suspect the new. That, in sum, helps explain why South Carolina was among the last of the states to abolish branding, to cease burning Negroes at the stake, to stop public whipping of white women, and to erect a State-administered prison. These blunt facts, despite the comparative excellence of the judicial machinery, served to condemn South Carolina in the eyes of many of her neighbors.

VI. The Continuing Theme

THE STUDY OF THE ANTE-BELLUM SOUTH CAROLINA CRIMINAL, his capture, trial, and punishment, has broader implications than those which are suggested by a delineation of criminal acts, police chases, courthouse scenes, and public hangings. When considered as a continuing theme in the history of the State, the account of the criminal and his treatment aids in evaluating certain personality traits of South Carolinians, a people who have done more than their share toward shaping the destiny of their section and of the nation.

Most prominent among South Carolina attributes emphasized by the study of the criminal are individualism, class consciousness, and conservatism. Individualism especially is indicated. The unwillingness of citizens to take their personal differences to court is an illustration of this attitude. Sessions records offer a dearth of libel and slander suits; contrariwise, contemporary sources of all types comment on the excess of personal affrays, serious and non-serious, formal and informal. The widespread practice of carrying weapons; the acceptance of murder by duel on the "field of honor" as a misdemeanor, or as no crime at all; and the appearance in grand jury presentments of such statements as "Hating the Law he did not prosecute," are cases in point.

Typical, in this connection, is the deposition of G. G. DeWalt, a citizen of Newberry, who reported that a group of men had fired several rounds into his house and that he had returned the fire. He wanted no police action, he said, for he was well able to defend himself. "We got no names of parties from him," commented the grand jury foreman who reported the case.[1]

Citizen acceptance of this individualism as being both right and proper is illustrated by such isolated episodes as that in Anderson where a sheriff and his posse swore an oath to keep forever secret the name of their member who killed, in cold blood apparently, an unpopular resident; or that in Darlington where "fifty-four highly respectable" gentlemen agreed to a similar vow under somewhat similar circumstances.[2]

The rapid and general growth of anti-abolitionist vigilance committees after 1840 brings out the point most clearly. These bands of non-deputized citizen police were never really needed. Regular officers of the law were ready, able, and certainly willing to go after and arrest abolitionists. In the eyes of numerous Americans it would have been much better had they been allowed to do so. But in the vigilance committee movement the people collectively were giving sanction to extra-legalism, to near anarchy perhaps, an example of individualism in the extreme.

The class-consciousness indicated by the study of crime and punishment in South Carolina takes at least three forms. It is expressed first in the obvious differences of opinion which arose between heterogeneous grand juries and aristocratic, planter-lawyer legislatures concerning such matters as the need for a new penal code or the desirability of a state penitentiary. Second, it is evidenced in the varying character of the punishments awarded "persons of quality," who were fined almost invariably, and "citizens of little respectability," who received public lashings and served the jail terms. Third, it is displayed in the general evaluation of misdemeanors by the better classes as innocent amusement or understandable self-defense; whereas similar missteps on the part of lower-ranked citizens were designated as crimes against the State.

Little if any dissatisfaction with these obvious class distinctions was publicly expressed by the people of South Carolina. If the grand jury presentments were ignored, the jurors indicated neither profound shock nor noteworthy anger. If judges dispensed justice in favor of the aristocrat, no energetic complaint from the less favored classes found its way into print, and apparently no criminal cases were appealed to higher courts on such a legal ground as discrimination. Some lawyers made good use of class-against-class arguments in their orations to petit juries, but these were rare and do not reflect any widespread hatred of the upper classes by the lower.

Social differences were, of course, part and parcel of the history of the Old South and would be expected to play their role in the various aspects of the criminal system. A man had his "natural station." He was expected to conduct himself in accordance with unwritten rules of his rank; and as long as he did, certain privileges were granted him, willingly it would seem. There is something of the air of English and French nobility in all this; something of the belief in and close adherence to an aristocracy by birth.

It is an aphorism that the existence of a ruling aristocracy in a society is conducive to conservatism. Despite such a seeming progressive step as the construction in the 1830s of the Charleston to Hamburg Railroad, or such supposed radicalism as State Secession, conservatism ruled in ante-bellum South Carolina. The railroad represented not progressiveness but an act of survival in the desperate fight for trade with neighboring Savannah; and Secession was not a radical departure as such, but a violent expression of complete inflexibility concerning slavery and the dying thesis of the sovereign rights of American states.

Beneath the surface of both actions may be found arch conservatism, and one illustration of its working is discovered in the passive approach of State leaders to criminal matters. The persistent, almost apathetic refusal of those leaders to revise their outmoded penal code is an example; their stubborn adherence to an inadequate, many-headed jail system is another. Abolitionism and a lack of funds were sometimes claimed in mitigation of the refusal of the legislators to act regarding these two needs of their criminal system, but such claims appear weak when one considers that other states in all sections of the nation made the necessary changes. Georgia and Alabama, for examples, had adopted sensible penal codes and were operating well constructed, humane penitentiaries by 1841. These states had slave and money problems similar to those in South Carolina.

For that matter, had there been agreement among South Carolinians concerning their claims of poverty and fright as factors forbidding the revision of the code and the establishment of a State penitentiary, explanation was still needed for the failure of the ante-bellum legislators even to codify the criminal laws. Regardless of pleas from sheriffs, magistrates, lawyers, and interested citizens generally, no systematic codification of penal statutes was undertaken until 1858, and then only half-heartedly. The "penal code" remained throughout the pre-Civil War years an ungrouped and poorly indexed mass of statutes dating from about 1712.

In addition to the foregoing conclusions there are several which relate to a comparison of the State's nineteenth and twentieth century criminal systems. The substance of such comparison is that crime was no less a problem in pre-Civil War South Carolina than in the present State; and that the moral fiber of the people, considered collectively, was not appreciably stronger nor weaker than it is today. Only in petit and grand larceny is there a higher percentage of criminal indictments in twentieth century South Carolina. Improved police methods for the apprehension of thieves may well account for this difference.

The pre-1860 South Carolinian was certainly not less prone to do physical violence; nor was he less apt to violate the code of conduct between the sexes. He fought, murdered, raped, and swindled about as much as his present-day counterpart; and this despite nostalgic claims which are sometimes made by those who derive their impressions of ante-bellum society from sentiment and tradition.

Other comparisons of the ante-bellum and present-day South Carolina criminal systems indicate that the criminals, then as now, were most often the poorer, less educated citizens; that police forces were less formally organized and administered in the 1790-1860 period but were undergoing a continuous improvement; that the defense and trial of indicted malfeasants was carried through with perhaps less regard for the rigid letter of statute law than at present; and that guilty verdicts were rarely appealed to higher courts in the ante-bellum decades. Finally, one notes that the punishment of convicted criminals, once the pillory, branding iron, and whipping post had been abolished, was the modern fine-and-jail type; and that no serious attempt was made during the ante-bellum decades to rehabilitate criminals, singly or in the mass.

Appendix

I. Unpublished Materials

A. *Manuscripts*

THE MANUSCRIPTS BASIC TO THIS STUDY WERE THE STATE PENAL Papers, in the possession of the South Carolina Archives Commission, Columbia, South Carolina. Dealing exclusively with problems of crime and law enforcement, they consist of correspondence of governors, attorneys general, magistrates, and sheriffs; the reports and accounts of jailers, constables, coroners, prison physicians, court solicitors, and court witnesses; the fines and forfeitures files which were kept by the several clerks of sessions courts; and the petitions and miscellaneous accounts of various citizens such as jurors and posse members. A large and bulky collection, the Penal Papers for the years 1800-1859 suggest a number of research possibilities in the social history of the State.

Also located in the Archives Commission building are the Legal System Papers. In addition to letters and papers of various types pertaining to general problems of the execution of law, these include the full presentments of many of the district grand juries. In turn, the presentments deal with all manner of topics concerning law and order. Taken in the aggregate, these presentments, which are important to any study of the plain folk of the State, are vital to an investigation of criminal matters.

A third manuscript source in the Archives Commission is the collection of "Miscellaneous Records of the State of South Carolina, 1790-1860." Bound in fifty-three large volumes and indexed by name only, these include pardon papers, notices of rewards offered for the capture of the criminals, and militia and posse orders.

Collections of private letters and papers were of little consequence to this study. Few contemporary correspondents concerned themselves with affairs of crime and punishment. Beyond mention of a robbery, a murder, a duel, or a public hanging, they avoided the subjects.

Worse, few lawyers wrote in detail concerning their sessions practice. A noteworthy exception was Benjamin F. Perry, Greenville unionist and barrister of exceptional ability. His letters, papers, financial accounts, and case digests are filled with information on his legal practice in the criminal courts. Some of his letters are in the Southern Historical Collection of the library of the University of North Carolina. Others are at the Duke University library and at the South Caroliniana Library of the University of South Carolina. Additional letters, as well as a volume of financial accounts (for law practice only) and many of his case reports, are in the Alabama State Department of Archives and History, Montgomery, Alabama.

Other than the Perry items, letter collections which were used were the Richard Dozier Papers at the University of North Carolina; and the Job Johnson Letters and Papers, the George McDuffie Papers, the Samuel Rainey Papers, the John Siegling, Jr., Papers, the John W. Simpson Papers, and the Waddy Thompson Papers at Duke University. Each of these collections is small for the ante-bellum period but each was of importance in connection with the study of the sessions court lawyer.

A few diaries and manuscript reminiscences were rewarding. Benjamin F. Perry's two volume manuscript diary (1832-1860) at the University of North Carolina was the outstanding item of its sort and is a rich mine of fact and observation on the sundry tribulations of the circuit-riding barrister.

A three volume manuscript journal, written by Jacob Schirmir, Charleston businessman and oft-time petit and grand juror, was of much value. Schirmir had a high interest in the crime which took place in his city and his journal describes all sorts of lawless acts. The readily legible, delightfully phrased journal, covering the years 1826 through 1877, is in the Charleston archives of the South Carolina Historical Society.

Filed with the same depository are two anonymously written lawyer's notebooks, dated respectively 1795 and 1840. Both contain entries useful to the study of crime and punishment but neither of the authors was a record-keeper such as Perry.

Two noteworthy diaries in the possession of the South Caroliniana Library are a single manuscript volume written by an unnamed traveler who visited Columbia in 1846, and twelve small manuscript volumes penned by John McLees, a Presbyterian minister. McLees wrote of his life and work in Columbia, Anderson, Abbeville, and

Greenwood, and his viewpoint on the morality of the citizens is an interesting aside to the story of crime. A diary containing similar material is that of James B. Grimball. A typed copy of this manuscript item is available at the Charleston Library Society.

Among the miscellaneous holdings of the South Caroliniana Library which were of importance to this study are the following: (1) the Reminiscences of Thomas Pinckney Lowndes, 1839-1899, which have scattered references to criminal matters; (2) the scrapbook of John L. Wilson, which contains numerous clippings and copied items dealing with the commission of unusual crimes; (3) the Yates Snowden Collection, which includes a typescript, unpublished article on duelling in South Carolina; and (4) the originals of a jury venire and several arrest warrants.

Two valuable manuscript items in the Charleston Library of the South Carolina Historical Society are the books of the Pineville (St. John's) Police Commission for the years 1823-1839 and the docket book of Oliver M. Smith, 1834-1839. The books of the St. John's Police Association include the financial accounts of this early vigilance-type group and the broken files of their meetings. Smith, a Charleston magistrate, outlines in his docket book a number of the sessions cases and misdemeanor causes in which he was officially interested. A similar book in manuscript, kept by Franklin William Fairy, another Charleston magistrate, for the years 1848-1860, is at the library of Duke University.

B. *Court Records*

The sessions courts' records for eighteen of South Carolina's twenty-eight ante-bellum judicial districts were used in this study. Few are complete for the period 1790-1860. Files were sometimes destroyed by fire, or lost when a court moved to a larger building, or allowed to deteriorate from neglect. Nonetheless, sufficient court journals and court minutes remain to make them an invaluable collection. In their original form these records are housed in various court buildings. As a result of a program carried through by the Works Progress Administration during the 1930s, all have been copied by typewriter, bound, and given to the South Caroliniana Library for safekeeping. These typescripts were used for this study.

It should be pointed out that the sessions courts' journals and minutes are not the full records of criminal trials, but rather the summaries of all sessions proceedings. The completed file of papers concerning any single criminal case is termed a "case roll," and few South Carolina courts have attempted to preserve these bulky documents for the pre-Civil War years.

The sessions journals and minutes contain, in addition to a summary of each case tried, complete lists of jurors, grand and petit, all orders of judges, all jury verdicts, and a name and title listing of all grand jury indictments, whether true-bill or no-bill.

Originally the coroners' inquest books were also a part of the sessions courts' records. The majority of these have, unfortunately, been destroyed. Two of them, one for Horry District (1849-1860) and one for Edgefield District (1844-1859), are in typescript at the South Caroliniana Library. They are valuable not only for their detailed testimony of witnesses to murders of white citizens, but to Negro murders as well. As evidence of white brutality toward refractory slaves these coroners' reports are unexcelled.

One volume of manuscript court records, "The District Court Records of Charleston, 1816-1823," is at the Duke University library. It includes both sessions and common pleas cases.

II.   Printed Materials

A.   *Correspondence, Memoirs, and Autobiographies*

Items in these allied categories were, with few noteworthy exceptions, of limited importance. The letters of Francis Lieber have been compiled by Daniel C. Gilman (ed.), *The Miscellaneous Writings of Francis Lieber* (2 vols., Philadelphia, 1881), and by Thomas S. Perry (ed.), *The Life and Letters of Francis Lieber* (Boston, 1882). Hext M. Perry (ed.), *Letters of my Father to my Mother . . . with Extracts from his Journal* (Philadelphia, 1889), is the best of the printed Benjamin F. Perry items. The son has edited the letters without attempting to remove those passages which do not place his father in the best light. This evaluation also applies to James Petigru Carson (ed.), *The Life, Letters and Speeches of James Louis Petigru, the Union Man of South Carolina* (Washington, 1920).

Of the several memoirs and autobiographical monographs consulted, two were outstanding. These were J. Marion Sims, *The Story of my Life* (New York, 1884), and Edwin J. Scott, *Random Recollections of a Long Life, 1806 to 1876* (Columbia, 1884). Both men were substantial citizens, the first a physician and the second a planter and lawyer. Each wrote skillfully. Scott, especially, includes in his account a wealth of carefully presented information on the less savory aspects of the social life of his generation.

Usable, but less valuable and generally less trustworthy, are Ebenezer S. Thomas' *Reminiscences of the Last Sixty-Five Years* (2 vols., Hartford, Connecticut, 1840); James B. Angell's *Reminiscences* (New York, 1912); William H. Sparks' *Memories of Fifty Years* (Macon, Georgia, 1872); and Joseph Johnson's *Traditions and Reminiscences . . . Including Incidents and Anecdotes* (Charleston, 1851).

Edwin De Leon's *Thirty Years of my Life on Three Continents* (2 vols., London, 1890) throws some light on South Carolina lawlessness, but the author's egotism is more impressive than his information. F. D. Srygley's *Seventy Years in Dixie: Recollections and Sayings of T. W. Caskey and Others* (Nashville, 1893) has the same weakness. Dave U. Sloan's *Fogy Days, and Now: or, the World has Changed* (Atlanta, 1891) is filled with contemporary observation, some of it presented in very bad blank verse.

"The Memoirs of Frederick Augustus Porcher" and "The Autobiography of William James Grayson," ably edited by Samuel G. Stoney, are published in the *South Carolina Historical Magazine*: the former in LXIV (April, 1943)-XLVIII (January, 1947), and the latter in XLVIII (July, 1947)-LI (April, 1950). Both are excellent memoirs, rich in information about many phases of ante-bellum life and culture. Both are illustrative of the opinions of the South Carolina upper classes toward the petty criminals; and the autobiography of Grayson is noteworthy in addition for its unrelenting attack on the work and character of the sessions court lawyer.

B. *Diaries, Journals, and Travel Accounts*

In common with those found in manuscript, printed diaries and journals were of widely ranging merit as sources for this study. Generally the travelers in the State and the short-term residents were more apt than natives to offer enlightening remarks and their remembrances are of the greater value. Two exceptional journals by natives are Alex S. Salley (ed.), "Journal of General Peter Horry," in the *South Carolina Historical Magazine,* XXXVIII (April, 1937)-XLVIII (April, 1947), and Paul R. Weidner (ed.), "The Journal of John Blake White," in *ibid.,* XLIII (April-July, 1942).

The travelers' accounts must be used with caution. Some of the visitors came to South Carolina looking for the worst and made wildly exaggerated statements concering any act of lawlessness which was brought to their attention. Others were prone to repeat hearsay, presenting it to the reader as firsthand observation. All were likely on occasion to arrive at their conclusions without due investigation.

For purposes of this study the best published diary of a visitor is that of Edward Hooker, 1805-1808, reprinted in *Report of the American Historical Association, 1896,* I, pp. 1880-1929. Connecticut born Hooker moved to South Carolina in 1805, following his graduation in law from Yale. For two years he lived in or near Columbia. His comments on the machinery of sessions courts, the rigors of circuit riding, and the actions of the crowds which gathered for court time are superior. He was a critical and at times an over-harsh observer.

An additional visitor's journal of merit is Giles J. Patterson, *Journal of a Southern Student 1846-1848 with Letters of a Later Period* (edited by Richmond C. Beatty, Nashville, 1944). Patterson was a student at the South Carolina College and despite his youth was a keen-eyed critic. His comments on gambling and on the brawling of the college boys are well chosen.

The printed journal of most immediate interest to a study of the methodology of the ante-bellum criminal is David T. Hines, *Life, Adventures, and Opinions* (New York, 1840). South Carolina's most famed scapegrace, Hines also operated in Georgia, Alabama, Louisiana, and Texas, and should be considered a visitor rather than a native. He writes with the pronoun "I" as the basic literary element, but he tells a good story of the swindler at work; and newspaper reports of his escapades make it clear that his journal is not excessively exaggerated. Indeed, several of Hines' deeds defy exaggeration. A copy of his rare journal is available in the South Carolina Room of the Clemson College Library.

The bulk of travelers' accounts consulted were written by American and English tourists. The latter are usually the more valuable. Aspects of society which might seem commonplace to the average American often appeared unusual to the inquiring Englishman and he granted them space in his travelog.

John Davis, William Faux, Adam Hodgson, and Basil Hall are typical of the English who toured the United States between 1790 and 1830 and each of them visited South Carolina. Davis was a tutor for Governor John Drayton's children and his volume, *Travels of Four Years and a Half in the United States of America* (Bristol, 1803), is of special interest concerning the early history of the State.

Faux's *Memorable Days in America* (London, 1823) includes in its early chapters information pertaining to duelling and other evidences of lawlessness which the author observed near Charleston; but Faux was something of an exaggerator. Basil Hall, an officer of the Royal Navy, was a more careful observer and was especially interested in the life and manners of rural citizenry. His two volumes, *Travels in North America 1827 and 1828* (Philadelphia, 1829), are highly critical but trustworthy. The acid-sharp letters of his wife, who toured with him, have been edited by Una Pope-Hennessy in a volume titled *The Aristocratic Journey* (New York, 1931). They, too, discuss the South Carolina "sandhiller." Adam Hodgson's *Letters from North America written during a Tour in the United States and Canada* (2 vols., London, 1824) are among the best of the journals penned by foreign travelers, both in style and in accuracy. Hodgson's volumes offer detailed information concerning Charleston.

English visitors were more numerous in South Carolina after 1830 and several of these wrote useful reports of their travel. Thomas Hamilton's *Men and Manners in America* (Philadelphia, 1833) is a brutal attack on all the State's institutions. James Stuart's *Three Years in North America* (second edition, revised, Edinburgh, 1833), contains brief items on punishments and on the work of police. Tyrone Power's *Impressions of America, During the Years 1833, 1834, and 1835* (2 vols., London, 1836) is perhaps the most readable of the travel accounts. Harriet Martineau's *Society in America* (fourth edition, 2 vols., New York, 1837) and *Retrospect of Western Travel* (2 vols., London, 1838) include scattered but pungent references to vigilance societies. James Silk Buckingham's *Slave States of America* (2 vols., London, 1842) is the fullest of all travel narratives, perhaps the most accurate, and the only one to consider in some detail the South Carolina Up Country. James Stirling's *Letters from the Slave States* (London, 1857) recounts hypercritical episodes of crime and punishment, some of them purely hearsay.

Two other foreign travelers who wrote memoirs of their visits to South Carolina were a German, Karl Bernhard (Duke of Saxe-Weimar Eisenach) and a Swede, Carl Arfwedson. Bernhard's *Travels Through North America During the Years 1825 and 1826* (2 vols., Philadelphia, 1828) is noteworthy in description of jails and jailers. Arfwedson's *The United States and Canada, in 1832, 1833 and 1834* (2 vols., London, 1834) has lucid paragraphs on the citizen police and on punishments generally.

From the list of travelogs written by Americans, four were helpful. Anne Royall's *Mrs. Royall's Southern Tour, or Second Series of the Black Book* (3 vols., Washington, 1831) includes a scathing and at times unfair condemnation of the citizens' morals and manners in Charleston, Columbia, and Camden. Frances A. Kemble's *Journal of a Residence on a Georgia Plantation in 1838 and 1839* (New York, 1863) has similar highly prejudiced statements regarding Charleston. Miss Kemble, then Mrs. Pierce Butler, was a native of England but became an American through her marriage. Louis Fitzgerald Tasistro's *Random Shots and Southern Breezes* (2 vols., New York, 1842) is as its sub-title indicates a "semi-serious" work; nonetheless, it accurately describes the brawling, petty fighting, and misdemeanor-type lawlessness of the plain folk of the State. Frederick Law Olmstead's *Journey in the Seaboard Slave States* (New York, 1856) and *Journey in the Back Country* (New York, 1860) are classics in the field of travel literature. Both works contain comments relating to the behavior of South Carolina citizens.

C. *Newspapers*

Contemporary newspapers were the most used printed sources for this study. Then as now editors as a group gave the subjects of crime and punishment considerable space. But some had a greater interest in such news than did others, and newspapers as a result do not necessarily reflect the amount or the character of lawlessness in a given locality. The Yorkville *Compiler,* Laurensville *Herald,* Sumter *Banner,* Edgefield *Advertiser,* and Lancaster *Ledger* were, for the purpose of this work, excellent sources. The Charleston *Observer,* Camden *Gazette,* Winyah *Observer,* and Columbia *Southern Chronicle* were less valuable. In general, the Charleston and Columbia newspapers were disappointing.

D. CONTEMPORARY PAMPHLETS

A number of items in this category were of special importance. Speeches of State legislators, attorneys general, judges, preachers, educators, and would-be-reformers on phases of crime and punishment were on occasion printed in pamphlet form. Many of these became effective propaganda weapons.

For the most part, pamphlets cited in this study may be found in the South Carolina Pamphlets Collection and the James Hammond Pamphlets Collection, both housed in the South Caroliniana Library.

Francis Lieber was a prolific pamphleteer. Two of his essays which dealt lucidly with criminals and with penal matters are *Remarks on the Relation Between Education and Crime, in a Letter to the Right Rev. William White, D. D.* (Philadelphia, 1835) and *A Popular Essay on Subjects of Penal Law, and on Uninterrupted Solitary Confinement at Labor* (Philadelphia, 1838). Lieber was also the translator of Gustave De Beaumont and Alexis De Toqueville's *Penitentiary System in the United States and its Application in France* (Philadelphia, 1833), which was sold throughout the United States.

Additional pamphlets of importance which treat of the penal codes or the desirability of a penitentiary system are Robert J. Turnbull's *Visit to the Philadelphia Prison . . . With Observations on the Impolicy and Injustice of Capital Punishments* (London, 1797), which was perhaps the earliest argument of any consequence for the general adoption of a State penitentiary; John L. Wilson's *Speech in the Legislature of South Carolina, on the Propriety and Expediency of Reducing the Laws of the State into a Code* (New York, 1827), being essentially a plea for a less severe body of criminal statutes; Isaac W. Hayne's *Report to His Excellency the Governor on Prisons, Prison Discipline, and the Criminal Law* (Columbia, 1852), which is a careful analysis of problems relative to jails and a group of strong recommendations concerning them; and Benjamin F. Perry's *Report of the Special Committee Appointed at the Session of 1838, on the Subject of the Penitentiary System* ([Columbia, 1840]), which was the most telling argument penned during the ante-bellum years for adoption of a State prison.

Samples of the numerous pamphlets which took issue with the circuit court system or with the judges and their work are "Black Sluggard," *The Proposed Alteration of 'The Judicial Tenure' in South Carolina* (Hamburg, S. C., 1844); "P", *The Present Judiciary System of South Carolina; its Defects Reviewed and Modes Suggested for its Improvement* (Charleston, 1850); and anonymous, *Proceedings of the House of Representatives of South Carolina, against Judge J. S. Richardson* (Charleston, 1848).

Three typical numbers from the mass of pamphlets written apparently to be sold at public hangings, each describing a murder trial and attempting evaluation of the character of the murderer, are S. C. Carpenter, *Report of the Trial of Richard Dennis the Younger* (Charleston, 1805); anonymous, *A Report (in Part) of the Trial of Thomas Gayner, for the Alleged Murder of his wife* (Charleston,

1810); and, anonymous, *Report of the Trial of Martin Posey for the Murder of his Wife* (n.p., 1850).

A pamphlet describing a public branding is Martin Strobel, *A report of the Trial of Michael and Martin Toohey, on an Indictment for the Murder of James W. Gadsden, Esq.* (Charleston, 1819).

Two anti-duelling pamphlets illustrative of the many printed between 1812 and 1860, are Nathaniel D. D. Bowen, *A Sermon; Preached October—1807, in St. Michael's Church, Charleston* (Charleston, 1823) and Arthur Wigfall, *Sermon Upon Duelling* (Charleston, 1856). A pro-duel pamphlet which includes the accepted rules of formal duelling is John L. Wilson, *The Code of Honor* (Charleston, 1858).

E. PUBLICATIONS OF STATE AND MUNICIPAL GOVERNMENTS

Materials printed by the State and city or town governments were used extensively in this study. Most of the items are statistical or documentary, but such materials as the governors' messages, the findings of legislative committees, and the reports of official boards mix fact and opinion.

The legislative journals of South Carolina for the ante-bellum period are, except for the years 1831 through 1838 when they were bound with the *Acts of the General Assembly,* printed in separate volumes bearing the titles, *Journal of the House of Representatives of South Carolina* or *Journal of the Senate of South Carolina.* Similarly, the *Reports and Resolutions of the General Assembly of South Carolina,* 1791-1860, which were bound with the *Acts* prior to 1839, are in separate volumes from that date. These *Reports and Resolutions* were especially valuable for their presentation of full figures concerning the cost of the administration of justice in each district.

The governors' official messages are a part of the legislative journals, but many of them were also printed as separate documents. Many of these separates, in turn, are included with the South Carolina Pamphlets Collection at the South Caroliniana Library.

The *Statutes at Large of South Carolina* for the pre-Civil War years are in twelve volumes, each indexed as to title and type of law. The constitution of 1790 is in volume one. The criminal statutes for the years 1786-1814 are in volume five, those for 1815-1838 in volume six, those for 1839-1849 in volume eleven, and those for 1850-1861 in volume twelve. Various digests of the *Statutes* are in print. These were useful for the years prior to 1836 since they offer explanation and background information concerning individual laws. Three such digests are Joseph Brevard, *An Alphabetical Digest of the Public Statute Laws of South-Carolina* (3 vols., Charleston, 1814); Benjamin James, *A Digest of the Laws of South-Carolina . . . designed, chiefly, for the Instruction and use of the Private Citizen . . . and Inferior Magistrate* (Columbia, 1822); and William Rice, *A Digested Index of the Statute Laws of South-Carolina* (Charleston, 1838.).

Useful digests of a more specialized nature are Benjamin Elliott and Martin Strobel, *The Militia System of South Carolina, Being a digest of the acts of Congress Concerning the Militia; Likewise of the Militia Laws of this State* (Charleston, 1835); A. E. Miller, *Miller's Compilation for the use of the South-Carolina Law Officer* (Charleston, 1848); and Benjamin C. Pressley, *The Law of Magistrates and Constables, in the State of South-Carolina* (Charleston, 1848). The laws relative to the pay of law enforcement officers were digested and printed about once in each ten years. The last such volume, prior to 1860, was *Digest of the Fees Allowed by the State to Sheriffs, Clerks, Magistrates, Constables, Coroners, and Secretary of State* (Columbia, 1857). Earlier editions bear similar titles.

The annual reports of such State administrative agencies as the civil and military engineering commission and the board of public works, both interested in the building and upkeep of jails and court-houses, are collected for the years 1817-1828 in David Kohn and Bess Glenn (eds.), *Internal Improvements in South Carolina, 1817-1828* (Washington, 1938). Unfortunately records seem not to be extant for the work of the district commissioners for public buildings which in 1828 took over the duties of the board of public works concerning jails and court buildings.

An additional group of official publications important to any study of the criminal history of the State are the forty-one volumes of case digests of the superior courts of law. These are printed under the common title (with slight variation during the ante-bellum years), *Reports of Cases at Law, Argued and Determined in the Courts of Appeals and Court of Errors of South Carolina*. The several volumes are cited not by title, but by the name of their editor, or editors. Where the court editor chose not to affix his name to the work, the volumes are cited as *South Carolina Reports*.

The ordinances and city council proceedings of Charleston and Columbia aid in evaluation of the special problems of crime and law enforcement within those urban areas. Consecutive *Ordinances of Charleston* from 1790 through 1854 are available in pamphlet form at the South Caroliniana Library. Various city mayors are listed as editors. Broken files of Columbia ordinances and mayor's reports are in the same depository.

F.   Histories of Cities, Counties, and Districts

The histories of South Carolina towns and districts are numerous. The bulk of them, however, were written as a labor of love by authors who had no larger plan in mind than the presentation of genealogical tables or the extolling in colorful prose of the ante-bellum peace and plenty. Exceptions to the above, few as they were, proved invaluable.

D. E. Huger Smith's *A Charlestonian's Recollections, 1846-1913* (reprint edition, Charleston, 1950) has scattered paragraphs touching the seamy side of life in the port city. Charles Fraser's *Reminiscences of Charleston* (Charleston, 1854) has similar merit and is a superior book. J. N. Cardozo's *Reminiscences of Charleston* (Charleston, 1866) is readable but the author is less trustworthy than Fraser on pre-Civil War episodes. Mrs. St. Julien Ravenel's *Charleston: The Place and the People* (New York, 1906) and William Oliver Stevens' *Charleston: Historic City of Gardens* (New York, 1940) have scattered items of interest to the researcher in lawless activity.

Julian A. Selby's *Memorabilia and Anecdotal Reminiscences of Columbia, S. C., and Incidents Connected Therewith* (Columbia, 1905) is a delightful potpourri of information concerning that city. The author made no effort to expunge from his text the less admirable events in Columbia's history, but he must be read with some caution since he did not authenticate many of his best tales. Helen K. Hennig (ed.), *Columbia: Capital City of South Carolina, 1786-1936* (Columbia, 1936) is a series of signed, documented historical articles dealing with several aspects of the government and social and economic life of the subject town. In the aggregate the articles are well written and useful. The best of them for the study of crime and punishment are Susan M. Fickling's "Ante-Bellum Columbia" and F. Carlisle Roberts' "Law and the Judiciary."

Two excellent works depicting the ante-bellum history of New-berry town and district appeared in 1890 and in 1895. John B. Carwile's *Reminiscences of Newberry* (Charleston, 1890) is the most fruitful as a source while *Annals of Newberry* by John Belton O'Neall and John A. Chapman (2 vols., Newberry, 1892) is the better written. Each is well above the average. George L. Summer's "New-berry County, South Carolina, Historical and Genealogical," as yet unpublished, is also of merit. The typed manuscript of this volume is in the library of the Charleston Library Society.

J. A. W. Thomas' *A History of Marlboro County* (Atlanta, 1897) is a poorly organized narrative dealing with its subject area, but offers select items of interest to a history of South Carolina crimes. Duncan D. McColl's *Sketches of Old Marlboro* (Columbia, c. 1916) is more readable.

Two informative monographs concerning Williamsburg District are Samuel D. McGill's *Narrative of Reminiscences in Williamsburg County* (Columbia, 1897) and William W. Boddie's *History of Williamsburg* (Columbia, 1923). Both authors have included colorful paragraphs in discussion of such events as court time, public hangings, and formal duels.

John A. Chapman's *History of Edgefield County* (Newberry, S. C., 1897) is the single work of merit dealing with the State's so-called "murder headquarters." Thomas J. Kirkland and Robert M. Kennedy's *Historic Camden* (2 vols., Columbia, 1926) is the only thorough history of that town and is a good one. Alexander Gregg's *History of the Old Cheraws* (New York, 1867) is an important study of the Pedee Basin area. For the most part, however, Gregg was interested in the history of the Colonial period.

Louise A. Vandiver's *Traditions and History of Anderson County* (Atlanta, 1928) is a loosely organized collection of tales, excellent and otherwise. More useful as a history of the Up Country is John B. O'Neall Landrum's *History of Spartanburg County* (Atlanta, 1900).

G. *Biography*

Biographical writing of interest and service to the study of crime and punishment deals almost exclusively with the lives of lawyers. John Belton O'Neall's *Biographical Sketches of the Bench and Bar of South Carolina* (2 vols., Charleston, 1859) and Ulysses R. Brooks' *South Carolina Bench and Bar* (Columbia, 1908) are works which offer short essays on lawyers and judges. O'Neall's two volumes are especially useful and contain material not readily found elsewhere. Benjamin F. Perry's *Reminiscences of Public Men* (second series, Greenville, S. C., 1889) is a similar type monograph, most noteworthy for well chosen anecdotal information.

William J. Grayson's *James Louis Petigru: A Biographical Sketch* (New York, 1866) devotes considerable attention to Petigru as a sessions court barrister. Theodore D. Jervey's *Robert Y. Hayne and His Times* (New York, 1909) contains information relative to Hayne's efforts to reform the penal system in the 1830s. Lillian A. Kibler's *Benjamin F. Perry, South Carolina Unionist* (Durham, 1946) is an excellent work and gives space to Perry's law practice and his attempts to establish a State-operated penitentiary system. Elizabeth Merritt's *James Henry Hammond, 1807-1864* (Balitimore, 1923) is generally disappointing but was of some value to this study. Essentially the same may be said of Mrs. St. Julien Ravenel's *Life and Times of William Lowndes of South Carolina, 1782-1822* (Boston, 1901). Charles M. Wiltse's *John C. Calhoun, Nationalist, 1782-1828* (New York, 1944) adequately treats of the short period during which Calhoun was engaged in law practice.

H. *Special Studies*

Serious histories dealing with crime and punishment in the United States are not numerous. A few monographs exist which provide background material for researchers. Harry E. Barnes, *The Repression of Crime* (New York, 1926) and *The Story of Punishment; A Record of Man's Inhumanity to Man* (Boston, c. 1930) are standard works, and Barnes is the pioneer American historian to treat extensively the criminal phases of legal and social history. John B. McMaster's "Old Standards of Public Morals," in the *American Historical Review*, XI (April, 1906) and Roscoe Pound's *Criminal Justice in America* (New York, c. 1930) also contain suggestive background items.

The best of the few state studies of crime and punishment is Arthur P. Scott's *Criminal Law in Colonial Virginia* (Chicago, 1930). Harry E. Barnes' *History of the Penal Reformatory and Correctional Institutions of the State of New Jersey* (Trenton, 1918) is meritorious. Paul Gratiot has completed at the University of Pennsylvania a dissertation entitled "Criminal Law in Ante-Bellum Kentucky."

The standard source on the development of American jails is Blake McKelvey's *American Prisons: A Study in American Social History Prior to 1915* (Chicago, 1936). Two earlier studies which have merit are Frederick H. Wines' *Punishment and Reformation: An Historical Sketch of the Rise of the Penitentiary System* (New York, c. 1895) and Orlando F. Lewis' *The Development of American Prisons and Prison Customs, 1776-1845* (Albany, N. Y., 1922). The story of South Carolina's State penitentiary is told by Alfred D. Oliphant in an article, "The Evolution of the Penal System of South Carolina from 1866 to 1916," in *The* (Columbia) *State,* February 18, 1916. Additional information is given in George W. Nicholson's "The South Carolina Penitentiary" (unpublished master's thesis, University of South Carolina, 1922). Hilda J. Zimmerman's "Penal Systems and Penal Reforms in the South Since the Civil War" (unpublished doctoral dissertation, University of North Carolina, 1947) is excellent in every respect.

A few monographs and articles on Southern history treat incidentally of crime and punishment. Most useful of these are Ulrich B. Phillips' *American Negro Slavery* (New York, 1918) and *Life and Labor in the Old South* (Boston, 1929). Both contain numerous references to Negro crime and to white crimes involving Negroes. William E. Dodd's *The Cotton Kingdom: A Chronicle of the Old South* (New Haven, 1921) contains a skillful evaluation of antebellum morals. Clement Eaton's *Freedom of Thought in the old South* (Durham, 1940) and *A History of the Old South* (New York, 1949) are each rich in information concerning the Southerner's proneness to violence. Charles S. Sydnor's *The Delevopment of Southern Sectionalism, 1819-1848* (Baton Rouge, 1948) has important generalizations respecting the conservatism of statute law in the South. Sydnor's conclusions on this and allied matters are better presented, perhaps, in an article, "The Southerner and the Laws," in the *Journal of Southern History,* VI (February 1940).

Monographs on special phases of crime and punishment are, like general studies of the allied subjects, few in number. Herbert Asbury's delightful *Sucker's Progress: An Informal History of Gambling in America from the Colonies to Canfield* (New York, 1938), John A. Krout's scholarly *The Origins of Prohibition* (New York, 1925), and Shields McIlwaine's sketchy *The Southern Poor-White from Lubberland to Tobacco Road* (Norman, Okla., 1939) all offer suggestions on the causes of crime. Jesse Macy's *The Anti-Slavery*

Crusade (New Haven, 1921) and Herbert Aptheker's *American Negro Slave Revolts* (New York, 1943) point out graphically how the fear of abolitionists and of Negro riots operated to stifle movements toward humanizing the criminal codes in Southern states. For South Carolina alone this is best done by Howell M. Henry, whose *Police Control of the Slave in South Carolina* (Emory, Va., 1914) is outstanding.

H. V. Redfield's *Homicide, North and South* (Philadelphia, 1880) and H. C. Brearley's *Homicide in the United States* (Chapel Hill, 1932) offer some basis for comparison of South Carolina murders with those elsewhere in the nation. Beatrice St. Julien Ravenel (ed.), *Charleston Murders* (New York, 1947), is a series of articles dealing with both ante-bellum and post-bellum killings. The editor's own contribution to the work, "Lovely Lavinia and the Drunken Hangman," is the best of the group, and Samuel G. Stoney's article, "The Footpad's Memorial," is meritorious.

James E. Cutler's *Lynch Law: An Investigation into the History of Lynching in the United States* (London, 1905) is, despite its age, still standard as a source for the ante-bellum years. Cutler should be read, however, with Clement Eaton's fine article, "Mob Violence in the Old South," in the *Mississippi Valley Historical Review,* XXIX (December, 1942).

Duelling has been the subject of much literary effort, most of it a mixture of truth and romantic fiction. Lorenzo Sabine's *Notes on Duels and Duelling, Alphabetically Arranged* (Boston, 1855) is still good. Thomas Gamble's *Savannah Duels and Duellists* (Savannah, c. 1923) is an accurate source and of interest to the South Carolina student. Thomas L. Stokes' *The Savannah* (New York, 1951) is readable both on duels and on general lawlessness in the area treated.

Any listing of printed materials dealing with a South Carolina subject must include David D. Wallace's *History of South Carolina* (3 vols., New York, 1934). This encyclopedic work is invaluable. An additional volume on South Carolina, Rosser H. Taylor's *Ante-Bellum South Carolina: A Social and Cultural History* (Chapel Hill, 1942) is praiseworthy and was most useful.

NOTES

Chapter I

[1]By way of comparison, the 1950 ratio of indictments to population was about 1 to 400. *See* "Report of the Attorney General" in *Reports and Resolutions of the General Assembly of South Carolina for 1950,* pp. 281-414. Statistics cited in this volume have been compiled from the sessions courts' records of eighteen of the State's twenty-eight ante-bellum districts (counties), and from manuscript records of sheriffs, clerks of courts, and grand juries.

[2]Isaac W. Hayne, *Report to his Excellency the Governor, on Prisons, Prison Discipline, and the Criminal Law* (Columbia: R. W. Gibbes, 1852), p. 4. *Also see* Lancaster *Ledger,* March 30, 1853, and Columbia *Daily South Carolinian,* November 21, 1853.

[3]For examples, *see* the following grand jury presentments: Chester, fall, 1812; Charleston, January, 1817; Anderson, spring, 1854; and Horry, fall, 1855.

[4]William Faux, *Memorable Days in America: Being a Journal of a Tour to the United States . . . Intended to Shew Men and Things as They are in America* (London: Simpkin and Marshall, 1823), p. 45.

[5]Anne N. Royall, *Mrs. Royall's Southern Tour, or Second Series of the Black Book* (3 vols., Washington: privately printed, 1831), III, pp. 4-5.

[6]Cited in Charles N. Wiltse, *John C. Calhoun, Nationalist, 1782-1828* (Indianapolis: Bobbs-Merrill Co., 1944), p. 41.

[7]Cited in Laurensville *Herald,* July 12, 1850.

[8]Charleston grand jury presentments, fall, 1821, and spring, 1847. *See also* Jacob Schirmir Journal (manuscript, South Carolina Historical Society, Charleston), December 9, 1849.

[9]Thomas L. Stokes, *The Savannah* (New York: Rinehart and Co., Inc., 1951), p. 330.

[10]*Reports and Resolutions for 1850,* pp. 209-210. Quoted material in this book contains numerous misspellings and the like. Unless otherwise stated, such errors appear in the original. Normally *sic* will not be used.

[11]Letter in Columbia *Daily South Carolinian,* June 26, 1854.

[12]Cited in Ulysses R. Brooks, *The South Carolina Bench and Bar. Vol. I* (Columbia: The State Co., 1908), p. 199.

[13]Benjamin F. Perry to his Wife, n.d., in Hext McCall Perry (ed.), *Letters of My Father to My Mother . . . With Extracts From His Journal* (first series, Philadelphia: Avil Printing Co., 1889), pp. 20, 57; Edwin J. Scott, *Random Recollections of a Long Life, 1806 to 1876* (Columbia: Charles A. Calvo, Jr., Printer, 1884), p. 98.

[14]Columbia *Daily South Carolinian,* January 16, February 15, 1855.

[15]Cited in *ibid.,* October 17, 1853. *Also see* John A. Chapman, *The Annals of Newberry* (Newberry: Aull and Houseal, 1892), pp. 502-503, 553.

[16]Lillian A. Kibler, *Benjamin F. Perry, South Carolina Unionist* (Durham: Duke University Press, 1946), pp. 41-42.

[17]Adam Hodgson, *Letters From North America* (2 vols., London: Hurst, Robinson, and Co., and A. Constable and Co., 1824), I, p. 38.

[18]Chester presentment, fall, 1827; Greenville presentment, spring, 1856.

[19]Entry of October 10, 1835, in Benjamin F. Perry Diary, 1832-1860 (manuscript, Southern Historical Collection, University of North Carolina); Lancaster *Ledger*, November 16, 1853.

[20]Benjamin F. Perry, *Reminiscences of Public Men, With Speeches and Addresses* (second series, Greenville: Shannon and Co., 1889), pp. 181-182; Ebenezer S. Thomas, *Reminiscences of the Last Sixty-Five Years* (2 vols., Hartford: Case, Tiffany and Burnham, 1840), I, p. 64; John B. O'Neall, *Biographical Sketches of the Bench and Bar of South Carolina* (2 vols., Charleston: S. G. Courtenay and Co., 1859), I, p. 37.

[21]Cited in B. F. Perry Diary, April 18, 1841.

[22]John B. O. Landrum, *History of Spartanburg County* (Atlanta: The Franklin Printing and Publishing Company, 1900), pp. 112-115; entry of February 23, 1838, in John McLees Diary, 1837-1857 (manuscript, South Caroliniana Library). James Silk Buckingham, English lecturer, is an example of a prominent person who came into the State to present a series of temperance talks. James S. Buckingham, *The Slave States of America* (2 vols., London: Fisher, Son, and Co., 1842), I, pp. 564-65.

[23]February 16, 1833. *Also see* B. F. Perry to his wife, n.d., in Perry (ed.), *Letters of my Father*, p. 89.

[24]Concerning whisky laws, *see Acts of the General Assembly of the State of South Carolina, 1791*, p. 50, *1801*, pp. 398-99, *1803*, p. 531; *Statutes at Large of South Carolina*, V, pp. 599-600, VI, p. 528, VII, pp. 142-43, XI, pp. 545-48; Alexander Edwards (comp.), *Ordinances of the City Council of Charleston . . . Passed Since the Incorporation of the City* (Charleston: W. P. Young, 1802), p. 148; *Ordinances of the City of Charleston From the 5th February, 1833, to the 9th May, 1837* (Charleston: A. E. Miller, 1837), p. 17; *Senate Journal, South Carolina General Assembly, 1846*, p. 37; *House Journal, South Carolina General Assembly, 1856*, pp. 180, 301.

[25]David Ramsey, *The History of South Carolina, From its First Settlement in 1670, to the Year 1808* (2 vols., Charleston: David Longworth, 1809), I, 391-92. *Also see* Samuel G. Stoney (ed.), "The Autobiography of William John Grayson," in *South Carolina Historical Magazine*, XLIX (January, 1948), p. 26.

[26]Cited in Pendleton *Messenger*, December 7, 1838.

[27]James Stirling, *Letters From The Slave States* (London: John W. Parker and Son, 1857), pp. 272-73; Carl D. Arfwedson, *The United States and Canada, in 1832, 1833, and 1834* (2 vols., R. Bentley, 1834), II, p. 40.

[28]*Senate Journal, 1844*, pp. 92-93.

[29]December 14, 1849. *Also see* Pendleton *Messenger*, July 17, 1833; Edgefield *Advertiser*, February 28, 1844; Charleston *Courier*, October 9, 1851.

[30]Concerning efforts to pass the concealed weapons act, *see Senate Journal, 1852*, pp. 74, 84, *1856*, pp. 27, 63, *1858*, pp. 69, 201; *House Journal, 1852*, pp. 115, 153; *Statutes at Large*, XII, pp. 634-35.

[31]B. F. Perry to his wife, January 4, 1837, in Perry (ed.), *Letters of my Father*, p. 20. *Also see* Giles J. Patterson, *Journal of a Southern Student, 1846-48 With Letters of a Later Period* (Nashville: Vanderbilt University Press, 1944), pp. 48-49, edited by Richmond C. Beatty.

[32]Basil Hall, *Travels in North America in the Years 1827 and 1828* (2 vols., Philadelphia: Carey, Lea and Carey, 1829), II, p. 194.

[33]Lancaster *Ledger*, November 9, 1853; Yorkville *Compiler*, August 1, 1840. *Also see* William W. Boddie, *History of Williamsburg . . . Until 1923* (Columbia: The State Company, 1923), p. 318; J. A. Thomas, *A History of Marlboro County* (Atlanta: Foote and Davis Co., 1897), pp. 144-45.

[34]S. A. Townes to George F. Townes, n.d. (manuscript, Townes Family Papers, South Caroliniana Library).

[35]For examples, *see* issues of December 27, 1851, and December 28, 1853.

[36]Laurensville *Herald*, January 4, 1850.

[37]*Diary of Edward Hooker, 1805-1808*, in *Report of the American Historical Association for 1896*, p. 862.

[38]Lancaster *Ledger*, March 19, 1856.

[39]For example, *see* the accounts of special constable James Walling of Fairfield, fall, 1828; and "Court Orders" in Horry Sessions Journal, spring, 1834.

[40]Cited in Rosser H. Taylor, *Ante-Bellum South Carolina: A Social and Cultural History* (Chapel Hill: University of North Carolina Press, 1942), p. 32.

[41]B. F. Perry Diary, October 1, 1837.

[42]Chester Sessions Minutes, fall, 1803; Barnwell Sessions Journal, spring, 1811.

[43]Yorkville *Compiler*, September 12, 1840; Charleston *Courier*, January 1, 1835.

[44]James L. Petigru to William Elliott, September 7, 1831, in James P. Carson (ed.), *Life, Letters and Speeches of James Louis Petigru* (Washington: Lowdermilk and Co., 1920), p. 85; Jacob Schirmir Journal, September 8, 1831; Charleston *Courier*, March 7, 1853.

[45]Camden *Gazette*, October 31, 1816.

[46]Greenville *Mountaineer*, January 12, 1833. *Also see* William J. Grayson, *James Louis Petigru* (New York: Harper and Brothers, 1866), pp. 108-109; Chauncey S. Boucher, *The Nullification Controversy in South Carolina* (Chicago: University of Chicago Press, 1916), pp. 132, 205-206.

[47]March 13, 1807. *Also see* Paul R. Weidner (ed.), "The Journal of John Blake White," in *South Carolina Historical Magazine*, XLIII (April, 1942), pp. 114-115.

[48]Susan S. Bennett, "The McCords of McCord's Ferry," in *South Carolina Historical Magazine*, XXXIV (October, 1933), p. 192.

[49]Lancaster *Ledger*, June 13, 1855; Charleston *City Gazette and Daily Advertiser*, September 24, 1808; Edgefield District Coroner's Book, 1846 (manuscript, Archives Commission), pp. 25-27.

[50]Lucius G. Moffatt and Joseph M. Carriers (eds.), "A Frenchman visits Charleston, 1817," in *South Carolina Historical Magazine*, XLIX (July, 1948),

p. 149. Louis F. Tasistro, *Random Shots and Southern Breezes* (2 vols., New York: Harper and Brothers, 1842), II, pp. 229-30.

[51]Edgefield *Advertiser,* February 14, 1844; Lancaster *Ledger,* March 9, 1953.

[52]*Ibid.,* March 28, 1860; Charleston *Courier,* September 26, November 7, 1853; Pendleton *Messenger,* March 16, 1831; Anderson *Gazette,* May 14, 1847.

[53]John A. Chapman, *The History of Edgefield County From the Earliest Settlements to 1897* (Newberry: Elbert H. Aull, Printer, 1897), pp. 158-59.

[54]Sumter *Banner,* May 20, 1854; Pendleton *Messenger,* July 17, 1833; Edgefield *Advertiser,* May 18, 1837; Charleston *City Gazette and Daily Advertiser,* October 31, 1807; Daniel W. Hollis, *University of South Carolina. South Carolina College* (Columbia: University of South Carolina Press, 1951), pp. 139-40; Buckingham, *Slave States,* I, p. 552.

[55]B. F. Perry Diary, April 18, 1841. *Also see* Jacob Schirmir Journal, March 20, 1852.

[56]Thomas Cooper to Thomas Jefferson, February 14, 1822 (manuscripts, Thomas Cooper Papers, South Caroliniana Library).

[57]Stoney (ed.), "Autobiography of Grayson," in *South Carolina Historical Magazine,* XLIX (April, 1948), pp. 91-92; Hollis, *South Carolina College,* pp. 187-189, 197-200; Columbia *Telescope,* June 26, 1829.

[58]Benjamin C. Pressley, *The Law of Magistrates and Constables, in the State of South Carolina* (Charleston: Walker and Burke, 1848), pp. 3, 310-15.

[59]Yorkville *Compiler,* June 27, July 4, 1840.

[60]Cited in Thomas S. Perry (ed.), *The Life and Letters of Francis Lieber* (Boston: James R. Osgood and Co., 1882), p. 126. Lieber did not name the youth.

[61]"J" to Robert Y. Hayne, March 22, 1834 (Governors' Correspondence, Penal Papers); *State* v. *Gibson Foote,* Edgefield Sessions Minutes, spring, 1824.

[62]For typical sentences, *see State* v. *Milly Vaughan,* Spartanburg Sessions Minutes, fall, 1812; *State* v. *Elizabeth Berry,* Barnwell Sessions Journal, spring, 1830; *State* v. *Elizabeth, Ann, and Jane Runnells,* Greenville Sessions Journal, fall, 1858; *State* v. *Margaret Weeks,* Union Sessions Minutes, fall, 1821.

[63]Charleston District Court Records, 1823 (manuscripts, Duke University); Barnwell Sessions Journal, spring, 1810.

[64]*Ibid.,* fall, 1815; Lancaster Fines and Forfeitures (Penal Papers).

[65]O'Neall, *Sketches,* II, p. 65.

[66]Beatrice St. Julien Ravenel (ed.), *Charleston Murders* (New York: Duell, Sloan and Pearce, [1947]), pp. 43-68. *Also see State* v. *Martin Fowler* and *State* v. *Polly Garrett,* Spartanburg Sessions Minutes, spring, 1806; *State* v. *Mary Reynolds,* Darlington Sessions Journal, spring, 1840; *State* v. *Elizabeth Martin,* Union Sessions Minutes, fall, 1819; *State* v. *Elrod,* 12 Richardson 662 (1860).

[67]*State* v. *Catherine Hallman,* Barnwell Sessions Journal, spring, 1807; B. F. Perry Diary, May 7, 1843; Jacob Schirmir Journal, May 27, 1853; *State* v. *Cynthia Simmons,* 1 Brevard 6 (1794); *State* v. *Mary Clark,* 2 Bailey 66 (1830); *State* v. *Elizabeth Green,* 4 Strobhart 128 (1836).

[68]Shields McIlwaine, *The Southern Poor-White From Lubberland to Tobacco Road* (Norman, Okla.: University of Oklahoma Press, 1939), p. 123.

[69]Scott, *Recollections,* pp. 59, 71, 84; Kibler, *Perry,* pp. 118-20; Tyrone Power, *Impressions of America, During the Years 1833, 1834, and 1835* (2 vols., London: Richard Bentley, 1836), I, pp. 100-101; *State v. Dill, Ford, and Hindman,* 3 Strobhart 517 (1839).

[70]*State v. William Gradin,* Barnwell Sessions Journal, spring, 1834.

[71]*State v. Joseph Bell and Jordan Carden,* Spartanburg Sessions Minutes, spring, 1806.

[72]Cited in B. F. Perry Diary, October 1, 1837.

[73]For examples of crimes committed by insane persons *see State v. Joseph Webster,* Chester Sessions Minutes, fall, 1815; Pendleton *Messenger,* January 10, 1815; Anderson *Gazette,* February 25, 1852.

[74]*Diary of Edward Hooker,* pp. 872-73. For Lieber's observations on the subjects, *see* his *Remarks on the Relation Between Education and Crime* (Philadelphia: privately printed, 1835), pp. 3-14.

[75]David D. Wallace, *The History of South Carolina* (3 vols., New York: The American Historical Society, Inc., 1934), III, p. 103.

[76]Cited in Chapman, *Edgefield County,* p. 77.

[77]Francis C. Adams, *Manuel Pereira: Or the Sovereign Rule of South Carolina* (Washington: Buell and Blanchard, 1853), pp. 135-36. For comments of foreign travelers on poverty and crime *see* Una C. Pope-Hennessy (ed.), *The Aristocratic Journey: Being the Outspoken Letters of Mrs. Basil Hall Written During a Fourteen Months' Sojourn in America 1827-1828* (London: Ernest Benn, Limited, 1929), p. 236; Frances A. Kemble, *Journal of a Residence on a Georgia Plantation* (New York: Harper and Brothers, 1863), p. 146; Thomas Hamilton, *Men and Manners in America* (Philadelphia: Carey, Lea and Blanchard, 1833), p. 347.

[78]Camden *Gazette,* May 30, 1818; Charleston *City Gazette and Daily Advertiser,* June 13, 1824; Pendleton *Messenger,* October 24, 1827; Yorkville *Compiler,* June 8, 1840; Charleston *Evening News,* January 26, 1847.

[79]Chapman, *Edgefield County,* p. 97; Scott, *Recollections,* pp. 127-28; Sumter *Banner,* February 17, 1847, citing the Columbia *Southern Chronicle;* James Douglas to Samuel Dunlap, October 9, 1809 (Magistrates' Correspondence, Penal Papers).

[80]David W. Johnson to Edward C. Johnson, August 2, 1853, in *Proceedings of the South Carolina Historical Association, 1939,* p. 31; Charleston *Courier,* November 11, 1853. *Also see* B. F. Perry Diary, October 24, 1835; *State v. Smith,* 2 Strobhart 77 (1847).

[81]Charleston *Courier,* April 16, 1803, January 9, 1834; Camden *Gazette,* May 30, 1816; Yorkville *Compiler,* May 7, 1841; Lancaster *Ledger,* March 9, 1856.

[82]*State v. Brown,* 3 Strobhart 508 (1849); *State v. James Anderson, alias James Smith,* Fairfield Sessions Minutes, spring, 1823; *State v. Daniel Dease, alias Daniel Graham, alias Daniel Rodgers,* Edgefield Sessions Minutes, 1844.

[83]Lancaster *Ledger,* October 19, 1853. *Also see* Pendleton *Messenger,* October 2, 1835; Cheraw *Gazette,* January 5, 1836.

[84]Sumter *Banner,* October 17, 1849; *State v. James and Mildred Carver,* Spartanburg Sessions Minutes, fall, 1804.

[85]Charleston *Mercury*, November 19, 1856; Pendleton *Messenger*, September 3, 1841; Columbia *Daily South Carolinian*, June 21, 1854; Charleston *Courier*, March 17, 1852; *State* v. *Winningham*, 10 Richardson 257 (1857).

[86]On the title page of his *Life, Adventures, and Opinions* . . . (New York: Bradley and Clark, 1840), Hines introduces himself as "David Theo. Hines, of South Carolina;—Master of Arts, and, Sometimes, Doctor of Medicine;— Alias Dr. Hamilton, Col. Hamilton, Dr. Haynes, Col. Hayne, Dr. Porcher, Col. Singleton, Rev. Mr. Bowman, Rev. Dr. Baker, Col. Allston, Maj. Parker, Col. Benton, Maj. Middleton, Lieut. Pringle, Capt. Rutledge, Col. Pinckney, Dr. Brandreth, Major Moore, &c. &c. &c."

[87]Lancaster *Ledger*, September 14, 1853. *Also see* Charleston *Courier*, April 5, 14, 1852; York *Miscellany*, May 1, 1852; Sumter *Banner*, May 11, July 27, 1852; Columbia *Daily South Carolinian*, November 15, 1852; Miscellaneous Records, Book 5-M, p. 112 (manuscripts, Archives Commission).

CHAPTER II

[1]Laurens grand jury presentment, fall, 1820; Chester grand jury presentments, spring, 1825, and fall, 1830.

[2]For examples, *see* Darlington Sessions Journal, 1806-1826, and Barnwell Sessions Journal, 1816-1826.

[3]October 19, 1853. *Also see* Pendleton *Messenger*, October 31, 1827; Jacob Schirmir Journal, May 22, 1840.

[4]Riots ("sett-toos") were fights involving more than two persons and were treated by sessions courts as assault and battery cases. About five per cent of assault and battery cases were riots and about one per cent were attempts to kill. For legal comment on riots, *see* Benjamin James, *A Digest of Laws of South Carolina, Containing the Public Statute Law of the State, Down to the Year 1822* (Columbia: The Telescope Press, 1822), p. 541.

[5]Cited in Laurensville *Herald*, January 18, 1850.

[6]Chapman, *Annals of Newberry*, 524-25.

[7]Edgefield *Advertiser*, January 4, 1860. *Also see* Samuel D. McGill, *Narrative of Reminiscences in Williamsburg County* (Columbia: The Bryan Printing Co., 1897), p. 76.

[8]James, *Digest of Laws*, pp. 88-89; Wallace, *History, II,* p. 465; *State* v. *Joseph Floyd*, Horry Sessions Journal, fall, 1837.

[9]B. F. Perry Diary, June 24, 1836, October 1, 1837. *Also see* Thomas J. Kirkland and Robert M. Kennedy, *Historic Camden: Nineteenth Century* (Columbia: The State Co., 1926), p. 227.

[10]Cited in O'Neall, *Sketches*, I, p. 55.

[11]Typical rape cases are *State* v. *Hugh Gourly*, Fairfield Sessions Minutes, July, 1795; *State* v. *George Rabon,* Horry Sessions Journal, spring, 1825; *State* v. *Peter Williams*, Edgefield Sessions Minutes, spring, 1834; *State* v. *Osborn Holloway*, Edgefield Fines and Forfeitures, fall, 1815.

[12]November 1, 1836.

[13]Pendleton *Messenger*, February 20, 1828. *Also see* Charleston *Courier*, January 12, August 18, September 22, 1806, and October 22, 1853.

[14]Stirling, *Letters*, p. 269. *Also see* Faux, *Days in America*, pp. 45-46.

[15]Ravenel (ed.)., *Charleston Murders*, pp. 7, 43-68.

[16]Horry County Inquest Book, 1849-1860; Edgefield District Coroner's Book, 1844-1859 (typescripts, South Caroliniana Library).

[17]For examples, *see* Laurensville *Herald*, May 24, 31, 1850; Lancaster *Ledger*, June 1, September 7, 1859; *Statutes at Large*, XII, pp. 712-13.

[18]*Ibid.*, V, pp. 671-72.

[19]Professor Howell M. Henry, in his *Police Control of the Slave in South Carolina* (Emory, Va.: Vanderbilt University, 1914), found only five such cases. The disallowance of Negro testimony against them was also a loophole through which murderers of Negroes escaped punishment. The law on murdering Negroes is in *Statutes at Large*, VI, p. 158. Typical cases are *State v. E. & R. Smith*, 1 Nott and McCord 13 (1817); *Arthur v. Wells*, 2 Mill 314 (1818); *State v. Fleming*, 2 Strobhart 464 (1848).

[20]Robert Bunch to J. B. Bergne, January 11, 1854, in Laura A. White, "The South in the 1850s as seen by British Consuls," in *"Journal of Southern History,* I (February, 1935), p. 33.

[21]Edgefield District Coroner's Book, 1844-1859; *State v. Gee*, 1 Bay 163 (1791); Barnwell grand jury presentment, fall, 1812; Henry, *Police Control of the Slave*, p. 71.

[22]For examples, *see State v. Cynthia Simmons and Lawrence Kitchen*, 1 Brevard 6 (1794); *State v. Mrs. Green*, 3 Strobhart 128 (1836); *State v. Martin Posey*, 4 Strobhart 103, 142 (1849).

[23]William L. King, *The Newspaper Press of Charleston, S. C.* (Charleston: Edward Perry, 1872), pp. 164-66; Camden *Gazette*, September 22, 1817.

[24]Faux, *Days in America*, pp. 47, 89-90; Buckingham, *Slave States*, I, p. 552, II, pp. 3-4.

[25]The official rules for duelling were compiled by John L. Wilson, later a State governor. John L. Wilson, *The Code of Honor; or Rules for the Government of Principals and Seconds in Duelling* (Charleston: James Phinney, 1858). An earlier edition was printed in 1838.

[26]*See* William Rice, *A Digested Index of the Statute Laws of South-Carolina From the Earliest Period to the Year 1836, Inclusive* (Charleston: J. S. Burges, 1838), p. 104; B. F. Perry Diary, October 24, 1836; Lancaster *Ledger*, November 11, 1857.

[27]James, *Digest of Laws*, pp. 87-90, 443-46; *Statutes at Large*, VI, pp. 393-94, 508. For typical cases, *see State v. John Price*, Darlington Sessions Journal, fall, 1811, and *State v. Hardy Miles*, Fairfield Sessions Minutes, fall, 1821.

[28]Edgefield *Advertiser*, March 9, 1837. *Also see* Columbia *Southern Courier*, July 27, 1842; Lancaster *Ledger*, May 4, 1859; Pendleton *Messenger*, March 20, 1846; King, *Newspaper Press*, p. 115.

[29]The soup ladle notices are in Charleston *Courier*, August 30, 1806, March 3, and April 22, 1824. *Also see* Camden *Gazette*, January 2, 1817; Yorkville *Compiler*, September 26, 1840; Sumter *Banner*, November 6, 1846.

[30]Lancaster *Ledger*, August 17, 1853; Yorkville *Compiler*, June 8, 1840; Royall, *Southern Tour*, III, pp. 10-11; John B. O'Neall, *The Annals of Newberry* (Newberry: Aull and Houseal, 1892), p. 80.

[31]Sumter *Banner,* November 11, 1851; "Report of the Chief of Police" in *Annual Report of the Mayor of Columbia, With the Reports of City Officers, March 31, 1860* (Columbia: R. W. Gibbes, 1860), n.p.; Charleston *City Gazette and Daily Advertiser,* April 10, 1824.

[32]Columbia *Daily South Carolinian,* January 17, 1855.

[33]Sumter *Banner,* December 13, 1854; *also see* Lancaster *Ledger,* March 30, 1853, January 28, 1857.

[34]Charleston *Courier,* March 20, 1852, May 1, 1854; Sumter *Banner,* March 3, 1847; Columbia *Daily South Carolinian,* January 16, 1855. For an account of a bank robbery, *see* Julian A. Selby, *Memorabilia and Anecdotal Reminiscences of Columbia, S. C., and Incidents Connected Therewith* (Columbia: The R. L. Bryan Co., 1905), p. 146. Legal distinctions between burglary, housebreaking, and lesser crimes against property are pointed out in James, *Digest of Laws,* pp. 87, 443-44, 515-16.

[35]Charleston *City Gazette and Daily Advertiser,* February 13, 1824.

[36]Pendleton *Messenger,* February 11, 1824; Charleston *Courier,* March 26, 1852; Sumter *Banner,* July 5, 1854.

[37]Edgefield *Advertiser,* October 28, 1857.

[38]*Statutes at Large,* V, p. 139, VI, p. 413.

[39]For examples, eighteen horse thieves were tried in Chester District between 1800 and 1810; thirteen in York between 1800 and 1839; and seven in Barnwell between 1841 and 1855. A Newberry horse thief had the distinction of being the first white man officially hanged there after the adoption of the 1790 Constitution. *See* O'Neall, *Annals of Newberry,* p. 79. Typical horse stealing notices in newspapers are Camden *Gazette,* April 8, 1819; Pendleton *Messenger,* March 20, 1822; Edgefield *Advertiser,* July 20, 1837; Lancaster *Ledger,* November 30, 1859.

[40]*Statutes at Large,* V, pp. 140-41. Concerning cattle, hog, and poultry stealing, *see* Benjamin F. Perry to his wife, October 25, 1837, in Perry (ed.), *Letters of my Father,* p. 61; Chesterfield constable Neil Campbell's accounts, March, 1824; Scott, *Recollections,* p. 110; Alex S. Salley (ed.), "Journal of General Peter Horry," in *South Carolina Historical Magazine,* XXXIX (October, 1838), p. 159.

[41]Horry Sessions Journal, fall, 1835.

[42]*Statutes at Large,* VII, p. 426. But "harbouring a slave" (depriving an owner temporarily of the use of his Negro) was punishable by fine only. *Ibid.,* p. 460.

[43]Darlington Sessions Journal, fall, 1816. *Also see* Charleston *Courier,* May 27, 1809; *State* v. *Baldwin,* 3 Brevard 309 (1813).

[44]Henry, *Police Control of the Slave,* pp. 109-110.

[45]Herbert Aptheker, *American Negro Slave Revolts* (New York: Columbia University Press, 1943), p. 257, citing the New York *Evening Post,* July 18, 1816. *Also see Mitchell* v. *DuBose,* 1 Mill 360 (1817); *City Council* v. *Cohen,* 2 Speers 408 (1844).

[46]Jacob Schirmir Journal, June 1, 7, 8, 1838; Charleston *Observer,* June 2, 1838; Columbia *Daily South Carolinian,* January 29, March 5, 1853.

[47]For noteworthy announcements, *see* Charleston *City Gazette and Daily Advertiser,* November 14, 1823; Cheraw *Gazette,* February 9, 1836; Yorkville *Compiler,* December 24, 1840; Columbia *Daily South Carolinian,* January 29, 1853.

[48]*Niles Register,* XXIX (February 4, 1826), p. 369; Jacob Schirmir Journal, June 1, 1838; Henry L. Pinckney, *A Report, Containing a Review of the Proceedings of the City Authorities, From the 4th September, 1837, to the 1st August, 1838* (Charleston: Thomas J. Eccles, 1838), p. 37; Columbia *Daily Telegraph,* May 4, 1849.

[49]Pendleton *Messenger,* June 27, 1845.

[50]Thomas Wilder to Robert Y. Hayne, April 20, 1834 (Governors' Correspondence, Penal Papers); King, *Newspaper Press,* p. 114; Sumter *Banner,* January 20, 1847.

[51]Pendleton *Messenger,* October 7, 1829; Sumter *Whig,* February 9, 1832; Charleston *Mercury,* May 9, 1853. Concerning insurance companies, *see* J. N. Cardozo, *Reminiscences of Charleston* (Charleston: Joseph Walker, 1866), pp. 27-28.

[52]Pendleton *Messenger,* February 14, 1821; Charleston *City Gazette and Daily Advertiser,* May 11, 1824; Yorkville *Pioneer,* November 15, 1823; Anderson *Gazette,* June 29, 1847; Sumter *Banner,* January 27, 1847, February 9, 1848, December 9, 1851, March 22, 1853, November 8, 1854; Lancaster *Ledger,* February 3, 1858.

[53]*Statutes at Large,* V, p. 28, XI, pp. 366-67.

[54]Charleston *Courier,* March 17, 1852. *Also see* Edgefield *Advertiser,* February 22, 1842, November 22, 1843.

[55]*Statutes at Large,* V, pp. 177-78, 397-98, VI, pp. 26-28; *State* v. *Mark Hasty,* Spartanburg Sessions Minutes, spring, 1811.

[56]Benjamin F. Perry to his wife, n.d., in Perry (ed.), *Letters of My Father,* p. 85.

[57]Lancaster *Ledger,* May 30, 1855; Charleston *Observer,* October 3, 1835.

[58]Columbia *Daily Telegraph,* November 4, 1848; Charleston *Courier,* January 18, 1803; Pendleton *Messenger,* July 9, 1807; Charleston *Observer,* October 31, 1835, September 16, 1837.

[59]Columbia *Southern Chronicle,* November 12, 1845.

[60]Duke de la Rochefoucauld-Liancourt, cited in Herbert Asbury, *Sucker's Progress: An Informal History of Gambling in America from the Colonies to Canfield* (New York: Dodd, Mead and Co., 1938), p. 134.

[61]Reminiscences of Thomas Pinckney Lowndes, 1839-1899 (manuscripts, South Caroliniana Library), p. 2.

[62]Charleston *Observer,* October 3, 1835.

[63]George A. Buchanan, Jr., "Government: Municipal, State and Federal," in Helen K. Hennig (ed.), *Columbia: Capital City of South Carolina, 1786-1936* (Columbia, R. L. Bryan Co., 1936), pp. 72-73.

[64]*Ibid.,* p. 73.

[65]Selby, *Memorabilia,* p. 75.

[66]Cited in Edwin L. Green, *A History of Richland County, 1732-1805* (Columbia: R. L. Bryan Co., 1932), 143.

[67]J. Marion Sims, *The Story of My Life* (New York: D. Appleton and Co., 1884), p. 87.

[68]Edward Broughton to William L. Felder, n.d. [1835] (manuscript, South Caroliniana Library). *Also see* Lancaster *Ledger,* March 29, 1854; Columbia *Daily South Carolinian,* December 29, 1855; Rosser H. Taylor, "The Gentry of Ante-Bellum South Carolina," in *North Carolina Historical Review,* XVII (April, 1940), pp. 128-29.

[69]Harriet H. Holman, "Charleston in the Summer of 1841; the Letters of Harriet Horry Rutledge," in *South Carolina Historical Magazine,* XLVI (January, 1945), p. 3.

[70]Pendleton *Messenger,* May 26, 1810. *Also see State* v. *Robert Mathews,* Fairfield Sessions Minutes, fall, 1825.

[71]Hines, *Life, Adventures and Opinions, passim.*

[72]Edgefield *Advertiser,* May 3, 1843.

[73]Charleston *Evening News,* January 19, 1859.

[74]Laurensville *Herald,* August 1, 1851.

[75]Lancaster *Ledger,* November 30, 1853.

[76]Cited in *ibid.,* March 29, 1854.

[77]Selby, *Memorabilia,* 76; Sumter *Banner,* April 19, 1853; Camden *Gazette,* January 21, 1819; Lancaster *Ledger,* May 27, 1857.

[78]Charleston *Times,* February 2, 1804.

[79]Horry Sessions Journal, spring, 1819; Fairfield Sessions Journal, fall, 1837; Spartanburg Fines and Forfeitures, November, 1816.

[80]Darlington Sessions Journal, spring, 1844; Barnwell Sessions Journal, spring, 1845; Fairfield Sessions Minutes, July, 1794; Chester Sessions Minutes, fall, 1833; Pickens Sessions Journal, spring, 1841.

[81]June 12, 1828. *Also see* Pendleton *Messenger,* May 28, June 4, 1823.

[82]*State* v. *Bryant Weathersbee,* Barnwell Sessions Journal, 1841-1856, p. 37.

[83]Horry grand jury presentment, fall, 1845. *Also see* Richard B. Morris, "White Bondage in Ante-Bellum South Carolina," in *South Carolina Historical Magazine,* XLIX (October, 1948), pp. 191-207.

[84]Cited in B. F. Perry Diary, April 9, 1836.

[85]Barnwell Sessions Journal, fall, 1829.

[86]Cited in Wallace, *History,* II, p. 509.

[87]One example is the account of the execution of "Slave Dan" in Lancaster *Ledger,* September 7, 1859. *Also see* Benjamin F. Perry Law Cases, 1841-1845 (manuscripts, Alabama State Archives), pp. 226-29.

[88]This is discussed in an anonymous "Law Notebook, Charleston, 1795" (manuscript, South Carolina Historical Society).

[89]Grand jury presentment, Horry Sessions Journal, spring, 1831.

[90]Spartanburg Sessions Minutes, fall, 1806; Barnwell Sessions Journal, spring, 1808.

[91]Pickens Sessions Journal, spring, 1843; Greenville Sessions Journal, fall, 1856; presentments of the Barnwell grand jury, fall, 1805, Orangeburg grand jury, spring, 1828, Union grand jury, fall, 1824.

[92]*House Journal, 1844,* pp. 34, 57, 64, 106, 152; *1856,* p. 248.

[93]Fall, 1858. *Also see* Barnwell Sessions Journal, spring, 1855.

⁹⁴Letter to the editor, August 29, 1835.

⁹⁵*Statutes at Large,* VI, pp. 554-55.

⁹⁶*Ibid.,* V, pp. 41-43.

⁹⁷James, *Digest of Laws,* pp. 105-106, 356-57.

⁹⁸Frederick L. Olmstead, *A Journey in the Back Country* (New York: Mason Brothers, 1860), p. 413; Ulrich B. Phillips, *American Negro Slavery* (New York: D. Appleton and Co., 1918), p. 512; Charles S. Sydnor, "The Southerner and the Laws," in *Journal of Southern History,* VI (February, 1940), p. 12.

CHAPTER III

¹For examples *see* Pendleton *Messenger,* February 27, 1808; Camden *Gazette,* April 25, 1816; Lancaster *Ledger,* November 30, 1853.

²Pendleton *Messenger,* May 19, 1837. *Also see* Charleston *Courier,* February 9, 1830; Sumter *Banner,* November 6, 1846.

³Lancaster *Ledger,* January 24, 1855.

⁴Edward P. Cantwell, "A History of the Charleston Police Force" in *Year Book, City of Charleston, 1908,* pp. 8-9.

⁵Proclamation of Governor James H. Adams, April 23, 1855 (Governors' Correspondence, Penal Papers); Pendleton *Messenger,* June 3, 1824.

⁶April 11, 1855. *Also see* Thomas Wilder to Robert Y. Hayne, April 20, 1834 (Governors' Correspondence, Penal Papers); Thomas R. McClintock to Andrew Pickens, October 27, 1819, and John Donovant to the South Carolina Senate, December 18, 1819 (Accounts, Penal Papers).

⁷*Statutes at Large,* VI, p. 28, VII, p. 422; 2 Bay 565 (1804); 2 Bailey 541 (1831); 1 Speers 305 (1843); Spartanburg Fines and Forfeitures, fall, 1815; Edgefield Fines and Forfeitures, Spring, 1816; Sumter Fines and Forfeitures, fall, 1818 (Penal Papers).

⁸Williamsburg presentment, spring, 1815, in Sessions Minutes; Lexington presentment, fall, 1807 (Legal System Papers); Newberry presentment, fall, 1852, in Sessions Journal.

⁹Pendleton *Messenger,* August 26, 1829.

¹⁰Harriet Martineau, *Society in America* (fourth edition, 2 vols., New York: Saunders and Otley, 1837), I, p. 228.

¹¹For example *see* the endorsement of refusal on the request of P. R. Bobo, December, 1838 (Accounts, Penal Papers).

¹²Typical examples are found in Charleston *City Gazette and Daily Advertiser,* July 11, 1832; Charleston *Courier,* November 24, 1851, December 7, 1853; Jacob Schirmir Journal, December 15-16, 1842; *State* v. *David Redhead,* Charleston District Court Records, 1823. For examples of citizens who caught murderers *see Senate Journal, 1844,* p. 22, and Samuel G. Stoney, "The Footpad's Memorial," in Ravenel (ed.), *Charleston Murders,* p. 13. For the capture of a horse thief by a citizen *see* Isham Clements to Members of the Legislature, December 13, 1845 (Penal Papers).

¹³James Stuart, *Three Years in North America* (second edition, revised, 2 vols., Edinburgh: Robert Cadell, 1833), II, p. 178.

[14]Elly Godbold to Members of the State Senate, November 22, 1856, and Report of Constable Robert Byars, June 17, 1824 (Accounts, Penal Papers).

[15]Concerning the patrol, see Benjamin Elliott and Martin Strobel, The Militia System of South Carolina . . . Also the Patrol and Quarantine Laws (Charleston: A. E. Miller, 1835), pp. i-lxxxiv, 1-157. For an excellent account of the patrol at work, see Henry, Police Control of the Slave, pp. 31-44.

[16]Samuel G. Stoney (ed.), "Memoirs of Frederick A. Porcher," in South Carolina Historical Magazine, XLIV (April, 1945), p. 81.

[17]For an account of a militia unit on the trail of a murderer see report of William Mescheck, November 20, 1822 (Accounts, Penal Papers).

[18]Elizabeth H. Jervy (ed.), "Marriage and Death Notices in the Charleston City Gazette and Daily Advertiser," in South Carolina Historical Magazine, XXXIII (January, 1932), p. 66.

[19]Edgefield Advertiser, February 22, 1842.

[20]Ravenel (ed.), Charleston Murders, pp. 42-44; Niles Register, XXV (October 18, 1823), p. 112.

[21]Chapman, Annals of Newberry, pp. 497-98.

[22]Yorkville Compiler, June 8, 1840.

[23]Statutes at Large, XI, pp. 30-44; James, Digest of Laws, pp. 363-64; Anonymous, Digest of the Fees allowed by the State to Sheriffs, Magistrates, Constables, Coroners, and Secretary of State (Columbia: R. W. Gibbes, 1857), p. 9.

[24]Concerning the sheriffs' fees and his difficulty in collecting them see Nathaniel G. Cleary to James L. Petigru, October 5, 1825 (Attorney Generals' Correspondence, Penal Papers); John C. Allen to Members of the State Senate, November 28, 1805, and Allen Barksdale to Members of the State Senate, November 24, 1805 (Petitions, Penal Papers); Senate Journal, 1848, p. 69; House Journal, 1856, pp. 73-248. For criticism of the sheriffs see reports in Barnwell Sessions Journal, fall, 1842; "Court Orders" in Horry Sessions Journal, fall, 1833; State v. Hugh McClure, Chester Sessions Minutes, fall, 1801; "Impeachments, Documents Concerning, 1810-1812" (Legal System Papers); George W. Featherstonhaugh, Excursion Through the Slave States, From Washington on the Potomac to the Frontier of Mexico (2 vols., London: John Murray, 1844), II, p. 347.

[25]Pendleton Messenger, June 25, 1807.

[26]James, Digest of Laws, 251; "Clerk's Report," Darlington Sessions Journal, fall, 1811; Edgefield Clerk of Court Record Book, n.d. (typescript, Archives Commission.)

[27]See reports of constables James Gillespie and Thomas Godfrey, September, 1800 (Accounts, Penal Papers). For examples of extradition requests see Wilson Lumpkin to Robert Y. Hayne, December 13, 1833, and James H. Adams to William F. Arthur, January 17, 1855 (Governors' Correspondence, Penal Papers).

[28]Constables' Accounts, Penal Papers.

[29]Charleston Mercury, July 16, 1860. Also see reports of Lexington constable James Calk, November, 1822, and Lancaster constable Robert Thomson, October, 1822 (Accounts, Penal Papers).

[30]Barnwell Sessions Journal, spring, 1830; Scott, *Recollections,* pp. 129-30.

[31]Sumter *Banner,* July 13, 17, August 3, 1852; Pendleton *Messenger,* October 8, 1828; Barnwell Sessions Journal, spring, 1800.

[32]For examples *see* presentments of the Lancaster grand jury, fall, 1809; Abbeville jury, fall, 1810; and Chester jury, spring, 1815.

[33]B. F. Perry Diary, July 29, 1835.

[34]Hayne, *Report,* pp. 5-8; *Also see* "J", "The Penitentiary Question in South Carolina," in *Southern Quarterly Review,* XVIII (November, 1850), p. 366.

[35]On this point *see* James B. Grimball Diary, November 21-22, 1856 (manuscript, South Carolina Library Society, Charleston).

[36]*Ordinances of the Town of Columbia Passed Since the Incorporation of Said Town* (Columbia: D. and J. M. Faust, 1823), pp. 34-37; Columbia *Daily Telegraph,* May 15, 1848.

[37]Patterson, *Journal,* pp. 41-42.

[38]Hollis, *South Carolina College,* pp. 197-99.

[39]For examples *see* Karl Bernhard, *Travels Through North America During the Years 1825 and 1826* (2 vols., Philadelphia: Carey, Lea and Carey, 1828), II, p. 7; Tasistro, *Random Shots,* II, p. 135.

[40]Edwards, *Ordinances,* pp. 36, 298, 308-11, 375; Cantwell, "Charleston Police Force," in *Charleston Year Book, 1908,* pp. 3-4; Henry L. Pinckney, *A Report Containing a Review of the Proceedings of City Authorities, From First September, 1838, to First August, 1839* (Charleston: W. Riley, 1839), p. 37.

[41]*Ordinances of the City of Charleston, From the 24th May, 1837, to the 18th March, 1840* (Charleston: B. R. Getsinger, 1840), pp. 11-12.

[42]Cantwell, "Charleston Police Force," in *Charleston Year Book, 1908,* pp. 4-11.

[43]H. Pinckney Walker, *Ordinances of the City of Charleston From the 19th of August, 1844, to the 14th of September, 1854* (Charleston: A. E. Miller, 1854), pp. 25-26, 60, 85, 95-96; *Mayor's Report on City Affairs. Submitted to Council at a Meeting Held Tuesday, September 29th, 1857* (Charleston: n.p., 1857), p. 42; Clarence M. Smith, Jr., "William Porcher Miles, Progressive Mayor of Charleston, 1855-1857," in *Proceedings of the South Carolina Historical Association, 1942,* pp. 31-33.

[44]*Mayor's Report, City of Charleston, for the Period from September, 1856, to September, 1857* (Charleston: Walker, Evans and Co., 1857), p. 41.

[45]*See* Charleston *Courier,* October 17, 1806; Jacob Schirmir Journal, January 2, 1832; Charleston *Standard,* May 3, 1855, April 8, 1857. For accounts of Levy's fame *see* Edgefield *Advertiser,* October 30, 1844; Pendleton *Messenger,* February 13, 1846; Laurensville *Herald,* November 28, 1851.

[46]Charleston *Courier,* May 1, 1854, August 30, 1833; Laurensville *Herald,* July 12, 1850; Charleston *Courier,* September 3, 1833; Charleston *Mercury,* December 10, 1835.

[47]Pinckney, *Proceedings of City Authorities, 1838-1839,* p. 45.

[48]Cantwell, "Charleston Police Force," in *Charleston Year Book, 1908,* pp. 7-9.

[49]*Reports and Resolutions, 1840,* pp. 42-60, *1845,* pp. 110-129, *1852,* pp. 151-59, *1860,* pp. 322-30, 451-72; Constables' Accounts, Penal Papers.

CHAPTER IV

[1]The construction of an official courthouse was one of the first governmental activities undertaken in any judicial district. Twenty-five such buildings, in varying stages of repair, existed in 1800. The aggregate was thirty-one in 1860, but this does not mean that only six were built during the sixty intervening years. Fires and the normal ravages of time and weather necessitated a continuous rebuilding program. Beginning during the 1820s courthouses were generally constructed of brick or stone so as to prolong their existence. These two-story structures, some of them standing today and a few still in use, averaged thirty by fifty feet, and cost at the time of construction from four to ten thousand dollars each. See *Report of the Board of Public Works to the Legislature of South Carolina, for the Year 1820*, reprinted in David Kohn and Bess Glenn (eds.), *Internal Improvements in South Carolina, 1817-1828* (Washington: privately printed, 1938), pp. 25-31.

[2]Laurensville *Herald,* November 7, 1851; Charleston *City Gazette and Daily Advertiser,* March 9, 1824; Charleston *Courier,* November 3, 1853; Columbia *Daily South Carolinian,* October 25, 1854; B. F. Perry Diary, June 10, 1836; Duncan D. McColl, *Sketches of Old Marlboro* (Columbia: The State Co., [1916]), pp. 39-44.

[3]Columbia *Daily South Carolinian,* February 11, 1856, citing the Charleston *Standard.*

[4]Darlington Sessions Journal, spring, 1812; Chester Sessions Minutes, spring, 1835. For the laws on contempt of court, *see* James, *Digest of Laws,* p. 222.

[5]A. E. Miller, *Miller's Compilation for the use of the South-Carolina Law Officer* (Charleston: Miller and Browne, 1848), pp. 63-64; O'Neall, *Sketches,* I, pp. lx-xii; Robert Mills, *Statistics of South Carolina* (Charleston: Hurlbut and Lloyd, 1826), pp. 195-96; *Statutes at Large,* IV, p. 661, VII, p. 211, XII, p. 647.

[6]For examples *see* presentments of the Richland grand jury, fall, 1827, Lexington jury, fall, 1828, and Spartanburg jury, fall, 1927; *Charleston City Gazette and Daily Advertiser,* May 15, 1824; Charleston *Courier,* April 19, 1852; "P", "The Judiciary System of South Carolina," in *Southern Quarterly Review,* XVIII (November, 1850), pp. 3-24.

[7]Benjamin F. Perry to his wife, n.d., in Perry (ed.), *Letters of My Father,* p. 121; O'Neall, *Sketches,* I, p. 242; Brooks, *S. C. Bench and Bar,* pp. 2-3; *Proceedings of the House of Representatives of South Carolina Against Judge J. B. Richardson* (Charleston: Walker and Burke, 1848), *passim;* Wallace, *History,* II, pp. 456-57.

[8]Brooks, *Bench and Bar,* p. 19; *also see* O'Neall, *Sketches,* I, pp. 41-42.

[9]B. F. Perry Diary, October 17, 1835; *Diary of Edward Hooker,* pp. 903-904; Anderson *Gazette,* April 23, 1847; Barnwell Sessions Journal, spring, 1802.

[10]Laurensville *Herald,* June 16, 1848, November 16, 1849; Lancaster *Ledger,* October 28, 1857; B. F. Perry Diary, April 9, 1836.

[11]O'Neall, *Sketches,* I, p. 130; Alexander Gregg, *History of the Old Cheraws* (New York: Richardson and Co., 1867), p. 479.

[12]Anderson *Highland Sentinel,* January 28, 1842; *Diary of Edward Hooker,* p. 885.

[13]Lancaster *Ledger,* April 4, 1855.

[14]David Johnson to Waddy Thompson, November 28, 1827 (manuscript, Waddy Thompson Papers, Duke University). *Also see Diary of Edward Hooker,* pp. 862-63; B. F. Perry to his wife, n.d., in Perry (ed.), *Letters of my Father,* p. 85.

[15]*Statutes at Large,* XI, pp. 16-28, 384; Pressley, *Law of Magistrates,* pp. xvi, 402-408. A typical petition urging enlargement of magistrates' jurisdiction is in Lancaster grand jury presentment, fall, 1809, and York grand jury presentment, spring, 1824. An opposed view is in Sumter grand jury presentment, spring, 1846.

[16]*Diary of Edward Hooker,* p. 863; "P", "The Judicial System of South Carolina," in *Southern Quarterly Review,* XVIII, pp. 482-83.

[17]Cited in Brooks, *Bench and Bar,* p. 199.

[18]Nathaniel G. Cleary to James L. Petigru, October 5, 1825 (Sheriffs' Correspondence, Penal Papers).

[19]Lancaster *Ledger,* November 7, 1855. Despite such high-handed procedures, juries often took days to decide a case. For examples *see* B. F. Perry Diary, June 10, 1836, and Charleston *Courier,* April 7, 1851.

[20]*Diary of Edward Hooker,* p. 863.

[21]Chester Sessions Minutes, spring, 1801; Darlington Sessions Journal, spring, 1853; Horry Sessions Journal, fall, 1857; *State v. Kindred Griffis,* Darlington Sessions Journal, spring, 1844.

[22]Hayne, *Report,* p. 6.

[23]*Acts of the General Assembly of South Carolina, From December, 1795, to December, 1804,* pp. 242-45; *Statutes at Large,* XII, p. 466.

[24]Newberry Sessions Minutes, 1830-1840; Jacob Schirmir Journal, January 21, 1832, July 8, 1834, June 4, 1840, September 10, 1840.

[25]James B. Grimball Diary, June 10, 1832. *Also see* entries for July, 1857.

[26]Edgefield Fines and Forfeitures, 1810 (Penal Papers); Chester Sessions Minutes, fall, 1803.

[27]Sumter Sessions Journal, spring, 1823.

[28]Grand jury presentment in Spartanburg Sessions Minutes, spring, 1811. *Also see* presentments of Richland jury, fall, 1804, Newberry jury, fall, 1809, Fairfield jury, fall, 1810, Pendleton jury, fall, 1813, and Williamsburg jury, spring, 1853.

[29]Spartanburg Sessions Minutes, spring, 1808, fall, 1812. *Also see* Jacob Schirmir Journal, August 4, 1832; *State v. John Collins,* Spartanburg Sessions Minutes, spring, 1808; *State v. Joseph Webster,* Chester Sessions Minutes, fall, 1815; *State v. Gibson Foote,* Edgefield Sessions Minutes, spring, 1824.

[30]*State v. John Hudspeth,* Union Sessions Minutes, spring, 1821.

[31]Cited in O'Neall, *Annals of Newberry,* p. 47. *Also see* Columbia *South Carolina State Gazette,* March 31, 1827; Jacob Schirmir Journal, April 10, 1850.

[32]Hayne, *Report,* p. 6; Pendleton *Messenger,* May 8, 1822; "J", "The Penitentiary Question," in *Southern Quarterly Review,* XVIII, p. 366.

[33]B. F. Perry Diary, June 10, 1836.

[34]Charleston *Evening News,* July 11, 1859; Lancaster *Ledger,* August 15, 1855.

[35]Calhoun *Highland Sentinel,* December 10, 1841; Sumter *Banner,* February 17, 1847.

[36]Cited in Grayson, *Petigru,* pp. 89-90.

[37]Laurensville *Herald,* February 25, 1859.

[38]Wiltse, *Calhoun, Nationalist,* p. 43.

[39]These cases are in B. F. Perry Diary, June 10, 1836. *Also see* Benjamin F. Perry to his Wife, October 24, 1837, in Perry (ed.), *Letters of my Father,* p. 59.

[40]Wiltse, *Calhoun, Nationalist,* p. 43; Mrs. St. Julien Ravenel, *Life and Times of William Lowndes of South Carolina, 1782-1822* (Boston: Houghton, Mifflin and Co., 1901), pp. 62-63.

[41]Stoney (ed.), "The Autobiography of William J. Grayson," in *South Carolina Historical Magazine,* XLIX (October, 1948), pp. 223-24.

[42]Edgefield *Advertiser,* May 5, 1858.

[43]Sumter *Banner,* April 11, 1849; Laurensville *Herald,* March 15, 1850.

[44]January 23, 1850. *Also see* O'Neall, *Annals of Newberry,* p. 46; Yorkville *Compiler,* March 12, 1841.

[45]January 7, 1819.

[46]Lancaster *Ledger,* July 18, 1855.

[47]October 22, 1856.

[48]March 1, 1850.

[49]June 7, 1850.

[50]May 17.

[51]March 29, 1850.

[52]Lee W. Ryan, *French Travelers in the Southeastern United States, 1775-1800* (Bloomington, Ind.: The Principia Press, Inc., 1939), p. 57 [citing Ferdinand-Marie Bayard].

[53]O'Neall, *Sketches,* II, pp. 599-614; John Livingston (comp.), *The United States Lawyer's Directory, and Official Bulletin for 1850* (New York: privately printed, 1850), pp. 65-66.

[54]John Siegling Papers, A. L. Taveau Papers, Job Johnson Letters, 1810-1863 (manuscripts, Duke University); "Sketch of my Life" in B. F. Perry Diary; anonymous, *History of the Bar of Richland County, 1790-1948* (n.p., n.d.), pp. 184-85.

[55]Stoney (ed.), "Autobiography of Grayson," in *South Carolina Historical Magazine,* XLIX (April, 1948), p. 88; James D. B. DeBow, "Law and Lawyers," in *DeBow's Review,* XIX (October, 1855), p. 398.

[56]For examples *see* Brooks, *Bench and Bar,* p. 10; "Anonymous Diary of a Visit to Columbia, S. C., May 3-6, 1846" (manuscript, South Caroliniana Library), May 4, 1846.

[57]Faux, *Days in America,* pp. 48-49; "Sketch of my Life" in B. F. Perry Diary.

[58]Stoney (ed.), "Autobiography of Grayson", in *South Carolina Historical Magazine,* XLIX (October, 1948), p. 223.

[59]*A Report (in Part) of the Trial of Thomas Gayner, for the Alleged Murder of his Wife* (Charleston: privately printed, 1810), pp. 11-37; Calhoun *Highland Sentinel*, November 5, 1840. *Also see* Benjamin F. Perry Law Cases, 1841-1845 (manuscripts, Alabama State Archives), pp. 8-32, 195-96.

[60]Cited in Carson (ed.), *Letters of Petigru*, pp. 55-57.

[61]Laurensville *Herald*, November 15, 1850.

[62]Diary entry of April 9, 1836.

[63]Benjamin F. Perry Law Cases, 1841-1845, p. 146; Carson (ed.), *Letters of Petigru*, p. 56.

[64]Grayson, *Petigru*, pp. 157-58; B. F. Perry Diary, November 4, 1833; Scott, *Recollections*, p. 134.

[65]Lancaster *Ledger*, April 4, 1855.

[66]Perry, *Reminiscences*, pp. 124-25.

[67]*See State* v. *Cantey*, 2 Hill 614 (1835); *State* v. *John Zeigler*, Barnwell Sessions Journal, spring, 1835; *State* v. *Susan Chavous*, Barnwell Sessions Journal, fall, 1848.

[68]Laurens presentment, fall, 1824.

[69]Lancaster *Ledger*, April 4, 1855. *Also see* Grayson, *Petigru*, p. 156.

[70]August 15, 1855.

[71]Illustrative cases are *State* v. *Jesse Williamson*, Darlington Sessions Journal, fall, 1812; *State* v. *Thomas Wood* and *State* v. *Bridget McKinney*, Charleston District Court Records (manuscripts, Duke University).

[72]B. F. Perry Diary, July 29, 1853. *Also see* Anonymous Law Notebooks, 1795, 1840 (manuscripts, South Carolina Historical Society); Docket Book of Oliver M. Smith, 1834-1839 (manuscript, South Carolina Historical Society); Benjamin F. Perry Common Law Cases, 1827-1834 (manuscripts, Alabama State Archives); George McDuffie Papers (manuscript, Duke University).

[73]Diary entries, March 9-April 9, 1836, September 3, 1837.

[74]Benjamin F. Perry to his wife, May 8, 1838, in Perry (ed.), *Letters to my Father*, p. 73; Perry, *Reminiscences*, p. 36; Carson (ed.), *Letters of Petigru*, pp. 52-53; *Diary of Edward Hooker*, pp. 859-60.

[75]For examples *see* Laurensville *Herald*, November 30, 1849; Perry, *Reminiscences*, pp. 164-65.

[76]Benjamin F. Perry to his wife, October 16, 1837, in Perry (ed.), *Letters of my Father*, p. 54; "Sketch of my Life," in B. F. Perry Diary; Charles Fraser, *Reminiscences of Charleston* (Charleston: I. Russell, 1854), pp. 71-86.

[77]B. F. Perry Diary, July 29, 1835, October 3, 1841.

[78]Benjamin F. Perry Common Law Cases, 1827-1834, *passim.*

[79]For general information concerning lawyers' fees, *see* Brevard, *Digest*, I, p. 47; James, *Digest of Laws*, p. 51; Miller, *Law Officer*, p. 105; Docket Book of Oliver M. Smith, 1834-1839; presentments of the Marlborough grand jury, spring, 1821, and the Laurens grand jury, fall, 1822.

[80]Benjamin F. Perry Common Law Cases, 1827-1834, *passim;* B. F. Perry Diary, June 10, 1836.

[81]Cited in Brooks, *Bench and Bar*, p. 251.

CHAPTER V

[1]Wallace, *History*, II, p. 467; *Message of His Excellency W. B. Seabrook, Read to Both Houses of the Legislature of South Carolina, on Tuesday, November 27, 1849* (Columbia, A. S. Johnson, 1849), p. 23; Benjamin F. Perry, *Report of the Special Committee, Appointed at the Session of 1838, on the Subject of the Penitentiary System* (Columbia: privately printed, c. 1840), pp. 24-25. Six capital crimes currently remain on the State's statute books.

[2]*Laurensville Herald,* June 14, 1850.

[3]*See* accounts of sheriff A. C. Bomar, November 20, 1839 (Penal Papers).

[4]Ravenel (ed.), *Charleston Murders,* pp. 61-62. *Also see* George L. Summer, "Newberry County, South Carolina, Historical and Genealogical" (typescript, South Caroliniana Library), p. 21; Roberts, "Law and the Judiciary," in Hennig (ed.), *Columbia,* p. 168; Charleston *Courier,* September 13, 1833; Yorkville *Compiler,* May 21, 1854; Lancaster *Ledger,* March 15, 1854.

[5]Pendleton *Messenger,* August 18, 1824; February 27, 1828.

[6]Charleston *City Gazette and Daily Advertiser,* January 30, 1813; Sumter *Banner,* July 26, 1848; Charleston *Mercury,* January 15, 1853; Anderson *Highland Sentinel,* March 31, 1843; Selby, *Memorabilia,* p. 63; Scott, *Recollections,* p. 17; McColl, *Sketches of Marlboro,* pp. 43-44.

[7]Selby, *Memorabilia,* p. 97.

[8]Pendleton *Messenger,* February 27, 1828; Ravenel (ed.), *Charleston Murders,* pp. 64-66; Taylor, *Ante-Bellum South Carolina,* p. 79; John B. Carwile, *Reminiscences of Newberry* (Charleston: Walker, Evans and Cogswell Co., 1890), pp. 200-261.

[9]"Governor's Message No. 1," in *Senate Journal, 1852,* pp. 23-24.

[10]*House Journal, 1844,* pp. 62, 152.

[11]*Message No. 1 of His Excellency, R. F. W. Allston, Governor of South Carolina, to the Senate and House of Representatives, at the Session of 1857* (n.p., n.d.), p. 13.

[12]Thomas Goodman to Members of the Legislature, [1825] (Accounts, Penal Papers); *Niles' Register,* XXVIII (August 27, 1825), p. 416.

[13]Camden *Gazette,* March 18, 1819.

[14]Patrick Noble to Maxmillian Laborde, February 20, 1839 (Governors' Correspondence, Penal Papers).

[15]Abbeville Presentment, spring, 1845. *Also see* Columbia *Southern Chronicle,* November 12, 1845.

[16]Hayne, *Report,* pp. 7-8.

[17]*State* v. *Sam Barber,* Chester Sessions Minutes, fall, 1801; *State* v. *Samuel Brown,* Edgefield Sessions Minutes, fall, 1824; *State* v. *Josiah Guin,* Barnwell Sessions Journal, spring, 1853.

[18]Chapman, *Annals of Newberry,* p. 500. *Also see* Edgefield *Advertiser,* March 11, 1841.

[19]For examples *see* J. W. Hayne to Robert Y. Hayne, January 7, [1833], John Vaughan to Robert Y. Hayne, May 3, 1834, and W. C. Moragne to Whitemarsh B. Seabrook, April 7, 1850 (Governors' Correspondence, Penal Papers).

[20]"J" to Robert Y. Hayne, March 22, 1834 (Governors' Correspondence, Penal Papers). The felon was pardoned: see Manuscript Records of South Carolina, Book 5-N, p. 521 (Archives Commission).

[21]J. E. Bobo and others to Robert Y. Hayne, January 26, 1834 (Governors' Correspondence, Penal Papers); Pendleton *Messenger,* December 12, 1845.

[22]Chester Sessions Minutes, fall, 1803. *Also see* Edgefield *Advertiser,* October 30, 1844; Benjamin F. Perry to his wife, n.d., in Perry (ed.), *Letters of my Father,* p. 128.

[23]Louise A. Vandiver, *Traditions and History of Anderson County* (Atlanta: Ruralist Press, 1928), p. 29. *Also see* Jacob Schirmir Journal, January 15, 1848; *State* v. *Mary Fuller,* 1 McCord 178 (1821); *Niles' Register,* XXII (September 28, 1822), p. 64; Lancaster *Ledger,* April 21, 1858. For an example of a man who chose a jail sentence rather than a pardon which stipulated banishment *see* Sara E. Holleman, "Contributions of Benjamin Ryan Tillman to Higher Education for White Men of South Carolina" (unpublished master's thesis, Clemson College, 1952), p. 23.

[24]For examples *see Statutes at Large,* V, pp. 184-85; *State* v. *James and Wiley Chancellor,* Darlington Sessions Journal, spring, 1847; *State* v. *John Lambert,* Barnwell Sessions Journal, fall, 1855.

[25]Vandiver, *Traditions,* p. 12.

[26]Darlington Sessions Journal, March, 1809.

[27]Martin Strobel, *A Report of the Trial of Michael and Martin Toohey* (Charleston: privately printed, 1819), p. 160. Typical branding cases are *State* v. *John Stone,* Chester Sessions Minutes, fall, 1816; *State* v. *Robert Creight,* Barnwell Sessions Journal, fall, 1805; *State* v. *Thomas Hardwick,* Horry Sessions Journal, fall, 1823; *State* v. *Archibald McAchin,* Barnwell Sessions Journal, fall, 1817.

[28]Bernhard, *Travels,* II, p. 9.

[29]Horry Sessions Journal, fall, 1824. *Also see State* v. *J. W. Rheuarch,* Horry Sessions Journal, spring, 1836; *State* v. *James Cassells,* Chester Sessions Minutes, spring, 1840; Charleston *Courier,* December 5, 1853.

[30]Columbia *Daily South Carolinian,* November 8, 1852; Charleston *Courier,* February 8, 1826; *State* v. *Robert Laing,* Barnwell Sessions Journal, fall, 1834; *State* v. *John Thompson,* Edgefield Sessions Minutes, fall, 1855.

[31]For instances, *see* the Horry and Edgefield Coroners' books.

[32]"Governor's Message No. 1," in *Senate Journal, 1852,* p. 24. *Also see* Selby, *Memorabilia,* p. 131.

[33]Hayne, *Report,* p. 8.

[34]Charleston *Courier,* December 5, 1853. For typical cases of women sentenced to the whipping post *see State* v. *Martha Fowler,* Spartanburg Sessions Minutes, fall, 1806; *State* v. *Milley Vaughan,* Spartanburg Sessions Minutes, fall 1812; McColl, *Sketches of Marlboro,* p. 85.

[35]"Governor's Message No. 1," in *Senate Journal, 1852,* p. 24.

[36]Chester Sessions Minutes, spring, 1816.

[37]*State* v. *Hiram Kennington,* Darlington Sessions Journal, fall, 1826.

[38]Barnwell Sessions Journal, fall, 1834.

[39]Calhoun *Highland Sentinel,* December 3, 1841. *Also see* in Barnwell Sessions Journal, spring, 1842, the bail notice concerning John Hickson. For laws on bail *see* James, *Digest of Laws,* p. 438. For examples of bail jumping *see* Barnwell Sessions Journal, 1801; Edgefield Sessions Minutes, 1830; and Charleston *Observer,* April 7, 1838.

[40]For examples *see* State v. *Allen Patterson* and State v. *James Macaulley* Chester Fines and Forfeitures, spring, 1823 (Penal Papers); State v. *John Polaskey,* Barnwell Sessions Journal, spring, 1818.

[41]For instance *see* in *Statutes at Large,* XI, p. 190, an act directing that Julius Pardue's fine be given to Daniel Price's widow.

[42]Barnwell Sessions Journal, fall, 1854.

[43]"State Cases" in Franklin William Fairey's Magistrate's Book, 1848-1860 (manuscript, Duke University). Fairey was a Magistrate at Branchville, South Carolina.

[44]For a verdict of each type *see* State v. *D. Conner* and State v. *J. T. Sessions,* Horry Sessions Journal, fall, 1829.

[45]Fines and Forfeitures, Horry District, March, 1814, and Abbeville District, October, 1818 (Penal Papers).

[46]For descriptions of early jails *see* Wallace, *History,* I, pp. 268-69; O'Neall, *Sketches,* I, p. 32; McColl, *Sketches of Marlboro,* p. 83; P. F. Henderson, "The Early Days of Aiken County," in *Centennial Celebration Pamphlet* (Aiken, S. C.: privately printed, 1935), pp. 9-10.

[47]*Report of Board, 1821,* in Kohn and Glenn (eds.), *Internal Improvements,* p. 121.

[48]Architecturally, the new jails followed a plan drawn up by a buildings committee of the board of public works in 1820. *See* Kohn and Glenn (eds.), *Internal Improvements,* pp. 37-38. Descriptions of the new jails are in Laurensville *Herald,* December 28, 1849; Columbia *Daily South Carolinian,* June 26, 1854; and *Reports and Resolutions, 1852,* pp. 169-74, 212-14.

[49]Typical jail sentences are in State v. *Gill,* Barnwell Sessions Journal, spring, 1801; State v. *Arthur Smith,* Horry Sessions Journal, spring, 1825; State v. *Alfred D. Hinds,* Sumter Sessions Journal, fall, 1845.

[50]Adams, *Manuel Pereira,* pp. 130-32, 146. For further comment on the Charleston Negro work house *see* Royall, *Southern Tour,* III, pp. 24-25, and Bernhard, *Travels,* II, p. 9.

[51]*Report of Board, 1820,* in Kohn and Glenn (eds.), *Internal Improvements,* pp. 28-29.

[52]*Ibid.,* pp. 108-109. *Also see* H. Arthur to Robert Y. Hayne, August 19, 1833, and John Harrelson to Robert Y. Hayne, October 2, 1833 (Governors' Correspondence, Penal Papers).

[53]Cited in Grayson, *Petigru,* pp. 69-70.

[54]For typical examples *see* reports of physicians Freeborn Adams, November 10, 1809, John A. Johnson, October 11, 1846, and Louis V. Hout, July 15, 1855 (Accounts, Penal Papers).

[55]November, 1824 (Accounts, Penal Papers).

[56]Adams, *Manuel Pereira,* p. 133.

[57]E. L. Henagan to Robert Y. Hayne, October 28, 1833 (Governors' Correspondence, Penal Papers). *Also see* Nathaniel G. Cleary to James L. Petigru, October 5, 1825 (Sheriffs' Correspondence, Penal Papers).

[58]Debtors were treated as civil prisoners and not as criminals; hence they do not fit into the scope of this study. Debtors were jailed until 1868, but from 1788 they were granted extensive jail-bounds privileges and their imprisonment was in fact a legal fiction.

[59]Fall, 1825. *Also see* Hayne, *Report*, pp. 9-10.

[60]"Governor's Message No. 1 [John H. Means]," in *Senate Journal, 1852*, pp. 23-24; Charleston *Courier*, December 10, 22, 1855, January 10, March 6, May 29, June 12, July 3, 1856.

[61]Hayne, *Report*, pp. 8-9; *Statutes at Large*, V, pp. 78-79, VI, p. 438, XI, p. 167.

[62]James, *Digest of Laws*, pp. 378-79; Pressley, *Law of Magistrates*, pp. 332-37; reports of jailers Samuel Dunlap, 1800-1808, John Gibbes, 1855, and Elly Godbold, May-December, 1855 (Accounts, Penal Papers).

[63]John Clarke Impeachment Papers (Penal Papers); grand jury presentment, Edgefield Sessions Minutes, spring, 1845; *State* v. *Carma Parnell*, Darlington Sessions Minutes, fall, 1846. *Also see State* v. *Robert Turner* (Impeachments, 1810-1812, Penal Papers); *State* v. *Wiley Floyd*, Darlington Sessions Minutes, fall, 1846.

[64]For examples *see* reports of jailers James Carroll, September, 1814, and Peter Cauble, November, 1825 (Accounts, Penal Papers).

[65]"Message No. 1," in *Senate Journal, 1858*, pp. 16-17.

[66]Lancaster *Ledger*, June 11, 1856, March 4, 1857, April 14, 1858, and August 8, 1860; Charleston *Courier*, October 1, 1805; Sumter *Banner*, July 19, August 9, 1854; Edgefield *Advertiser*, July 27, 1837; Lancaster *Ledger*, May 9, 1855.

[67]James L. Petigru to Jane Petigru North, December 2, 1854, in Carson (ed.), *Petigru*, pp. 530-31; Sumter *Banner*, July 12, 1854; Lancaster *Ledger*, January 11, October 24, 1860; Edgefield *Advertiser*, December 21, 1859; Clement Eaton, "Mob Violence in the Old South," in *Mississippi Valley Historical Review*, XXIX (December, 1942), pp. 351, 369-70.

[68]For examples *see* Pendleton *Messenger*, August 7, 1835; Charleston *Observer*, August 23, 1835; Anderson *Highland Sentinel*, February 4, 1842.

[69]King, *Newspaper Press*, p. 150; Jacob Schirmir Journal, August 21, 1835; O'Neall, *Sketches*, I, p. 36; Vandiver, *Traditions*, p. 202.

[70]Cited in Perry, *Reminiscences*, p. 14.

[71]For typical examples *see* Columbia *Southern Times and State Gazette*, October 8, 1831; Sumter *Banner*, July 12, 1854; St. John's Police Association Book of Proceedings (manuscript, South Carolina Historical Society).

[72]Cited in Lancaster *Ledger*, October 10, 1860.

[73]"Governor's Message No. 1," in *Senate Journal, 1858*, p. 17.

[74]James L. Petigru to Jane Petigru North, November 20, 1860, in Carson (ed.), *Letters of Petigru*, p. 362.

[75]White, "The South as Seen by British Consuls," in *Journal of Southern History*, I, p. 44. For accounts of tarring and feathering *see* Laurensville

Herald, August 25, 1848; Selby, *Memorabilia,* p. 131. For an instance of a whipping *see* Lancaster *Ledger,* September 26, 1860. For an account of a rail-riding, *see* letter from the Kingstree Vigilance Society, in Lancaster *Ledger,* March 30, 1859.

[76]Letter printed in Lancaster *Ledger,* November 21, 1860.

[77]Letter from Branchville Vigilance Society, in Charleston *Courier,* December 31, 1859; Laurensville *Herald,* October 18, 1850; Abbeville *Banner,* November 23, 1859.

[78]Stirling, *Letters,* pp. 282-83.

[79]*Rhodes* v. *Bunch,* 3 McCord 66 (1825).

[80]James L. Petigru to Jane Petigru North, December 2, 1854, in Carson (ed.), *Letters of Petigru,* pp. 350-51.

[81]Frederick H. Wines, *Punishment and Reformation; an Historical Sketch of the Rise of the Penitentiary System* (New York: T. Y. Crowell and Co., 1895), p. 147; Hilda J. Zimmerman, "Penal Systems and Penal Reforms in the South Since the Civil War" (unpublished doctoral dissertation, University of North Carolina, 1947), pp. 13-20; Adelaide M. Hunter, "Punishment of Crime in Virginia, 1775-1820" (unpublished master's thesis, Duke University, 1947), p. 54-74; Edwin Bruce Thompson, "Humanitarian Reforms in Tennessee, 1820-1850"; (unpublished master's thesis, Vanderbilt University, 1935) *passim;* Robert J. Turnbull, *A Visit to the Philadelphia Prison* (London: James Phillips and son, 1797), *passim.*

[82]Nathaniel G. Cleary to James L. Petigru, October 5, 1825 (Sheriffs' Correspondence, Penal Papers).

[83]*Message of His Excellency, David Johnson, Read to Both Houses of the Legislature of South Carolina on Tuesday, November 23, 1847* (Columbia: 1847), p. 4.

[84]York Sessions Minutes, spring, 1818.

[85]*Message of His Excellency Charles Pinckney, to Both Branches of the Legislature* (Columbia: privately printed, n.d.), p. 7; Wallace, *History,* II, p. 467; Thomas Lehere to James B. Richardson, November 21, 1803 (Sheriffs' Correspondence, Penal Papers). *Also see Speech of the Hon. John L. Wilson, Senator in the Legislature of South Carolina, on the Propriety and Expediency of Reducing the Laws of the State into a Code* (New York: Gray and Bunce, 1827), *passim.*

[86]Concerning Lieber *see* Daniel C. Gilman (ed.), *The Miscellaneous Writings of Francis Lieber* (2 vols., Philadelphia: J. B. Lippincott and Co., 1881), I, p. 21, II, pp. 470-94; Francis Lieber, *A Popular Essay on Subjects of Penal Law, and on Uninterrupted Solitary Confinement at Labor* (Philadelphia: privately printed, 1838), *passim.* Concerning Perry, *see* Kibler, *Perry,* pp. 54-55, 220-31; and Perry, *Report,* pp. 25-32.

[87]"Black-Sluggard," *The Proposed Alternation of "The Judicial Tenure" in South Carolina* (Hamburg, S. C.: The Republican Office, 1844), p. 3. *Also see* letters of "J.D." in Sumter *Banner,* March 22, April 5, 19, 1848.

[88]Daniel W. Hollis, "James H. Thornwell and the South Carolina College," in *Proceedings of the South Carolina Historical Association,* 1953, pp. 23, 24.

[89]Hollis, *South Carolina College,* pp. 189-190.

[90]"Message of Governor James Richardson," in Calhoun *Highland Sentinel,* December 10, 1841; *Message of Governor Whitemarsh Seabrook, 1849,* p. 23; "Message of Governor William Aiken," in Sumter *Banner,* December 2, 1846; *Senate Journal, 1854,* pp. 33, 56, *1856,* p. 63.

[91]*Statutes at Large,* VI, pp. 413, 438, 489, XI, pp. 447-48, XII, pp. 602, 712-13.

[92]*See* these grand jury presentments: Barnwell (fall, 1812), Chester (fall, 1816), Newberry (fall, 1817), Charleston (fall, 1849), Anderson (spring, 1854), and Horry (fall, 1855). *Also see* Elan Lynds to Benjamin F. Perry, February 12, 1839, and Edward G. Palmer to Benjamin F. Perry, August 2, 1839 (Miscellaneous Correspondence, Penal Papers).

[93]Columbia *Daily South Carolinian,* June 3, 1854.

[94]For examples *see* a Pendleton petition of November 15, 1802, and a "petition of Sundry South Carolina Citizens," November 24, 1811 (Petitions, Penal Papers).

[95]Laurensville *Herald,* February 16, December 7, 1849; Columbia *Daily South Carolinian,* November 21, 1853.

[96]*Message of Governor Whitemarsh Seabrook, 1849,* p. 23.

CHAPTER VI

[1]Cited in Summer, "Newberry County," p. 21.

[2]Vandiver, *Anderson County,* p. 202; Darlington *Family Friend,* March 24, 1858.

INDEX

Abbeville (town): police force established, 70; public hanging, 103; insecure jail, 114

Abbeville District: grand jury presentments, 4, 10, 114; low crime rate in, 6

Abbott, Barton: accused of bastardy, 54

Abolitionism, 120-22, 125, 130. *See also* Vigilance societies

Accessory to crimes, 62

Adams, James H. (Governor): reward offered by, 62

Adams, Jesse: freed of murder charge, 93

Adultery, 55-57

Aiken: poverty, 25; gunfight near, 66; police force established, 70

Aiken, William (Governor): liberal pardon policy, 104; urges acceptance of new penal code, 130

Alabama: new penal code adopted, 127; state penitentiary established, 131; penal reforms noted, 135

Alexander, Elizabeth: charged with adultery, 56

————, Nelson: robbed and beaten, 39

Aliases, use of, 28, 29

Allen, Hugh: jailed for contempt of court, 76

Allman, Abel: indicted for incest, 55

Allston, R. F. W. (Governor): deplores public executions, 103-04; discusses jail-breaks, 120; criticizes vigilance society movement, 123

Alston, Joseph (Governor): urges penal code reforms, 128

Anderson: brawling, 32; pillory, 107; posse, 133

Appleton, Charles W.: poses as preacher, 51

Arfwedson, Carl D.: discusses carrying of weapons by citizens, 10

Aristocracy, importance of in criminal matters, 134-35

Arnold, A. B. (physician): attends prisoners in jail, 117

Arson: by women, 22; feared by citizens, 44; cases, 44-45; belief that Negroes are guilty, 44-45

Arsonist: large reward offered, 62

Ashe, John: murdered in Charleston, 15

Assault and battery: in Charleston, 2; in up country, 6; women involved, 20-22; beneath dignity of better classes, 23-24; amount in state, 31; public acceptance, 31; citizens complain, 32-33; punishment, 110. *See also* Brawling

Baggett, Jesse: charged with adultery, 56

————, Mary: involved in brawl, 21

Bail, 110-111

Bailey, William: murder of, 16

Banishment: as punishment for immigrant criminals, 17; use by vigilance societies, 27; as punishment for vagrancy, 58; court procedures, 106; popularity as punishment, 106, 111

Banks, robbery, 41

Barber, Sam: receives pardon, 105

Barnwell District: grand jury presentments, 4, 7, 51, 56-57; brawling, 21; poverty, 25; adultery, 56-57; robbers caught, 68-69; sessions court journal, 84; jury service, 84-85; horse stealing, 160*n39*

Barnwell, Robert W.: urges improved educational facilities, 25

Bartholomew, Alexander: organizes posse, 65-66

Bastardy: in up country, 6; lack of public interest, 53; prevalence in

177

state, 53-54; punishment, 54-55; frequency of convictions, 55; decline, 55

Batts, Summerfield: shooting, 10-11

Bawdy houses. *See* Prostitution, houses of

Baxley, Sabria: charged with infanticide, 62

Bay, Elihu H. (Judge): sentence by, 33; influence, 78

Beaufort District: grand jury presentments, 78, 114; condition of jail, 114, 116

Beccaria, Cesare: writings on reform noted, 126

Benefit of clergy, 101

Benson, Jeremiah: court trial, 83

Bentham, Jeremy: reform activities noted, 126

Bible: kissing by jurors, 79-80; references by lawyers, 93-95

Bigamy, 55-56

Bishop, Emily: charged with prostitution, 57

Blackstock, Richard (constable): report of, 68

Blackstone, William, 92

Bloodhounds, use of, 64, 65

Bomar, A. C. (sheriff): accounts, 114

Bonds: required of sheriffs, 69; posted by Charleston police, 74. *See also* Peace bonds

Boyles, Charles (constable): injured in line of duty, 69

Bradley, Charles: jail record, 26-27

————, Robert: refuses to sit on jury, 84

————, Sarah: involved in brawl, 21

————, William: charged with bastardy, 54

Branding: as punishment, 101; unpopularity, 106-08; instances, 107-08, 119; method, 107-08; law against, after 1833, 130

Brasington, George: beaten, 15

Brawling: instances, 11-12, 13-15, 21, 22, 32, 37; prominent people involved, 23-24; excuse for, 39; among prisoners in jail, 117; law-

suit concerning, 125. *See also* Assault and battery

Brooks, Preston S., 3

Broughton, Edward: purchases lottery chances, 50

Brown, James: steals slaves, 28

————, Thomas: posts peace bond, 112

————, Vincent: charged with bastardy, 54

Buckingham, James S.: notes poverty in South Carolina, 26; discusses duelling in South Carolina, 37

Buggery. *See* Sodomy

Bunch, Robert: criticizes vigilance society movement, 123-24

Burglars, 40, 41. *See also* Robbers; Larceny

Burke, Aedanus (Judge): denounces use of whisky, 8; refuses to sentence swine thief, 24; admonishes jury, 33; eloquence, 79; witnesses mob murder, 121-22

Burning at stake, case of, 104

Butler, Andrew P. (Judge): influence, 78

————, Pierce M. (Governor): discusses weapons carrying by citizens, 9-10

Calendars, court: crowded, 31

Calhoun, John C.: notes crime in Charleston, 2; gives reason for quitting law practice, 88

Cambridge: evidence of mayhem, 33

Camden: duelling in, 37; robberies near, 39; arson, 44, 45; swindlers, 52; police force established, 70

Capital punishment. *See* Punishment, capital

Carden, Jordan: convicted of larceny, 24

Carrying of weapons, by citizens, 9-11

Carter, Ephraim: publicly whipped, 108

Carver, James: gang member, 28

————, Mildred: gang member, 28

Cattle, thievery, 42

Elections, brawling, 14-15
England: criminals thought to be in Charleston, 17
"E-O" (gambling game): 49
Epting, Jacob: jury service record, 83
Escapes: frequency from South Carolina jails, 64, 119-20
Evans, Josiah J. (Judge): dignity, 79
Extradition, requests for, 164n27

Fairfield District: grand jury presentment, 4; bastardy, 53
Faro (gambling game), 48
Farelly, Charles: involved in brawl, 15; alias, 28
Faux, William: meets duellists, 37; criticizes lawyers, 92
Fines: difficulties of collecting, 25, 67, 112; usual amount, 110-11; disposition, 111; returned by Governors, 113
Fisher, Lavinia: murders travelers, 22, 35; public hanging, 22, 35, 103
Fisticuffs: at militia musters, 12; during elections, 14-15; indictments, 21; gentlemen not to engage, 37. *See also* Assault and battery; Brawling
Flemming, Archibald: involved in brawl, 12
Florida: failure to establish state penitentiary noted, 131
Food: thievery, 42; cost, 117
Foote, Gibson: steals horse, 20
Ford, Henry: avoids jury duty, 84
Foreigners, in South Carolina, 16-17
Forgery: youth involved, 18; punishment, 47
Fornication, 56-57, 61
Frederick William IV: reforms noted, 126
Freeholders. *See* Magistrates and freeholders courts
French Alley (Charleston): crime, 3
Frost, Edward (Judge): influence, 78

Gadberry, J. M.: introduces penal code legislation, 130
Gaffney, William: kills Negroes, 27

Gallows: superstitions, 102; attitude of felons, 103
Gamblers, professional: criticism, 47-48; in Charleston, 48-49, 73; in Columbia, 48-49; methods used, 49-50; punishment, 111
Gambling, 47-50. *See also* Lotteries
Gambling houses, 48-49
Gandy, Mary: bastardy charge brought by, 54
Gangs, 2, 28-29, 41, 46, 73
Gantt, Richard (Judge): denounces evils of whisky, 8; eloquence, 79; humor, 79; leniency in court, 94
Gayner, Thomas: freed of murder charge, 93
Georgetown: police force established, 70
Georgia: penal code adopted, 127; state penitentiary established, 131; penal system reform noted, 135
Gibbes, Hasell (Judge): impeachment, 78
Gill, John: attacks constable, 69
Godbold, Elly (constable): work, 64
Good-Bye Alley (Charleston): crime, 3
Gouging, 33. *Also see* Mayhem
Graham, Mary: charged with prostitution, 57
Grand juries. *See* Juries, grand
Grand larceny. *See* Larceny
Grave robbers, 40
Grayson, William J.: expresses low opinion of college student morals, 19; criticizes lawyers, 88-89; admits lack of oratorical ability, 93; describes Coosawhatchie jail, 116
Greenville (town): amount of crime, 5-6; bastardy, 53; police force established, 70; escapes from jail, 120
Greenville District: grand jury presentment, 57; fines and forfeitures files, 113
Gregg, William: discusses poverty in state, 25
Gregory, Jackson: involved in brawl, 12

Imprisonment, solitary: urged by reformers, 126, 128-29
Incendiaries. *See* Arson
Incest, 55
Individualism of South Carolinians, 133-134
Infanticide: cases, 22, 54, 62; woman hanged, 22
Informers, 62-63
Inquests. *See* Juries, coroners'
Insanity of criminals, 20, 25, 27-28
Involuntary servitude, of white men, 54-55, 130
Ivey, Temperance: bastardy charge brought by, 54

Jackson, Evander: murder, 18
Jailers: sheriffs as, 67; administer public whippings, 109; work, 116-19; money allowance, 117; criticism, 119
Jailing: popularity as punishment, after 1820, 113
Jails: overcrowding, 3; in Edgefield, 4, 116; sentences, 22, 114; burning, in Camden, 45; in Charleston, 113-115; in Horry District, 113; poor condition, 113-18; improvement during 1850s, 114; discomforts, 114-18; in Beaufort District, 116; at Coosawhatchie, 116; at Lexington, 116; brawling, 117
James, William D. (Judge): removed from office, 78
Jefferson, Thomas, 127
Jenkins, Shadrack: involved in brawl, 21
Johnson, David (Governor): notes crowded docket at Charleston court, 80; speaks against changes in penal code, 128
Jones, Gavin: murder reported, 62
Jordan, Adam: fine returned, 113
Judges, 69, 76-78. *Also see* names of individual jurists
Judicial districts: historical sketch, 77
Juries, coroners': lack of skill, 34; verdicts, 34, 36, 38
————, Grand: protest high crime rates, 1, 3; deplore weapons carrying by citizens, 10; criticize use of court time for hearing misdemeanor cases, 31; protest widespread adultery, 56-57; call attention to prevalence of prostitution, 57; examples of presentments, 62-63; request investigations, 62-63; urge bonding of constables, 69-70; influence of judges, 78; membership, 80; true bills found, 80; work, 80; criticize condition of jails, 113-14; urge penal code reforms, 127-28; urge establishment of state penitentiary, 130-31. *See also* names of Districts; Jurors, grand
Juries, petit: leniency of, 19-20, 27, 38, 85-87, 100-101; attitude toward prominent defendants, 23-24; severity, 39-41, 43; attitude in bastardy cases, 55; protest crowded court dockets, 80; work, 80-87; use of two at each court, 81-83; pardons requested, 105-106. *See also* Jurors, petit; Jury service
Jurors, grand: swearing in, 79; oath taken, 79-80; social status, 80; pay, 85. *Also see* Juries, grand; Jury service
————, Petit: swearing in, 79; oath taken, 79; deplore heavy work loads, 81-82; number on duty at court session, 82-83; refuse to serve, 84-85; leave court before end of term, 84-85; drink while on duty, 84-85; pay, 85; bribery, 86-87; instances of improper acts, 86-87. *See also* Juries, petit; Jury service
Jury service: qualifications, 79, 83; dislike by citizens, 83-85. *See also* Jurors, grand; Jurors, petit
Justices of the peace. *See* Magistrates
Juvenile crime, 18-20, 58, 71, 118

Kelly, James: jailed for contempt of court, 76
Kentucky: revised penal code noted, 127
Kershaw District: grand jury presentments, 4, 28, 113; criminal gangs, 28; insecure jail, 113

Kidnapping of slaves: cases, 28, 43, 86; prevalence, 43; punishment, 43

King, William L.: lists Charleston duels, 37

Kleptomania, 17

Landsford: Vigilance society, 124

Lancaster: riot in, 12; murder, 27; robbery, 40; swindlers, 51-52; escapes from jail, 120

Lancaster District: grand jury presentment, 27; posses, 51-52

Larceny: prevalence in Charleston, 2, 63; amount in low country, 6; during court sessions, 12; by juveniles, 18-19; by women, 20, 22, 86; by member of legislature, 24; poverty as cause, 25-26; repeaters, 26-27; distinctions between grand and petit, 39; laws, 39; newspaper reports, 39; public attitude, 39; punishments, 39; typical articles stolen, 39-40; at Columbia, 40; at Yorkville, 40; of ladles, 40; jury severity, 85. *Also see* Robbery

Lashing, public. *See* Whipping, public

Laurens (town): temperance societies, 8; swindlers, 51; insecure jail, 113; jailer, 119

Laurens District: grand jury presentments from, 31, 113, 128

Law, criminal. *See* Code, criminal

Law enforcement, cost of, 73, 74

Lawyers, criminal court: belief in skill by defendants, 87-88; adverse criticism, 87-90; defense of the guilty, 88-89; favorable publicity granted, 90-91; number in ante-bellum South Carolina, 91; training, 91; licensing, 91-92; pay, 96-98; circuit riding, 97; competition, 97-98; brawling, 97-98; social acceptability, 99

Lee, Thomas (Judge): denounces evils of drinking whisky, 8

Levy, Moses: captures criminals, 73

Lewdness, 56-57. *Also see* Adultery; Fornication

Lexington (town): locks not used, 4-5; murder, 27; jail, 116

Lexington District: grand jury presentment, 116

Lieber, Francis: recounts instance of juvenile crime, 20; considers lack of education to cause crime, 25; urges penal code reforms, 128-29; suspected as favoring abolitionism, 130; urges establishment of state penitentiary, 130

Locks, use of, 4-5, 42

London Inns of Court, 91

Lotteries, 50

Low Country: larceny, 6; murder, 6; swine thievery, 42; swindlers, 51-52

Lowndes, William: gives reason for quitting practice of law, 88

Lowry, James: charged with bastardy, 54

Lynch law: instances, 27, 65, 121-22, 133-34; applied to abolitionists, 120-21, 125; criticism, 122-23. *See also* Vigilance society movement

McCarna, Mary: charged with infanticide, 54

McClennan, Polly: charged with prostitution, 57

McCord, David J. (Judge): hot temper, praised, 16

McCormick, John: charged with bastardy, 54

McDaniell, John: involved in brawl, 14

McKenna, John: involved in brawl, 15

McKenzie, C. C.: poses as physician, 51

Mackey, John: involved in brawl, 23

————, Thomas J. (Judge): humor, 4, 82

McKinney, Bridget: involved in brawl, 21

McLeod, Daniel: tried for murder, 83

————, David B.: charged with drunkenness, 84

McMurphey, Mitchell: involved in brawl, 14

Magistrates, duties, 66, 75, 81

185

scribed, 60-61; lawyers criticized, 89-90

New York: criminal in South Carolina, 16; public executions ended, 127

Ninety-Six: lynch mob, 121

Noble, Patrick (Governor): pardon blanks requested, 104

Non-support, 53-54

North Carolina: criminals said to be in South Carolina, 28-29; swindlers chased into, 52; failure to establish state penitentiary, 131

Nott, Abraham (Judge): influence, 78

Nuisances, 58-59

Nullification controversy, violence caused by, 15

Nunn, Elijah (sheriff): murder of, 65

Oliver, James: murder by, 16

Olmstead, Frederick L.: notes similarity of South and West, 59

O'Neall, John B. (Judge): charges juries, 7; leads Sons of Temperance, 7-8; recounts story of brawling woman, 22; influence, 78; severity of sentences, 79, 94; urges establishment of state penitentiary, 130-31

Orangeburg: insecure jail, 113

Oratory: importance to criminal court lawyers, 92-95

Pardons: granted to prominent persons, 24; adverse criticism, 104-105; style, 104-105; reservations attached, 104-106; procedures for obtaining, 105-106; requests by juries, 105-106; of woman sentenced to public lashing, 109

Parnell, Carma (jailer): corrupt activities, 119

Patrol, 64

Patrols, in cities, 72

Peace bonds, 21, 58, 112

Pearson, Philip: aids victim of gamblers, 49

Penal code: attempts to reform, 125-30, 132, 135; influence of noted writers on reform of, 126; influence of other states on reform of, 126-

27, antiquated language of, 127-28; legislative interest in reform of, 128; opposition to reform of, 129-30; changes in, 130; severity of, 132

Pendleton (town): robbery in, 41; swindlers in, 52; public hangings in, 102-103; insecure jail in, 114

Pendleton District: public warning by constable in, 67; grand jury presentment from, 114; vigilance society in, 122

Penitentiary, state. See State penitentiary

Pennsylvania: penal reforms in, noted, 126-27; public executions ended, 127

Perjury, 96

Perry, Benjamin F. (lawyer): remembers Greenville crime, 5; discusses causes of crime, 7; defends counterfeiter, 18-19; defends an infanticide, 22; meets mayhem victims, 33; defends forger, 47; criticizes constables, 70; recalls instance of jury dishonesty, 86; defends guilty felons, 88; discusses importance of oratory to lawyers, 92-93; discusses reputations of judges for severity of sentences, 94; circuit ridden by, 97; fees charged by, 98; law business of, 98; urges penal code reforms, 128-29; proposes new penal code, 129; urges establishment of state penitentiary, 130

————, James B.: introduces bill for acceptance of revised penal code, 130

Person, crimes against the, 31-38, 40-41, 59

Perversion, sexual, 17

"Peterson's Counterfeit Detector," 46

Peitgru, James L. (lawyer): criticizes vigilance society movement, 123; wins law suit, 125

Petit juries. See Juries, petit

Petit larceny. See Larceny

Petitions, citizen: ask higher pay for constables, 70; ask pardons for convicted criminals, 105

186

Phillips, Ulrich B., 59

Physicians: criminals pose as, 26, 50-51; rob grave, 40; attend prisoners in jails, 117

Pickens District: vigilance society, 122

Pickpockets: at public festivals, 11; *modus operandi,* 26, 40; gang, 29; at Charleston, 40, 63, 73; at Columbia, 40; at Hamburg, 40; at railroad depots, 40; at Sumter, 40; change in law concerning, 130

Pillory, 106-07

Pinckney, Charles (Governor): urges reform of penal code, 128

Platts, Sarah: bastardy charge brought by, 54

Poison: fear by white people, 36; law against use, 36, 130; use by criminals, 41

Police: numbers in South Carolina, 60, 71-72; volunteers, 60; militiamen, 64-65; administration, 66; areas served, 70; in Columbia, 70-71; in Charleston, 72-74. *See also* Constables

Political campaigns: brawling, 14-15

Porcher, Samuel: work as militia officer, 64-65

Posses: chases, 51-52, 64-66, 133; need, 60, 64; criminals punished, 63-64; distinguished from mobs, 64; types, 64-66

Poultry thieves, 42

Poverty: thought to cause crimes, 17, 25-26

Preachers: involved in brawl, 23; criminals pose as, 51; attend court sessions, 75; attend public executions, 103

Pressley, Samuel P.: preaches funeral discourse at gallows, 103

Prince, Thomas: murder by, 16

Prison bounds: laws concerning, 118; allowance, 130

Prisoners: treatment in jails, 116-19; brawling among, 117; feeding, 117; medical care, 117, 119; solitary confinement, 118; torture, 119; chaining, 119-20; escapes, 119-20

Professional gamblers. *See* Gamblers, professional

Professional men: criminals pose as, 26, 46, 50-52

Professors: swindlers pose as, 51; accused of bad behavior, 58

Property, crimes against, 39-53, 59

Prostitutes: lack of jury sympathy, 20; punishment, 21, 58; grand jury presentments concerning, 57; in Charleston, 58; in Columbia, 58; classified as vagrants, 58

Prostitution, houses: locations, 57-58; punishment for keepers, 58

Public executions. *See* Hanging, public

Public whipping. *See* Whipping, public

Punishment: for receiving stolen goods, 21; of women, 21-22, 58; for mayhem, 33; of animal thieves, 42; of Negro kidnapper, 43; of counterfeiter, 46; of forger, 47; of swindlers, 47; for bastardy, 54-55; for bigamy, 56; for sodomy, 56; for keepers of houses of prostitution, 58; of vagrants, 58; for accessory to crimes, 62; by posses, 63-64; for manslaughter, 85, 111; of Negroes, 109; of misdemeanants, 114; of debtors, 118, 173n58; by vigilance societies, 120-25, 133-34. *See also* Punishment, capital

Punishment, capital: of women, 22; penal code, 100; leniency of juries, 100-101; by hanging, 101-104; by burning at stake, 104; plea for end, 126, 128-29; ending, in other states, 127

Punishment, extra-legal, 27, 65, 120-25, 133-34

Rabon, John: steals animals, 43

"Race Week": crime during, 11

Railroad depots: pickpockets, 40

Rall, Jacob (constable): arrests crazed man, 69

Ramsey, Edward: charged with fornication, 56-57

Rape: amount in state, 33-34; Negroes thought guilty of, 34; publicity given to, 34

Rapist, burning of, 104

Ratcliffe, Charlotte: involved in brawl, 21

Receiving stolen goods: punishment, 21

Rehabilitation of criminals, 136

Rewards: instances, 15, 61-62; collection, 62

Reynolds, J. L. (preacher): involved in brawl, 23

Rhett, Albert (lawyer): proposes severe punishment for drunkards, 8-9

Rice, William, son of: involved in murder, 18

Richardson, James B. (Governor): urges penal code reforms, 128

————, James P. (Governor): urges acceptance of revised penal code, 130

————, James S. (Judge): impeachment of, 78

Richland District: grand jury presentments, 4, 118

Riots: in Greenville, 5; at the Columbia races, 11; in Lancaster, 12; in Yorkville, 13; in Spartanburg, 14; during "court time," 14; during elections, 14-15; law concerning, 32, 158n4; by students in Columbia, 71

Robbery: of luggage, 39; of mail bags, 39; on public roads, 39; of stagecoaches, 39; of trains, 39; of a grave, 40; at Lancaster, 40; of businesses, 40-41; in Charleston, 41; in Columbia, 41; of ships, 41; in Sumter, 41; newspaper accounts, 41; in Pendleton, 41; in Edgefield, 41-42; of banks, 41, 160n34; of smokehouse, 42. See also Larceny; Robbers

Robbers: gang in Charleston, 29; tools used, 41-42. See also Burglars; Thieves

Rock Hill: vigilance society, 122

"Rowly-Powly" (gambling game), 48

Roy, James (murderer): ignorance of described, 28

Royall, Anne N.: denounces Charleston as city of crime, 2; has notebook stolen, 40

Rupel, Polly: operates gaming house, 48

Sabbath, violations, 59, 111

Sadism: violence resulting, 27

St. Bartholomew, gentry of: mistreat Northerner, 125

Sanders, Thomas (constable): shot in line of duty, 69

Sandiford, Joseph: charged with adultery, 56

Schirmir, Jacob: jury service record, 83

Seabrook, Whitemarsh B. (Governor): urges acceptance of revised penal code, 130; explains state's failure to establish penitentiary system, 131

Secession, 135

"Self arson": suggestion of, 45

Servitude, involuntary: as punishment in bastardy cases, 54-55; legal end, 55, 130; as punishment for vagrants, 58

Shaffer, M. C.: discusses prostitution in Columbia, 58

Sharpers. See Swindlers

Shaver, W. K.: newspaper notice, concerning criminal, 61

Sheriffs: work, 66-67, 109; bond required, 69; duties at meetings of sessions courts, 75-76

Ship, robbery, 41

Shultz, Henry: pardoned after murder conviction, 24

Siegling, John: studies law, 91

Sims, David G.: hanging, 103

Singleton, Margaret: charged with bigamy, 56

————, Mary: charged with bigamy, 56

Slave owners: influence in South Carolina, 43

Slave sales, pickpockets at, 29

189

by, 22; whisky sold by, 22; as members of gangs, 28; rape of, 33-34; murder of, 36; gaming house operated, 48; involved in swindles, 52, 55; bastardy cases brought by, 53-54; involved in sexual promiscuity, 55-57, 62; seduction, 60, 61, 95; attend court as spectators, 76; public whipping, 108, 109, 132; peace bonds requested, 112; jailing, 117-18

Wosdon, Thomas: charged with fornication, 56-57
Wythe, George, 127

Yancey, William L.: pardoned by Governor
Yaun, Charles: release from jail petitioned, 116
Yorkville: riot, 13; thievery, 40; shooting, 69; police force established, 70; horse stealing, 160$n39$